Chris Sidwells is a freelance author, editor and photographer who specialises in all aspects of cycling. He has contributed over 1000 features to magazines and websites, including *Cycling Weekly, Cycle Sport, Tour* magazine, *Cycling Plus, GQ, Men's Fitness, The Sunday Times* and the BBC. He has previously written 19 books on cycling. Chris is currently working on his own publishing brand, Cycling Legends: www.cyclyinglegends.co.uk.

'An intriguing read for almost any reader, not only those who are interested in cycling' *Tuam Herald*

'[An] engaging and accessible account of the race's history' *Sunday Business Post*

'*The Call of the Road* is the definitive story of cycle road racing . . . Sidwells dissects the seemingly ever-present question of doping, and brings the story of road racing completely up to date' *The Sports Book Club*

THE CALL OF THE ROAD

THE HISTORY OF
CYCLE ROAD RACING

WILLIAM
COLLINS

William Collins
An imprint of HarperCollins*Publishers*
1 London Bridge Street
London SE1 9GF

WilliamCollinsBooks.com

First published in Great Britain by William Collins in 2018
This William Collins paperback edition published in 2019

1

A catalogue record for this book is available from the British Library

ISBN 978-0-00-822080-8

Typeset by Palimpsest Book Production Ltd, Falkirk, Stirlingshire

Printed and bound by CPI Group (UK) Ltd, Croydon CR0 4YY

MIX
Paper from
responsible sources
FSC C007454
www.fsc.org

This book is produced from independently certified FSC™ paper to
ensure responsible forest management.

For more information visit: www.harpercollins.co.uk/green

Contents

1

Call of the Road

A road race is many things. It includes many aspects of life, but magnified; a maelstrom of ambitions, plans, desire, cooperation and treachery. A road race ebbs and flows through the countryside like a living thing, a kaleidoscope of colour, a visceral mass of muscle and machine, a chess game played on wheels. And it doesn't matter what level: whether it's the Tour de France or evening league, road races share the same basic qualities. Only speed, distance, stakes and the sophistication of the game are different.

Road races are battles, pure battles where social norms are replaced by personal or cohort needs. Basic needs like food and drink to re-fuel and shelter to save energy, and higher needs like peer approval, money, victory and admiration. It's rare to experience physical battles in everyday life, and on that level the fight to succeed brings out something primitive, making road racing wonderful to experience and wonderful to watch.

But the best professionals raise road racing to an art; the art of warfare maybe, the art of a hunter perhaps, but still art and glorious to behold and appreciate. Especially since road racing is not played out in stadiums or on pitches, but on incredible natural canvases. Some are stark, set on the cobblestone roads and brutish hills of northern Europe. Others are stunning, like races in the great mountain ranges of Italy, France and Spain. But all are beautiful in their unique way.

There are single-day road races and stage races. Some single-day races have more history or more notable terrain, and they are called the classics. Of the classics five are the biggest and the best, and they are known as the 'monuments' of cycling. Stage races are at least two or three days long, most are around one week, but the biggest stage races last for three weeks. They are the Grand Tours: the Giro d'Italia, the Vuelta a España, and the biggest and oldest of them all, the Tour de France.

The Tour de France is not just the biggest bike race in the world, it's the biggest annual sports event in the world, only ever surpassed by football's World Cup and the Olympic Games. Figures from 2011 show that the Tour de France, or simply the Tour as it's referred to in cycling, was covered by seventy radio stations, four thousand newspapers and press agencies, and seventy websites, who between them sent 2,300 journalists from thirty-five countries to the race. The Tour de France website, www. letour.fr had 14 million unique visitors that year. Over 100 TV channels broadcast the race to 190 countries in 2011, sixty of them receiving live pictures. And that's just the media coverage, which has grown since 2011; the Tour de France has a truly worldwide audience today.

The number of roadside spectators is harder to gauge, but the Tour organisers Amaury Sport Organisation (ASO) reckon that a staggering 12 to 15 million people watch the race pass by at some point each year. And that's one of the big attractions of road racing: it goes to the places where people live, it comes down their roads and past their houses. Still, many spectators want to see the race on a famous mountain climb, and they must either walk or bike there on the day of the stage, or they must drive there two or three days beforehand to get any chance of finding a place to park. Many camp on the mountainside, turning their visit into a holiday.

By the time the race gets there the crowds on mountain roads are huge. Police estimated that half a million people stood on Alpe d'Huez to watch a time trial stage in 2004. The atmosphere is always electric and often a little bit mad. Some fans wear bizarre costumes, and so many spill out onto the road that the race leaders often face a wall of hysterical humanity, which parts just ahead of them, leaving only the narrowest gaps to ride through. It's an incredible sight, and unforgettable to be part of. So let's look at a typical mountain stage of the Tour de France.

The race fills almost any place where it starts or finishes. Parking anywhere near the start is impossible, so planning ahead is vital if you are to see anything. The focus is the Village de Départ, a temporary structure erected by a travelling team, then taken down as soon as the race leaves town, and transported to wherever it's needed next.

In Tours gone by everybody had access to all areas, but the race has outgrown the charming informality it once had. Riders, race officials, accredited media and VIPs are the only people allowed in the Village now. Everybody else stands behind barriers, people-watching and star-spotting, and there are plenty of both to see. Old champions and former team-mates meet for a coffee in the Village, where they gossip about the old days; celebrities are shown around by sponsors or race officials, while members of the media pretend to check their smart-phones but are continually looking for somebody, anybody, to interview. They don't find many current riders, just the few who are sent out by their teams to keep the press happy.

The Tour de France has changed a lot. It was always big, always serious for the top riders, but now it's very big and ultra-serious for every rider. Everybody takes their A-game to the Tour de France – they have to; anything less won't do. Riders don't mingle much with the public now; they are cocooned behind black glass in massive team buses. Inside they chat in air-cooled calm, or get lost in i-pods and laptops, but they are all focusing on the day ahead. The last team briefing is done. Everybody knows their job, their part in the team's stage plan has been explained. This is their quiet time before battle.

Some of the more garrulous riders emerge from the buses first, sign autographs and pose for selfies. Some like the attention, the interaction, but they are rarely the contenders, who stay in their bus shells until the last minute. They want to avoid questions from news-hungry press. How do they feel? What do they think will happen today? Is this a crucial stage? Things the top guys know, or hope they know, but are unwilling to talk about because they don't want input from anybody else, or in case they are just plain wrong. Contenders emerge in time to wave, nod politely at well-wishers, and head for the signing on. They have a job to do in the race, and it takes all they've got to do it. There's no spare capacity to answer questions, not now, not before the stage. Afterwards they'll talk at length.

Signing on for a stage is a cycling tradition. In days gone by it served to inform officials which riders were still in a race, but now it's used as a device for the race speaker to introduce the riders to the spectators, so they know who is who and what they've won. One at a time the riders mount the steps to the speaker's stage, walk stiffly to where they sign, wave to the crowd and by the time they've gone the speaker has been through their career in detail, and maybe had a word or two from them. The speaker never asks difficult questions, that's his side of the bargain. It's all done quickly and professionally, then the riders head for the start line and the race rolls out.

Tour de France stages have two starts; a nice smiley ceremonial one in the middle of town, then the real one when the race gets out in the countryside. The man in charge, the Tour de France director, the ultimate word on the race, Christian Prudhomme is driven ahead in a distinctive red car. The riders follow it closely, crowding its back bumper. Prudhomme emerges through the sun-roof, a red flag stretched between his hands. The riders watch it, waiting for him to drop it, and when he does all hell breaks loose.

The director's car accelerates away, and the riders always attack. It's like the cork coming out of a Champagne bottle, the start of each team's stage plan, a release of pent-up energy as every rider is anxious to play his part. Tour stages need breakaways, more often referred to as breaks. On stages that suit sprinters their teams work to ensure the whole bunch is together for the finish, but part of doing that involves letting a group go ahead early and stay ahead for a while. The early attackers are trying to form such a breakaway.

In professional road races an early break creates order where otherwise there would be chaos. Breakaways provide a focus for the race; they give it shape so long as there's nobody in them who threatens somebody else's plan. Breakaways stop races becoming a free-for-all for the whole distance, with attack after attack until the peloton is cut to ribbons. The trick is not to let a break-away get so far ahead it can't be caught later. Just keep it there, keep the gap, then reel it in before the finish. Pro teams have that down to an art.

But this isn't a sprinter's stage, this is a mountain stage with other agendas going on. A breakaway still brings order, but the riders trying to get in today's break come from two distinct groups. One is trying to win the stage, and the other is made up of riders trying to help their team leaders win the race overall. I'll talk more about both groups in later chapters, but for now let's look at how a breakaway forms at this level of racing.

For a start the other riders don't say, 'Go on, lads, you go ahead and we'll see you later.' Quite the opposite, and there's an incredible scrap before a breakaway forms. Its mix must be right, and the other riders won't let anything go until it is. For example, if an outside favourite for overall victory or a high overall placing tries to slip into a breakaway unnoticed, it won't happen. It will be noticed, and the other teams will pounce on it and snuff it out.

Neither will the other favourites' teams let one of their

rivals get too many team-mates in a breakaway. If they did that, they could find themselves outnumbered later in a stage. So there will be attack and counter-attack, embryo breakaways forming and being brought back, until the right combination is allowed to go. Then things calm down, and the break is on.

But if all that sounds too choreographed, many things can spoil the script. Crosswinds, early steep climbs and other factors can and do upset the course of all the above. Early difficulties in a race provide opportunities for the strongest riders or teams to attack early and turn everything on its head. It happens a lot, especially in single-day races, but that's another thing I'll cover later in the book.

The British rider Steve Cummings is a current top dog at spotting the right combination of riders for a breakaway to succeed, and when a stage suits him he'll be in it. 'I focus totally on the first ninety minutes of a stage I know I can do well in,' he says. 'I don't even think about the rest of it, I just psyche myself up for the first ninety minutes, because that's when you have to give everything you've got to ensure you get in. Once I've done that, and I'm in, then I think about the rest of the stage.'

Cummings's preference is for rolling terrain, or medium mountains in cycling parlance, a route with several quite long climbs, but not the big mountains of the Alps and Pyrenees. The stage I'll try to describe here isn't like that. It's a typical, if imagined, stage in the Alps. One that finishes on top of one of the famous climbs: Alpe d'Huez, say, or the Col du Galibier.

Okay, on with the stage. Let's say an early break has formed, so now the race leader's team by tradition assumes control at the front of the peloton, trying to go fast enough to discourage further attacks but not so fast that the breakaway is caught early. If it is caught, the attacks will start all over again.

With the race leader's team in control, the race is in perfect balance, and will stay that way for a while. Time to consider the physical presence of the Tour de France, because it's immense. For a start there's the Caravane Publicitaire, the procession of vehicles that precedes the riders, and it's spectacular and weird in equal measure.

If you watch the Tour de France by the roadside – and everybody should do it once because it's an incredible experience, very different from seeing the race on TV – the first race vehicles start zooming past you at least two hours before any cyclist is seen. They might be media or logistics vehicles on the way to the stage finish, vehicles involved with safety or official duties; cars, lorries, motor-bikes and buses all zoom by. Then, after a short pause, the Caravane arrives.

Have you seen a giant fibre-glass insect lying on a flat-bed truck, or a man driving a huge gas canister or a giant wheel of cheese? Or have you been pelted with cheap plastic knick-knacks flung from a float by moon-lighting students? Well you will; you'll see them all, along with more elaborate creations, in the Caravane Publicitaire. All are products of the imaginations of publicists or design agencies, who embrace the maxim 'weird is wonderful', and weirder is always better for the Tour de France.

The Caravane takes forty-five minutes to pass. Some vehicles stop to better distribute their branded plastic tat, while those in others just chuck it in the direction of spectators as they drive by. Woe betide you if you try to race a French granny for a free Esso keyring. She will trample you down and her grand-kids will dance on your spine.

Once the Caravane has gone there's another lull, an even shorter one punctuated by waves of motorbikes and cars, all part of the Tour, all speeding to where they are needed next. To marshal the race, maybe, or man one of the feed stations. They pass like squally showers, with an increasing number of French police connected to the race mixed in. Team vehicles too. Each passing batch is greeted with enthusiasm. Is this the race? Are the riders coming now? No. You can't mistake it when they do.

First there's a Mexican wave of noise. It's been noisy so far but the noise has been random, without any order to it. This noise has order, and depth, and it grows louder and louder. On flat stages the noise travels from village to village towards you, drowning the throbbing of the helicopters above the race at first, but then they get too near to be drowned out. There are always at least two helicopters above the riders, swapping with others, leap-frogging to provide total stage cover for TV directors to switch to. Nothing is better than a view from above to show what's happening in a road race.

You feel as well as hear the race long before you see it, but that feeling is magnified in the mountains. Go high and you might be standing directly above the race as it approaches. It ascends to you, passing thousands of spectators lining the route below you. The sound of their cheers and cries is trapped by the surrounding rocks and bounces off them, reverberating upwards. Alpe d'Huez, for example, is a natural theatre. The climb is named after a ski village at its summit, and it starts directly below the finish in Bourg d'Oisans. The road between the two places goes up in tier after tier, twenty-two hairpin bends and twelve straights, one piled on top of the other.

Standing, waiting for the race near the summit of Alpe

d'Huez or Mont Ventoux, as I have done, the sound rises up to meet you, to engulf you. The helicopters fly slowly upwards, their blades beating the air, sending pulses of sound pushed by thousands of shouting, screaming voices, rolling upwards like thunder, charging the air so it prickles with anticipation.

The riders get nearer and nearer, clawing their way upwards like a giant bellowing beast. Nearer and nearer, our anticipation growing. Cars, motorbikes, police whistles, revving engines, shouting and screaming. A solid wave of sound crashing up a rocky wall, rolling onwards and upwards. The anticipation grows stronger and louder, until …

They're here, the first riders, though you can't see them yet because people further down the road have rushed out to see them before you do. The early breakaway has been caught, and now the best in the race are fighting it out for the stage. They include most of the overall contenders.

Anticipation turns into hysteria now, and formerly responsible people with good jobs and old enough to know better go glassy-eyed. They jump up and down, shouting themselves stupid. Kids grab their parents' hands for reassurance. What's happening? Now you can taste the Tour, it's an actual physical thing, like a summer storm and the relief of rain.

People crowd the riders, some run alongside, roaring incoherently at them. They ignore everything that isn't a clear threat, but fans who get too close risk a slap from their hero, and possible rough treatment from the rest of the crowd.

The stage leaders' faces are masks of concentration. Only total commitment and solid self-belief keeps them where they are. Let go now, and it's over. There's a belief in pro road racing that everybody at the pointy end of a mountain stage in a Grand Tour is three minutes from letting go. That's how they get through, they hold on for these three minutes, then the next three, and the next, and the three after that, until they cross the finish line or they cross their physiological and/or mental thresholds.

Then, one by one, riders let go. That's what they call it. They say, 'I had to let go' or 'I blew' – another cycling word. The stage is over for them now, and all they can hope for is to limit their time losses.

Sometimes they lose ground slowly, agonisingly. They drop to the back of a group then fight forwards, drop back, then forwards again, then back until this time there's a gap to the back of the group, and it grows bigger. Limitations accepted, they join the group behind, promising to challenge later. It's not all over, they think. They will come back, they think. They seldom do, not at this stage. Others fail in a worse way. They go into the red, a zone of effort the body can't maintain. It goes into oxygen debt, a debt that can only be repaid by slowing down. And if they stay too long in the red, and some can because toughness is high up on a pro road racer's job description, they slow down rapidly and irretrievably.

All the above has played out on this final climb. We are three kilometres from the summit now. The front group of five looks good. Behind them more flog past where I stand, some don't look so good, but others have found something; they are chasing, eyes full of hope and fixed ahead. Ones, twos, little groups and bigger groups, pass until the last big one, known as the auto-bus.

That's where the sprinters live on mountain stages, helping each other get through and beat the time limit.

It's not easy, because their physiques, so powerful and so fast on the flat, work against them here, but they push on, trying as hard as the climbers at the front but with less encouragement.

The wave of emotion rolling up the mountain peaks with the passing of the first riders, then slowly ebbs away as the others pass. The sprinters get respect, they certainly deserve it, polite applause and encouraging words mostly. There's occasional abuse too, but even the front riders can get that. It comes from people who should know better, and some do, but alcohol has turned off their inhibitions. Considering the millions of people they pass, the riders don't get abused so much.

Up front the battle is on, war is being waged. Two kilometres to go now, and four riders are chasing one who has launched a decisive attack. Attacks must be 100 per cent, especially at this point in a stage. The best road racers in the world are fighting for the biggest road racing prize. Attacks in this company at this point must stick. If they fail, the rest will blow right by and the attacker will lose time, and probably any chance of winning the Tour de France this year.

But this attack looks good. This rider is on top of his game, at full stretch but totally in control, making a superhuman effort he can keep all the way to the finish line. His legs are on fire, but his will to win overrides them. Total concentration, his pain-face some call it, not strained, just set: a steely glare ahead. One kilometre to go, keep it going, this is good; this will work.

Push, push. At this point a rider might feel everything around him starting to fade. His peripheral vision is slowly fading, even the colours he sees become muted. His muscles are demanding so much oxygen that his body sends everything to them. His eyes can wait; his legs, lungs and heart can't. They must have oxygen now.

But there it is: the last corner, the final straight, the finish line. The noise is just as loud now as it was lower down, but crowds are corralled behind barriers for the final kilometres. Safety and space, the riders need both. He will win. The others aren't far behind, but they aren't closing, and they have started watching each other. They have lost time to one man, but can't afford to lose to another.

The leader knows now; he punches the air, still low over his bike, still absolutely on it. Pushing as hard as he can, determined to gain every precious second he can. Attacks like this cannot be mounted every day, so he has to make it count.

At last the stage is his, and depending on how much his attack has gained, the Tour de France might be too. Across the line, under the banner; a salute, two hands off the handlebars, but only briefly – he's given too much for joy to sustain him any longer. He falls into the arms of a team helper, a carer who has waited with colleagues from other teams, all looking for their man. They are the confessors of cycling, the first person a rider sees after a race, the person to whom they confide their unmitigated joy, or their disappointment, before they tone either down and put on a different face for the press and other team personnel.

That's road racing at its highest level: a sensory feast; a battle, raw and beautiful. It can even be noble at times, but it's always intensely human. This book tells its story, good and bad, from the first ever road race to road racing today, and seeks to explain its language and the way it works.

2

The First Road Races

There's debate about when the first ever bike race was held. Many quote a race in Parc St Cloud, Paris, on 31 May 1868. It was won by an Englishman, James Moore, but it was part of a series of races in the same park on the same day. The names of the other winners were lost, and only Moore's survived.

It's possible that other races pre-date the St Cloud meeting, although it can't have been by much. The first bike with pedals – the act of pedalling is what I think defines cycling – was made in 1864, and the first patent for a pedal-powered bicycle given in 1866. So there wasn't much time between those dates and the Parc St Cloud races.

But because they were held on a 2-kilometre lap of prepared cinder paths inside the park, not on the open road, they weren't the first ever road races. The first proper road race of which there is a record happened in November 1869. It went from Paris to Rouen on normal roads. But since James Moore also won that race, he is the father of road racing.

There are stories of races on the public roads of Europe in the spring and summer of 1869, but they weren't very long and only attracted local riders. For example, the writer and researcher Rosemary Southey discovered an account of a short bicycle race on the roads of what was then the English county of Cumberland, now part of Cumbria, in May 1869.

'The race is recorded on the 21 May 1869 issue of the *Carlisle Patriot* newspaper,' Southey says. 'Under the title "Grand Picnic and Sports at Keswick: A Velocipede Race".' The report continues: 'Perhaps the greatest novelty of the day was the bicycle race. The course was along the Lake-road to Portinscale and back. The winner took the lead at a rattling pace, was never headed, and came in victorious by a great distance. Much merriment was created as the defeated competitors returned through the streets, many of them not riding their "iron horses" but, puffing and flushed, one foot propelling them along to the point from which they had started. The greatest good humour, however, prevailed, as was evidenced by one of the disappointed, struggling at the tail of his "steed," replying to the badinage with which he was assailed, "Well, never mind, there's three more behind."'

'The results read "Velocipede Race: 1 Mr Irving, Carlisle. 2. Mr G Graham, Carlisle. 3. Mr Stalker, Carlisle." The Keswick event is the earliest I can find on the road in Cumberland, but there were others in the same year on the path,' Southey says. 'The path' was a 19th century term for a cycle track – like running tracks – surfaced with cinders or red shale.

Southey continues, 'Cycling seems to have taken off in the county very early on, though of course there were plenty of sceptics, and disapproving magistrates and horse owners. I have records of cycling clubs in around a dozen places. Carlisle for instance had three clubs in the 1890s.'

The first mass-produced bikes were called 'boneshakers' in Britain and *vélocipèdes* in France. They were made from wrought iron, had wooden wheels with iron bands around their circumference to reduce wear, and one rudimentary brake. The pedals were attached to the front wheel, so these early bikes were direct drive; one revolution of the pedals meant one revolution of the wheel. And because wheels with greater circumference cover more ground per pedal revolution, the front wheels of early bikes were slightly bigger than the rear.

A Paris blacksmith and coach builder called Pierre Michaux was the man who put pedals on a two-wheeled running machine of the type that had become very popular in Germany, France and Britain. Or it may have been his son, Ernest. Again, there are conflicting accounts. But by creating the first pedal cycle, Pierre and/or Ernest Michaux made France the birthplace of cycling. By 1869 there were around sixty bicycle manufacturers in Paris, and about fifteen in the provinces. But the possibilities of this new invention were quickly being discovered on both sides of the English Channel.

The first newspaper dedicated to cycling was also born in 1869 in France. It was called *Le Vélocipède Illustré*, and although there had been news sheets about bikes before, *Le Vélocipède Illustré* was professionally produced, lavishly illustrated and lavishly written. This is what the editor,

Richard Lesclide, also known by his pen name of Le Grand Jacques, wrote at the beginning of the first issue, which was published on 1 April 1869:

> The Vélocipède is rapidly entering our lives, and that is the only justification we need for starting this new magazine. And yet never has the famous phrase: 'People began to feel the need for a special organ devoted to a fashionable conveyance' been so appropriate.
>
> Indeed the Vélocipède is gaining ground at amazing speed, spreading from France to the rest of Europe, from Europe to Asia and Africa. Not to mention America, which has outstripped us and now has the advantage of us in the race for further improvements.
>
> The Vélocipède is not a mere flash in the pan, here today and gone tomorrow. As you can see from the fact that, as it obtains a footing in the fashionable world, the government and the major public services are using it for special duties. It has now won complete acceptance in France, and we are founding a magazine under its patronage in order to bring together, in the same fellowship, its adherents and believers.

His piece set the timbre of cycling journalism, or at least French cycling journalism, for the next 100 years. A few months after Lesclide wrote those words, the long association between the cycling press and race promotion began when *Le Vélocipède Illustré* organised the Paris to Rouen race. Or Paris–Rouen, following the accepted protocol that the 'to' in the names of place-to-place road races is always replaced by a dash.

It was 7 November 1869, and Paris–Rouen set a pattern of place-to-place road races that was copied and developed over the years as the template for some of cycling's biggest races. Thirty-one men and one woman gathered at 7.15 a.m. outside Le Pré Catalan, on the Route de Suresnes in the Bois de Boulogne for the first Paris–Rouen. Le Pré Catalan is now a restaurant with three Michelin stars, but was then an exhibition centre where a cycle show had been held for five days preceding the race.

According to James Moore's son, also called James, speaking to *Sporting Cyclist* magazine in 1968 on the occasion of the centenary of the historic Parc St Cloud race, before the inaugural Paris–Rouen his father announced: 'Unless I arrive first, they will find me lying beside the road.' Gritty, determined words that set the mood and mind-set for road racing that still dominates the sport.

The riders set off for Rouen at 7.25 a.m., and at 6.10 p.m. the same day Moore crossed a finish line drawn by members of the Rouen cycling club at the gates to their city. A fine drizzle fell, and it was dark when Moore finished. The first prize was 1,000 gold francs and a Michaux bicycle, the race having been organised by the Michaux brand owners, the Olivier brothers Aimé, René and Marius.

Roads outside cities were appalling. They were either made of bone-jarring hard-packed clay or stones, or were muddy tracks with puddle-filled ruts and holes. They were very muddy that November day between Paris and Rouen, and the mud sucked at the riders' heavy bikes. Even Moore walked up the hills, and he finished 15 minutes ahead of the next man. The female competitor, made mysterious by her pseudonym of Miss America, finished 12 hours after the winner, but she wasn't last. That honour fell jointly to E. Fortin and Prosper Martin, who crossed the line together 14 hours and 15 minutes after Moore.

Moore was to all intents a professional cyclist by 1869. His success in the Parc St Cloud race was followed by more victories on cinder cycle tracks, which was where cycle racing grew quickest at first. At the St Cloud event Moore raced on a standard Michaux *vélocipède*, with a front wheel slightly bigger than the rear, but by the time he won Paris–Rouen he was riding a prototype bike made under the direction of a Parisian manufacturer, Jules Suriray.

It was far lighter than Moore's original bike, had ball bearings to reduce friction in its hubs, and was custom-built in the workshop of Sainte-Pélagie prison in Paris.

Suriray invented ball bearings, but needed the forced labour of prisoners to make and polish the steel balls he needed. Moore's bike also had Clément Ader patented rubber tyres. Plus its front wheel measured 48.25 inches in diameter, while the rear was just 15.75 inches. It was one of the first 'penny-farthing' bikes, which were called 'ordinaries' or 'high-wheelers'.

There was a boom in French manufacturing during the late 1860s, but it was stopped dead by the Franco-Prussian War in 1870, and bicycle development switched to the UK. With the French bicycle industry stymied, investment flowed into what at first was just a few British bicycle companies, and they became big. New companies formed, and older manufacturers started including bikes in their product range. Some even changed their names, like the Coventry Sewing Machine Company, which became Coventry Machinists so it could manufacture bikes.

The French were still leaders in bike design, but the English bought patents on nearly everything they invented. For example, a major step forward affecting racing was made by Jules Truffault, who reduced the weight of bikes he made from 25 kilograms down to 15 by using a cheap consignment of steel scabbards (sword holders) that he had obtained. By adapting scabbards, Truffault manufactured hollow forks and wheel rims, but the British bike industry bought the patent on his idea, used it to manufacture their own bikes, and paid him a small royalty for each one sold.

Getting back to racing, even though Paris–Rouen sparked some interest in France, and later in surrounding countries, track cycling was the focus in Britain. Big crowds attended track meetings, and the first race billed as the world cycling championship was held on 6 April 1874, over one mile on a cinder track in Wolverhampton. James Moore won the race from John Keen in a time of 3 minutes and 7 seconds, setting a new world record for the distance.

Across the Channel confusion reigned for several years after the Franco-Prussian War ended in 1871. There were a few short road races in 1870, mostly in Paris and Toulouse. Leon Tarzi and Jean-Marie Léotard won them, but the longest race in France in this period was only 63 kilometres, and most were around the 30-kilometre mark. Not nearly long enough for road racing to capture people's interest and imaginations. Long place-to-place races did that, something people could compare their own journeys by train or by carriage to.

The first road race in Italy was in 1870: a time trial between Florence and Pistoia. It was won by an American, Rynner Van Heste. The first Italian bunched road race appears to have been in Milan in January 1871. It was just 11 kilometres long and won by Giuseppe Pasta. The next bunched race in Italy was 46 kilometres from Milan to Novara, held in December the same year. The winner was Giuseppe Bagatti Valsecchi. However, it's always possible that there were others that preceded these races.

Documentary evidence of road racing is thin after that. There could have been races in Italy during the next couple of years, but the next race about which there is certainty was the Milan–Piacenza race in 1873. It was 63 kilometres long and the winner, Valsecchi again, did the distance in 3 hours and 44 minutes. There were at least two more races in Italy that year, one in Florence and the other from Milan to Cremona. There's also evidence of a road race in Bagnères-de-Luchon, France.

After that the numbers of road races rose slowly until 1876 when Europe, and in particular France, was more settled. That was the year when road racing started to gain more interest, maybe because races were much longer by then. Angers–Tours–Angers, for example, was 222 kilometres long. It was won by M. Tissier, who beat a top track racer Camille Thibault using a light bike of Truffualt's design, to win in 11 hours and 25 minutes.

Another longer road race, one that still exists today, was born in 1876, this time in Italy. It went from Milan to Turin and was won by Paolo Magretti, who went on to be an eminent entomologist, discovering a number of new species of African Hymenoptera. Magretti was the best of just ten initial competitors, and the race wasn't run again until 1894. After that, editions were intermittent until 1913, when Henri Pelissier of France won. Apart from times of political upheaval, war, lack of sponsorship and on one occasion a flood, Milan–Turin has run fairly consistently ever since.

All the bikes used in races so far were penny-farthings, but racing on these was quite dangerous, given the road conditions. On a smooth track a penny-farthing is stable and not too bad to ride, but out on a road it's a different story. Hit a pothole with that big front wheel, or apply the brake a bit sharply, and you could be pitched straight over the handlebars. It was so common the term 'taking a header' was coined to describe it.

But then came the safety bicycle. Safety bicycles had two wheels of equal size, slightly smaller in diameter than most road bike wheels are today, and the rider sat balanced between them. Safety bicycles were much easier to ride than penny-farthings, so they were safer, hence the name, but the safety bicycle's appeal for racers was that they had gearing through a roller chain.

The safety bicycle was partly invented by an Englishman, John Kemp Starley. In the 1870s he was working for his uncle, James Starley, whose bike manufacturing business made one of the best penny-farthings, the Ariel. But Starley junior saw the danger in high-wheeled bikes, and the fact that they were tricky to get on and off and to handle. He thought there had to be a better, more stable, way to go cycling.

In 1876 John Lawson designed a bike with equal-sized wheels, where treadles transferred the rider's leg power to the rear wheel, but treadles are complicated and heavy. Starley thought that Lawson was on the right track, but treadles were the wrong way to drive the rear wheel, so along with fellow enthusiast William Sutton they came up with the 'Safety Bicycle'. Drive came from pedals on cranks turning a chain-wheel, or chainring as it's more commonly known today. The chain-wheel was connected by a roller chain to a sprocket on the bike's rear wheel, and the chain-wheel was bigger than the sprocket, so every pedal revolution meant several revolutions of the rear wheel. That is basic gearing, and it meant that for the first time a bike's potential speed was determined solely by the power its rider applied to the pedals, not a combination of that and the size of its direct-drive wheel.

Safety bicycles made cycling more popular because riders could place their feet on the floor while they were still seated on their bikes. This increased people's confidence in them. Once under way, safety bicycles were easier to ride and control than penny-farthings, which made them much safer. Safety bicycles saw an increased uptake of cycling among women, and they played a big part in the emancipation movement, which is well documented in other books.

Road racers first saw the benefits of safety bicycles in 1877, the year that Starley and Sutton founded their company, when a Bordeaux bike mechanic called Georges Juzan covered 100 kilometres from Bordeaux to Libourne and back in 4 hours and 40 minutes. He rode a French version of the safety bicycle, proving they were ideal for covering long distances. And long-distance rides were how road racing became well established.

People understood long-distance rides by comparing them with their own experiences. One hundred miles back then was like a thousand now. The less well-off rarely travelled far, while for the rich a 100-mile carriage ride, even a rail journey of that length, was an undertaking. By helping cyclists cover long distances relatively quickly the safety bicycle was pivotal in the development of road racing in Europe.

British cyclists already did long rides on penny-farthings, and 100 miles became the mark of the serious British cyclist. It's the same for cyclists today. One hundred miles is a challenge, but doable on a bike. The safety bicycle made 100 miles more accessible, and it provided a jump in performance for those who wanted it.

In 1878 Frank Dodds set a British 100-mile record on a penny-farthing of 7 hours, 18 minutes and 15 seconds. His time stood for six years before George Smith broke it riding a Kangaroo brand safety bicycle made by Hillman, Herbert and Cooper Ltd. The following year, on an improved version of the Kangaroo, Smith reduced his 100-mile record by nearly 6 minutes. Then, on 20 October 1885, Teddy Hale knocked almost half an hour off Smith's record by riding 100 miles, again on a Kangaroo safety bicycle, in 6 hours, 39 minutes and 5 seconds.

That sealed the reputation of the 'safety' for speed on the road, and more manufacturers started making them. To show it was best, and hopefully sell more, manufacturers employed top racers to ride their bikes, sowing the seeds of professional road racing. In 1886 the Rudge Bicyclette became the pre-eminent safety bicycle, due mainly to the efforts of H. O. Duncan. He was a British racer who settled in France to compete in a growing programme of long road races there, against a growing number of top riders – men like De Civry, Medinger and the first big star of road racing, Charles Terront.

Terront was born in St Ouen in 1857 and took up cycling with his brother Jules. Success came almost immediately. Charles won eight races in 1876, including Paris–Pontoise, where despite being only 19 years old he beat a well-established star in Camille Thuillet, covering 62 kilometres in 2 hours and 53 minutes. Terront was described in *Le Vélocipède Illustré* as wearing 'a spotted shirt, coloured breeches, black and white stockings and a magnificent red scarf flung over the top'.

Terront started racing on a Michaudine Vélocipède, similar to the one James Moore rode when he won the St Cloud race in 1868, and he graduated through the racing ranks by riding bigger and better penny-farthing bikes in road and in track races. But Terront switched to a safety bicycle as soon as they proved to be faster. His fame grew rapidly, and Terront's racing career coincided with a huge growth in interest in cycling. Soon books were being written on the subject, and more cycling newspapers were founded. The distances of races grew rapidly too.

Cycling fans loved reading about their champions struggling through long, gruelling races, defying the odds, suffering setbacks and yet still coming through to glory. The fascination was such that newspapers begin to vie for who could organise the longest, most gruelling race. This gave rise to two incredible road races, which in different forms still exist today. They aren't races now, but are long-distance challenge rides. They aren't run every year; one was so long it was never made into an annual event.

The first race is Bordeaux–Paris, a 572-kilometre slog from the southwest of France to the nation's capital, which was first held in 1891. It was a tough journey by train in those days, but unimaginable on a bike. And it was raced all in one go. The clock started in Bordeaux and it stopped in Paris; if riders stopped to eat or sleep the clock carried on, and the stationary period was included in their time. The roads were nothing like they are now, still stage-coach tracks. It sounds overwhelming, but there had already been a lot of long-distance track races, as well as the growing number on British roads.

Long-distance track cycling took a big jump in profile in 1878, when David Stanton, a gambler and a professional racer, bet that he could ride 1,000 miles inside six days. His attempt took place in the Agricultural Hall in London's Islington, and the man who took his £100 bet was called Davis. A flat, oval track was marked out inside the hall, and Stanton rode his penny-farthing bike round and round it.

Planning on riding up to eighteen hours a day, Stanton completed 172 miles on the first day, and 160 miles on each subsequent day until he hit 1,000 miles with 27 minutes left of the sixth day. His total riding time was 73.5 hours, giving an average speed of 13.6 miles per hour.

Watching a man ride in circles on a big bike at thirteen and a bit miles per hour doesn't sound like a spectacle now, but Londoners flocked to watch Stanton. Another six-day race was quickly organised in the Agricultural Hall, but with other competitors involved. They were cyclists and one horse rider, who won with 969 miles covered in six days. The first cyclist was 59 miles behind the horseman, and all the cyclists complained because the horseman was allowed to change mounts as each one grew tired.

The result stood, but no more horses were allowed in six-day races, while the Agricultural Hall became a regular venue. The next six-day race held there had ten cyclists competing, including Charles Terront, and a Sheffield rider called W. Cann, who won with 1,060.5 miles. His prize was £100, which is worth about £12,000 now. The public loved it, and in April 1879 a race billed as the six-day world championships was held at the same venue. George Waller of Newcastle won with 1,172 miles, including 261 miles ridden on the first day. Events came thick and fast after that. The six-day distance record grew and grew, and so did the riders' fame. Soon there were six-day races in other British cities, then in Europe and in America, where it really took hold.

But while that was going on inside halls and stadiums, British long-distance road races were growing in number. Many were run over set distances, 50 and 100 miles, but in the most popular races competitors rose as far as they could in 12 or 24 hours.

George Pilkington Mills quickly became the man to beat in all long-distance road races. He started cycling aged 12, and in 1885, when he was still only 18, Mills set a new British 24-hour record of 259 miles in the Anfield Cycling Club race, riding a penny-farthing.

Mills won the Anfield 24-hour again the following year, then between 5 and 10 July 1886 he rode from Land's End to John O'Groats, just over 900 miles in the days before bridges shortened it, in a new record of 5 days and 1 hour. Again, Mills rode a penny-farthing, but he was slowly changing his mind about what was the most efficient and fastest way to go racing. Mills set his last record on a penny-farthing on 5 August 1886, when he did 273 miles in 24 hours.

A few days later he started another 'End to End', as the Land's End to John O'Groats record is called. This time he rode a three-wheeled version of the safety bicycle, which some long-distance road racers preferred because of its stability. Mills set a new tricycle record of 5 days and 10 hours, but he still wasn't done for the year. In September 1886, along with his partner A. J. Wilson, Mills broke the British tandem tricycle records for 50 and 100 miles. Then on 5 October Mills switched to a safety bicycle and set a new 24-hour figure of 295 miles. Six long-distance records in one year must be a record in itself.

But as time went on, although still setting records, Mills was pushed hard by a club-mate: Montague Holbein, who broke a number of Mills's records as well as setting new ones of his own. That's why Mills and Holbein, along with Selwyn Edge and J. E. Bates, all members of the North Road Cycling Club, were invited to take part in the first ever Bordeaux–Paris race by its organisers, a newspaper called *Le Véloce Sport*.

When the British riders were invited, Bordeaux–Paris was scheduled to be a professional race, but Mills and the other Brits were amateurs. So the National Cycling Union (NCU), which like so many early British sporting bodies didn't approve of professionalism, asked the French organisers to change the race's status and only allow amateurs to enter.

They did, and the first ever Bordeaux–Paris, held on 24 May 1891, was a race for amateurs only. The 38 entrants started at 5 a.m. from the Pont Bastide in Bordeaux. As well as four British riders, there was one Swiss, one Pole, and the rest were French. All rode safety bicycles apart from 56-year-old Frenchman, Pierre Rousset, who rode a tricycle.

Holbein had recently set a new British 24-hour bicycle record of 340 miles, and a 12-hour record of 174 miles. The bookmakers were impressed and made him the race favourite. To ensure everybody covered the same course, and did so entirely by bicycle, or tricycle in Rousset's case, each competitor had a booklet with fourteen towns and villages in it, which had to be signed by race officials and stamped at the fourteen designated towns and villages. Gold medals and *objets d'art* were offered for the first ten to arrive in Paris. Silver medals and palm branches were given to each of the next finishers, if they arrived within three days of starting. Bronze medals were awarded to finishers inside four days, and there were diplomas for those inside five days.

The race started in the dark and fog. There were few spectators early on, but a big crowd awaited the riders at Angoulême, where the four Brits arrived together at

10.30 a.m. They had a good lead, and stopped for five minutes. They ate soup, replenished the stores of food they carried with them, had their control books stamped and signed by officials, then remounted and rode off into the grey gloom.

A Frenchman, Henri Coulliboeuf, was next to arrive at 10.55 a.m., then Joseph Jiel-Laval at 11 a.m. He was half an hour ahead of the next rider, and tricyclist Rousset rolled into Angoulême around 1.45 that afternoon.

Pacers could join the race at Angoulême, and after meeting his first one, Lewis Stroud, Mills tucked in behind him and drew away from his compatriots. By the time he reached Châtellerault, Mills led by half an hour from Holbein, then Edge, and then Bates. And so it went on, Mills drawing further ahead as pacemaker after pacemaker relayed him towards Paris, where Mills passed the finishing post 26 hours and 36 minutes after he'd set off from Bordeaux. The total distance ridden was 356 miles.

It was a very professional and disciplined display by the British amateur. As well as having fast pacers, Mills spent minimal time when he stopped at controls, just taking morsels of food. He carried anything else he needed with him. The race was big news in Britain, and several British newspapers followed it, placing journalists at various points along the route. At Tours the *Birmingham Daily Post* correspondent noted that 'Mills swallowed a dog-mouthful of finely-chopped meat and drank a bottle of specially-prepared stimulant.'

British riders took the first four places. Holbein was second in a time of 27 hours and 52 minutes, Edge was third in 30 hours and 10 minutes, and Bates was fourth, just 8 seconds behind him. The first French rider, Jiel-Laval, was fifth, nearly two hours behind Bates. And the stately Rousset? He finished 15th on his tricycle in 63 hours and 29 minutes.

The race was a great success, and Bordeaux–Paris soon became a professional race and a fixture in the pro calendar. For a while it was considered one of road racing's classics, especially from 1945 onwards, when competitors were paced for the last two-thirds of the race by men riding small motorbikes called Dernys, after their inventor Roger Derny. Pacing was preserved in Bordeaux– Paris long after similar marathon bike races died, because it meant they covered the distance in a reasonable time, but the race required specific and dedicated training which, as the sport developed, fewer riders were prepared to do. The last Bordeaux–Paris was in 1988.

Le Véloce Sport achieved a coup by staging Bordeaux– Paris, which was irksome to Pierre Giffard, the editor of *Le Petit Journal*. So in response he came up with something absolutely staggering, something he hoped would make *Le Véloce Sport*'s 572-kilometre race pale into insignificance, and for a while it did. Paris–Brest–Paris was the longest road race in the world. The trip from Paris to Brest, near the tip of the Breton peninsula, and back to Paris is close to 1,200 kilometre and, like Bordeaux–Paris, it was done all in one go. Riders could rest, sleep, sit down to eat, do what they liked, but the clock kept ticking, and any non-riding time was included in their finishing time.

Giffard called his race an *épreuve*, a French word that can mean test, trial or ordeal. He chose the word because he saw the race primarily as a test of bikes, something designed to show the durability and capability of what was still a fairly new invention. The founding rule of Paris–Brest–Paris was that competitors must complete the course on the same bike, which had to be delivered to the organisers before the start. Identifying seals were placed on each bike and on its parts, and the bikes were kept in *parc fermé* conditions until the start. That doesn't happen in cycling any more, but the French stuck with *épreuve* as a word to describe bike races. It helps convey the sense of bike races being tests of man or woman and machine.

When news of Paris–Brest–Paris got out, entries came from abroad and from a few women, but they were all refused. So, on 6 September 1891, a group of 207 Frenchmen set out from Paris and headed for Brest. There were ten riding tricycles, four on two tandems, and one die-hard listed as Monsieur Duval who was riding a penny-farthing. The other 192 competitors raced on safety bicycles. Amateurs and professionals were mixed together, but the pros were allowed up to ten pacers each to meet them at different points along the way. The pacers carried extra food and drinks for their riders. Racers weren't allowed to swap bikes with anybody, but they could make repairs, so long as they did them without help.

Charles Terront raced without sleep for 71 hours and 22 minutes to win the first Paris–Brest–Paris by almost eight hours. Ninety-eight riders battled through to finish behind him. Some competitors took days longer than Terront, sleeping in hotels overnight. It was a success. The race captured the imagination of people who lined the route and followed the riders' progress through newspaper dispatches and reports.

Ten thousand people welcomed Terront at the finish line in Paris, and Giffard waxed lyrical about the race in *Le Petit Journal*: 'For the first time we saw a new mode of travel, a new road to adventure, and a new vista of pleasure. Even the slowest of these cyclists averaged 128-kilometre a day for ten days, yet they arrived fresh and healthy. The most skilful and gallant horseman could not do better. Aren't we on the threshold of a new and wonderful world?'

Giffard was bewitched by cycling, and in 1896 he joined the cycling newspaper *Le Vélo* as joint editor with Paul Rousseau. *Le Vélo* was founded in December 1892, and was the pre-eminent source of cycling news and information in France until 1903. By then, though, it had picked a battle with a rival, which *Le Vélo* lost badly.

But going back to Paris–Brest–Paris, it was a victory for Terront, but also a victory for the bicycle, and for pneumatic tyres. The first two riders, Terront on Michelin and Jiel-Laval on Dunlop, both used pneumatic tyres, which were relatively new. They both had punctures, and took around one hour each in total to repair them, but the tyres were demonstrably faster than solid tyres when they were rolling. Above all, though, Paris–Brest–Paris was a victory for long-distance road racing.

The following year, 1892, saw the return of Bordeaux–Paris, and the race was repeated annually, apart from 1955, 1971 and 1972, and during the two World Wars, until 1988. Paris–Brest–Paris, however, because it was longer and harder to organise, was run only every ten years, the next edition being in 1901. By then the race was so famous the organisers commissioned a top pastry chef, Louis Duran, to invent a cake for it. It was called Paris-Brest and is still a popular dessert in France today. It's even been made by contestants of the *Great British Bake-Off* TV programme.

After a relatively slow uptake, by the last decade of the nineteenth century road racing was becoming a feature of European life. Races were analysed in the press, riders written about, their thoughts recorded and their performances and characters dissected and discussed. More long races were organised: Vienna–Berlin, Rennes–Brest, Geneva–Berne, Paris–Besançon and Lyons–Paris–Lyons. All have disappeared from the race calendar now, but some races born in the early days of road racing still exist.

Milan–Turin, first run in 1876, is the oldest race from this period still in existence. Two others born a little later have grown to become two of the five single-day races called the monuments of cycling. They are Liège–Bastogne–Liège in Belgium, and Paris–Roubaix in northern France.

Liège–Bastogne–Liège was first held in 1892, a race for amateurs that actually ran from Spa, close to the city of Liège, south through the green hills of the Ardennes to turn at Bastogne, then head back to Spa. Liège is the capital of the French-speaking Walloon region of Belgium, and according to legend Bastogne was chosen as the southern turnaround because it was the furthest point the Liège-based organisers and cycling officials could reach by train which would still allow them to check the riders through and return in time for the first riders to finish.

Liège soon replaced Spa as the start and finish, and the race became about its hills, which are anything from 1.5 to 3 kilometres long. They are very British hills; in fact, the Ardennes are a bit like the North York Moors or the Scottish border country. It took a while for the race to get the shape it has today, where the selection and order of the climbs vary only slightly from year to year. Then again, it took Liège–Bastogne–Liège a while to get going at all.

A Liège man, Léon Houa, won the first three editions, after which it was shelved from 1895 to 1907. Two more editions were run in 1908 and 1909, then nothing in 1910. After that there were three more, 1911, 1912 and 1913, then nothing for the whole of the First World War.

There is even some dispute about when professionals were first allowed to take part. Some authorities put it as early as 1894, others say as late as 1919.

The reason for the on-off start of Liège–Bastogne–Liège was because cycle racing in general went through a hard time in Belgium during the very early twentieth century. Velodromes closed in both the Walloon and Flanders regions. The number of road races dwindled, and the best Belgian riders had to compete in other European countries for foreign sponsors in order to make a living.

The next big race, Paris–Roubaix, was created to publicise a new velodrome. Track cycling had moved from flat cinder tracks, or indoor ovals, to tracks with straights and bankings, which allowed faster and more exciting racing. Some tracks were indoors, similar to new velodromes today, but bigger banked tracks of 400 to 500 metres a lap were in big open-air velodromes. There were a lot in northern France, and they were in competition with each other to get the paying public to come through their gates to watch their racing.

Many early road races finished in velodromes, but Paris–Roubaix is the only big one that still does, albeit on a newer track in a slightly different position to the original. The original Roubaix velodrome was at the junction of Rue Verte and the main road from Hem, not far from Paris–Roubaix's route into town today. It was built by two local textile magnates, Maurice Perez and Théodore Vienne, to make money.

Perez and Vienne needed to publicise races at their velodrome. When the Roubaix track opened in 1895, the legendary African-American sprinter Major Taylor made one of his first European appearances. Perez and Vienne had other big events planned, but needed publicity because velodromes in nearby Lille and Valenciennes put on good meetings too. They thought that hosting the finish of a big road race from Paris could grab attention away from their rivals. With the help of the major French cycling publication *Le Vélo*, Perez and Vienne put on the first Paris–Roubaix in 1896.

The route was different to today, but it was still a race of cobbled roads. The difference was that in 1896 the organisers didn't have to look for cobbles; all roads in the industrial north of France were cobbled. So the race went from Paris almost directly to Roubaix. It started outside the offices of *Le Vélo*, went due north to Amiens then continued to Doullens, where it veered northeast to Arras, then went north again to Roubaix. The total distance was 280 kilometres.

Almost all the roads used in 1896 are now tarmac or concrete, which is why a modern Paris–Roubaix starts north of Paris so it can seek out the back roads, those that still have cobbled surfaces. In fact the cobbled back roads the race uses now are protected, and they are maintained by a group called Les Amis de Paris–Roubaix. Going this way and that to find those roads, and not direct from Paris to Roubaix, is why the start is now a bit nearer Roubaix as the crow flies, but not as the race goes.

Good prize money, the winner receiving the equivalent of seven months' pay for a French miner, the number one industry around Roubaix, attracted a large entry. But most had entered blind and hadn't a clue what the race held in store for them. Come to that, neither did the organisers. Paris–Roubaix wasn't long by the standards of the day, but the roads were appalling, as the man charged with finding a route quickly found out.

He was a *Le Vélo* journalist called Victor Breyer. In

planning the race he simply drew a direct route on a map, then followed it. He drove the first leg from Paris to Amiens, where he stayed overnight. Next day he set off for Roubaix by bike, and by the time he got there he thought the idea of holding a race in this part of France was mad. He was cold, wet, muddy and exhausted, and determined to send a telegram next morning to his boss asking him to cancel the race. But after sleeping on it, Breyer saw the epic potential of Paris–Roubaix. A potential the race has lived up to ever since.

However, it did not have the most auspicious start. Many entrants for the first edition had never seen the roads of the north, and when word spread about Breyer's ride, and especially as there was a lot of rain just before the race, half the field didn't start. The professional riders were all there, though, with their eye on the big first prize. Professionals were allowed to use pacers, some riding tandems, to help them, and the field soon split up across the rolling roads of Picardie. Even a lot of the roads in Picardie were cobbled, and the cobbles and weather conditions grew worse as the riders went further north.

The reason they were worse, and the reason why there were so many cobbled roads in the first place, was that the north was the heart of heavy industry in France. Hundreds of coal mines, steel mills and factories, often barely 100 metres apart, belched fire and filth across the countryside. Mining subsidence buckled the roads and warped the houses, while heavy carts lifted loose stones and spread mud and coal dust wherever they went.

Josef Fischer of Germany won the race in a time of 9 hours and 17 minutes, which is an average speed of 30.162 kph (18.742 mph). He entered the Roubaix velodrome 25 minutes ahead of the next rider, Charles Meyer of Denmark.

And when Fischer arrived, the crowd, who were enjoying some track racing while being informed of the progress of Paris–Roubaix, were shocked by his appearance. He was covered from head to foot in coal dust and mud from the roads, and with dried blood from his frequent crashes.

Apart from Meyer, only two other riders finished within an hour of Fischer. The first of them was Maurice Garin, who would win Paris–Roubaix the following year and again in 1898; the other rider was a Welshman called Arthur Linton; and both would continue to feature in the story of early road racing.

Once he'd cleaned off the mud and muck, Fischer was remarkably casual about his victory. 'The race was quite easy for me,' he told reporters. 'You must be strong to ride so far over cobblestones, and I am strong. I know that about myself.' Given his domination, and how seemingly straightforward it was for Fischer to win, it's incredible that Germany had to wait 119 years for its next Paris–Roubaix winner, which was John Degenkolb in 2015.

Promoting and/or organising road races helped make the names of many newspapers and periodicals, but it also saw an intense rivalry grow between them. A rivalry that had them trying to outdo each other with longer, bigger and more attention-grabbing races. This inter-publication war moved the sport along, and it helped write the next page in the history of road racing, with the creation of the biggest road race in the world: the Tour de France.

3

The Tour is Born

By 1894 *Le Vélo*, the newspaper that organised the first Paris–Roubaix, was the leading cycling journal in France. It had an advantage over its rivals because as well as carrying news it was also the official voice of the governing body of French cycling. *Le Vélo* published the locations and start times of all official races in France, so cyclists and cycling fans alike needed to buy it, to read race reports and interviews, and to find out where future races were being held.

Everything was looking good for *Le Vélo*. Even if some advertisers grumbled when the newspaper hiked its ad prices up, it didn't affect their need to be seen in its pages. Then, just when it looked like *Le Vélo* had French cycling sewn up, its editor Pierre Giffard got involved in something outside of the sport that ended up costing his newspaper dearly. It was the Dreyfus affair, a *cause célèbre* in which a Jewish army officer called Alfred Dreyfus was framed for treason by a section of the French military and was convicted in 1895 on very dubious evidence.

Dreyfus was sent to the French penal colony, Devil's Island. His Jewish heritage and the fact that he was born in Mulhouse in Alsace, which was then part of Germany having been won during the 1870 Franco-Prussian War, were accepted as evidence that he had passed French military secrets to the Germans. Somebody had done so; there was no doubt about that, but no direct evidence implicating Dreyfus.

There was public disquiet, and even some of the French Army didn't believe in his guilt. One officer, Lieutenant-Colonel Picquart, conducted his own investigation, and he came up with credible evidence that the real traitor was a Major Ferdinand Esterhazy. The French high command wouldn't listen, and Picquart was transferred to Tunisia to keep him quiet, but the questions he and others raised wouldn't go away. Reports of a cover-up started appearing in the French press.

A campaign led by artists and intellectuals, including the novelist Emile Zola, gathered strength and eventually won a pardon for Dreyfus in 1899, but the case stirred deep emotions. It was a massive talking point in France, with everybody having a view. There were some very public arguments and demonstrations on both sides. At one protest an influential backer of *Le Vélo*, the Count de Dion, was arrested. He was demonstrating against the campaign to pardon Dreyfus, and was alleged to have hit the President of France, Emile Loubet, on the head with a walking stick he was waving about to emphasise his point.

Le Vélo's editor Giffard was pro-Dreyfus, and had high principles. Putting principle before business, he criticised De Dion in an article he wrote for a serious newspaper, *Le Petit Journal*. De Dion was outraged, and even though he was imprisoned when word of what Giffard had written reached him, he withdrew his support for *Le Vélo* as well as all of the money he'd invested in it. Then, still unhappy, De Dion went further.

When he was released from prison after a fifteen-day sentence in 1900, De Dion formed his own sports newspaper, which he called *L'Auto-Vélo*. It was funded by his businesses, and by those of his friends who either sympathised with his views or were unhappy with *Le Vélo*'s advertising rates. They included Edouard Michelin, the biggest tyre manufacturer in France.

The new venture needed an editor, and De Dion went for somebody young and ambitious who knew about cycling. He was Henri Desgrange, a 35-year-old former racer who ran the biggest velodrome in Paris, the Parc des Princes. Desgrange had a law degree, and had started his working life practising law, but he was too adventurous to spend his life in fusty courts arguing arcane cases. He was a racer first and a lawyer second, and he came unstuck when one of his employer's clients saw Desgrange speeding around a Paris park with his calves exposed. The client complained to Desgrange's boss, who promptly sacked him.

So Desgrange changed careers, quickly becoming the head of advertising for the tyre manufacturer, Clément et Cie. He continued racing, setting the first official World Hour Record in 1895, riding a distance of 35.325 kilometres on the Vélodrome Buffalo in Paris. There had been unofficial hour records before. James Moore rode

23.2 kilometres in 1873, and Frank Dobbs did 29.552 in 1876, but Desgrange's hour was the first recognised by the then governing body of world cycling, the International Cycling Association.

While working in advertising, Desgrange wrote articles about cycling for various newspapers, including *Le Vélo*. He also wrote a best-selling book on training called *The Head and the Legs*. By the time Desgrange left advertising to run the Parc des Princes he had a big following in French cycling, and influential friends. De Dion chose well.

It was 1900, the beginning of a new century, but starting a new publication is never easy even when there are good reasons to do so. Giffard and *Le Vélo* were in a very strong position. As well as the backing of the French Cycling Federation, *Le Vélo* still had a lot of advertisers because Giffard only put up rates for De Dion's associates. And Giffard held the moral high ground because of his stand over Dreyfus.

But still not willing to make life easy for his new rival, three years after *L'Auto-Vélo* was launched, Giffard instituted proceedings in the courts that forced it to drop the word *vélo* from its title. Giffard won, and *L'Auto-Vélo* had to call itself *L'Auto* from then on. The newspaper covered many new and adventurous pursuits, but focused on cycling, and now its title said it was about cars. Circulation hadn't been great since it was founded, so how would it hold up in future? Desgrange needed a marketing plan to cement *L'Auto*'s association with cycling, the sport people were interested in.

He tried printing the words 'Motoring and Cycling' underneath 'L'Auto', like a sub-heading to help reveal the paper's content. He also listed on the front page other adventurous pursuits *L'Auto* covered, but it was a bit clumsy. With sales falling and his advertisers taking their custom elsewhere, Desgrange needed a big gesture. He needed something that would link *L'Auto* in people's minds with cycling for the foreseeable future.

The pressure was on, but then Giffard cranked things up by goading Desgrange in print. Desgrange was furious and called his staff together, telling them they needed to come up with something that would switch attention from *Le Vélo* to *L'Auto*. 'We need to do something big, a big promotion. Something that will nail Giffard's beak shut,' he is reported to have said.

Géo Lefèvre was a young reporter who covered cycling and rugby, as well as taking part in both sports. He'd worked for *Le Vélo*, but Desgrange convinced him that he'd be better off with him. Now, though, Lefèvre had his back against the same wall as Desgrange. Giffard was unlikely to re-employ Lefèvre if *L'Auto* went under. Maybe Desgrange realised that, because he took Lefèvre out to lunch and asked him what he thought they could do.

The story goes that Lefèvre suggested promoting a six-day cycle race on the road. Six-day races on the track, although popular in Britain and America, were not yet so in France, but this was never-know-until-you-try time for *L'Auto*. Lefèvre suggested the route should be in the shape of a hexagon, the same shape as the outline of France. There are other versions of what happened at that meal too, and Lefèvre himself was always vague about it. Later, when the Tour de France was part of French life, he said in at least one interview that he only suggested a lap of France for want of something better to say when Desgrange asked him.

A lap of France, a Tour de France, already existed, and

it was part of life in the centre of the country. It was a rite of passage for apprentices. The tradition began in Provence and Languedoc, where boys who wanted to learn a trade went between towns around the edges of the Massif Central. Each boy was sponsored by the trade guild he wanted to join. In each town they learned different aspects of that trade, and were looked after by women called guild mothers – not always very well. It was a rough life.

There were other precedents. For example, there'd already been a motor-racing Tour de France in 1899, but Desgrange still wasn't sure. It couldn't be done in one go with the clock running and the riders resting only when they had to, as they did in the six-day track races or Paris–Brest–Paris. The race would have to be broken into stages. Desgrange appears to have only made up his mind when *L'Auto*'s company accountant, Victor Goddet, got behind the prospect. If the guy who controlled the money thought the Tour de France made sense, then maybe it did. So in late January 1903 Desgrange wrote in *L'Auto*, 'We intend to run the greatest cycling trial in the entire world. A race more than a month long; from Paris to Lyon, then to Marseille, Toulouse, Bordeaux, Nantes and back to Paris.'

Desgrange wanted a big spectacle, a route right around the outside of France. He said the race would be broken into different legs, or stages, and run over five weeks from the end of May until 5 July. Spacing the race out like that would give ample time to recover between each leg, and maybe Desgrange thought it would maintain interest for longer, but it was too long a period for any but the top professionals to commit to. It was also probably too long to hold the public's interest. Above all,

Desgrange needed his spectacle to have mass appeal, so he needed lots of racers to provide the stories to report on. To attract more entrants he cut the duration, but not the distance, to just under three weeks.

He also put the dates back, so the Tour de France ran at the same time as what would become a growing feature of French life, the country's annual two-week holiday. That was a great decision, and would be one of the reasons for the Tour's success. It came to mean summer in France, the holidays and happy memories, and that helped the race grow.

The first Tour de France was 2,428 kilometres long, split into six stages, with between two and four days separating each one. The shortest stage was 268 kilometres and the longest 471 kilometres. The long gaps between stages helped stragglers finish and still get some rest. And, going against the trend of other road races of the day, no competitors, professional or amateur, were allowed to have pacers. They had to make their own way around the route with no outside help.

Seventy-nine entered, a mix of professionals and weekend warriors, and sixty of them took the start outside the Réveil-Matin café in Montgeron at three o'clock in the afternoon of 1 July 1903. The café is still there, on the Rue Jean-Jaurès, and a little plaque outside records the event. The favourites for victory were Maurice Garin and Hyppolite Aucouturier. Garin had won the 1897 and 1898 Paris–Roubaix, and the second edition of Paris–Brest– Paris in 1901, which was the biggest road race in the world before the Tour de France. Garin had also won Bordeaux–Paris in 1902, while the younger man, Aucouturier, was the rising star, having won Paris–Roubaix earlier in 1903.

On the morning of the first stage Henri Desgrange wrote in his editorial: 'With the broad and powerful swing of the hand which Zola in *La Terre [The Earth]* gave to his ploughman, *L'Auto*, newspaper of ideas and action, is going to fling across France today those reckless and uncouth sowers of energy who are the great professional riders of the road.' Desgrange continued writing like that for the rest of his life.

Garin won the first stage, riding 467 kilometres from Paris to Lyons in 17 hours 45 minutes and 13 seconds, at an average speed of 26 kilometres per hour. Emile Pagie was just under a minute behind him, and the rest were spread out behind the first two. The last rider, Eugène Brange, took more than 38 hours to reach Lyons. Twenty-three riders didn't get there, including Aucouturier, who dropped out with stomach cramps. He was allowed to contest the next stage, which he won, although he was removed from the overall standings.

Although the 1905 Tour de France is often referred to as the first to venture into the mountains, when it went to the Vosges and climbed over the Ballon d'Alsace, there were low mountain passes in the first Tour de France in 1903. There was one on the first stage. Not far from Lyons the riders scaled the 712-metre (2,335-ft) Col des Echarmeaux. Then on the next stage, from Lyons to Marseilles, there was a longer and slightly higher climb, the Col de la République, just south of St Etienne. Aucouturier broke away on its slopes with Léon Georget to win the 374-kilometre stage to Marseilles, while Garin stayed close enough to preserve his lead.

Garin won two more stages to round off the first Tour de France, winning 6,000 gold francs, the equivalent to nine years' earnings for a miner from Lens in the north of France, where Garin lived. The French tax rate in 1903 was less than 10 per cent. So the Tour de France set Maurice Garin up quite nicely, and it did wonders for the sales of *L'Auto*.

Before the race the newspaper's circulation was around 25,000 copies per day, but it grew to 65,000 copies during the Tour. Ten years later *L'Auto*'s average daily circulation was 120,000 copies, which rose to a quarter of a million per day when the Tour de France was on. Apart from the *Sun* and *Daily Mail*, no mainstream British newspaper gets anywhere near those figures today. Newspapers were very big business at the turn of the twentieth century. For most people they were the only way to find out what was going on, not just in the world but in their own countries, and even in their own regions.

It had been a big adventure, both for the riders and for the organisers. On each stage after the starters were flagged away, Fernand Mercier of *L'Auto* set off in his car to drive to the finish, where he would liaise with the paper's local correspondent to look after and arrange accommodation for the riders who made it through, and who wanted to continue. There were also control stops along the way that Mercier had to check, where riders submitted their official race cards for the obligatory stamp to ensure they covered the whole route. Unfortunately they didn't all cover it by bike, as the following year's Tour would show.

Géo Lefèvre had dual responsibilities. He had to help at the finish of each stage, but he also had to report on the race. The story goes that Lefèvre did this by joining the competitors at the start of each stage with his bike, then riding with them a bit to get on-the-spot reports from the top men. After talking to the leaders he slowly dropped through the field, doing interviews as he went, until he arrived at the first major town with a train service that could take him to the finish. This enabled him to jump ahead of the race and help Mercier at the end.

Riders started some stages in separate groups, and with the race decided on time it wasn't always the first across the line who won the stage. Joseph Fischer was caught being paced by a motor vehicle on the first stage and a penalty was added to his time. There was also a bit of conflict on the fifth stage when Garin and Fernand Augerau came to blows, but all in all Desgrange was happy with the race. It was a success. There would be another Tour de France in 1904.

The route was the same as in 1903, but this time people outside the race got physically involved to help their local heroes. Hyppolite Aucouturier was the first to be affected. Even in the earliest races competitors understood the advantage of slipstreaming and riding in a group to share the pace setting, but there were big variations in their levels of fitness, experience and ambition, as well as variations in the bikes they raced on. Thanks to that and the awful road conditions, the fields thinned out quickly.

So, on stage one in 1904 a group of fans waited just south of Paris. The road was lonely, so there were few witnesses around, and the fans let the first few riders through, but then, just before Aucouturier arrived, they spread carpet tacks across the road. Of course he punctured, but he fitted a new tyre and carried on, only to ride into another patch of tacks and pick up another puncture. Aucouturier ended the stage two and a half hours behind the winner, Maurice Garin, not that Garin had a straightforward journey.

Later on the same stage he and Lucien Pothier were well ahead when somebody tried to run them off the road with a car. They survived, but Garin got into trouble for getting food outside of the stipulated feed zones. The organisers told him to stop, so he threatened to pull out of the Tour if they didn't allow him to carry on doing what he wanted. They let him carry on. Then after the stage there were reports of riders getting lifts in cars, even taking the train, and an allegation that one rider was towed by a car with a cord that he held between his teeth.

It was a rocky start, and the race continued in the same way. When the riders tackled the Col de la République on stage two, supporters from St Etienne, the city at the foot of the climb, decided to stop or at least delay everybody ahead of their favourite rider, a local called Antoine Fauré. They hid in the woods – the Col de la République is also called the Col du Grand Bois (big wood) – and when Garin arrived in the lead with an Italian, Giovanni Gerbi, the fans jumped out and beat both riders up. Race officials weren't far behind, but according to reports Desgrange had to fire a pistol into the air to disperse the attackers. Battered and bruised, Garin continued, but Gerbi's injuries were so bad he left the race.

There were many other incidents. On stage three some men from Ferdinand Payan's village barricaded the street once their man went through Nîmes. It took Desgrange and his gun to sort that one out as well. The Tour was on the verge of getting out of control, and only dogged determination and help from police got the race to Paris. And once there the organisers had another problem. They had already disqualified several riders for cheating, but stories began circulating that the first four finishers in the overall standings, plus others not already thrown off the race, had cheated as well.

The French governing body for cycling investigated the stories, and it found that there were solid grounds to disqualify the first four finishers, and others. There was proof that some riders had cut the route, and others had been towed by motor vehicles for long stretches. Some had even covered part of a stage by train. There were probably more culprits, but in December 1904 it was announced that the first four overall, Maurice Garin, Lucien Pothier, César Garin, who was Maurice's brother, and Hyppolite Aucouturier, had all cheated, and they were disqualified along with five others.

That left the rider previously placed fifth, Henri Cornet, as the winner. He was 19 years, 11 months and 20 days old when he crossed the finish line in Paris, and he remains the youngest ever winner of the Tour de France and the only teenager ever to win the race. He was a good rider, who went on to win the 1906 Paris–Roubaix and come second the same year in Bordeaux–Paris, but he never won the Tour de France again.

Garin was banned from racing for two years, ten others were banned for one year, and a few were banned for life. None admitted what they'd done, at least not at the time. Garin stuck to his denials for years, but later, as an older man running his garage business in Lens, he would laugh about it with his friends, saying: 'Of course I took the train, everyone did. I was young, the Tour de France was different then. It didn't matter as much as it does now.'

In public Henri Desgrange appeared worried about the Tour, even writing that it was dead, killed by the riders who competed in it and by the public who supported them. But it wasn't dead. And anyway, Desgrange was already planning the 1905 race. The route would start at the edges of towns and avoid built-up areas as much as possible, which meant fewer people would see the race, but it also meant that big groups of people travelling into the countryside would stand out and could be policed. Stages were shorter too, eliminating the need to ride at night, but their number nearly doubled to eleven. Finally, it was decided that the overall classification of the 1905 Tour would be decided on points rather than on time. But the organisers needed something else, a grand gesture to sweep away the memory of the 1904 race and the scandal surrounding it.

The Vosges mountains in the east were very significant in early twentieth-century France. They had been part of France, and are today, but after the 1870 Franco-Prussian War, Germany took over control of the eastern half of the Vosges. The highest peaks in the range became the new border between Germany and France, and the Ballon d'Alsace is one of those highest peaks.

France wanted the Vosges back. The mountains were referred to by serious journalists and politicians of the time as 'the peaks on a blue horizon', and their return to all-French rule was an object of national desire. Their significance had already been celebrated by a motorbike race between Brest and Belfort, the eastern city that refused to surrender during the Franco-Prussian War. So Desgrange looked to the Vosges, and to its German border, and wondered if a bold statement in that direction might be the grand gesture he needed to help his race.

Desgrange spoke about the mountains to his route planner, a young journalist called Alphonse Steinès: 'We don't have to go direct from Paris to Lyons,' he told Steinès.

'Instead, why don't we take a giant side step to the Vosges and run as close to the German border as we can?'

The idea appealed, Steinès was an avid cyclist and great adventurer. He wanted to see if the highest mountain passes could be crossed in a race. After all, some adventurous touring cyclists had done so already. The Vosges weren't the highest mountains in France, but they would do for now, and his research told Steinès that the ascent of the Ballon d'Alsace ran within metres of the German border. The climb would have huge significance with the French public, making a defiant gesture against the invaders and so helping to focus public attention on the Tour de France for the right reasons.

With the route decided, Desgrange got on with what he did best, influencing opinion with words. In *L'Auto* he wrote an impassioned 'advertorial' for his race: 'Am I putting my racers in danger?' he asked. 'Not only am I asking them to climb a mountain of more than 1,000 metres; I am asking them to do it right under the eye of the enemy.' To add to the drama perhaps, he also predicted that no rider would climb the Ballon d'Alsace without walking up its steepest pitches.

He was wrong about the last bit, but it was a dramatic claim that increased public interest in the race. And interest was at fever pitch when the 1905 Tour hit the Vosges on stage two, which went from Nancy to Belfort. Six riders reached the bottom of the Ballon d'Alsace together: Hippo-lyte Aucouturier, Henri Cornet, Louis Trousselier (who was doing military service and only had a 24-hour pass to start the race, so was AWOL), Emile Georget, Lucien Petit-Breton (who was really called Lucien Mazan but raced under an assumed name because his family were wealthy and consid-ered professional cycling beneath them), and René Pottier.

The riders stopped to change to lower gears at the foot of the climb. This involved removing their rear wheels and turning them around to engage the larger of two sprockets, one on each side of the hub. Petit-Breton was distanced because he messed up his wheel change – a tricky operation in the days before quick-release hubs – but the others bent their backs into the slope and made good progress.

The rest stuck together until 4 kilometres from the summit, where Cornet launched an attack and Trousselier was dropped. Cornet went again one kilometre later, this time shaking Georget loose. Then Aucouturier let go, and it was down to two, Cornet and Pottier, with Pottier just managing to get clear and cross the summit first. The press went into raptures. If climbing the Ballon d'Alsace was meant to capture imaginations, the swashbuckling way the best riders did it was even more impressive. One newspaper called Pottier the 'King of the Mountains', and the name stuck.

The northern ascent of the Ballon d'Alsace, the one used by the Tour in 1905 and usually since, starts in St Maurice-sur-Moselle, and at the time the German border ran a few metres to the left of the road. That land reverted to France after the First World War, and today the Ballon's summit is the border of three French regions; Franche-Comté, Alsace and Lorraine, and four *départements*. There's a memorial to René Pottier, who took his own life in 1907, close to the summit café, and a clearing in the trees reveals an outstanding 360-degree view over the Vosges, and beyond them to the Alps.

The southern descent of the Ballon d'Alsace is long and quite shallow, but it twists and turns through the trees before levelling out in Giromagny. That's where

Aucouturier finally caught back up to Pottier in 1905, before winning the stage a further 12 kilometres down the road in Belfort.

Once the Tour had conquered the Ballon d'Alsace, the French journalist Philippe Bouvet later wrote, 'The Tour de France left the hills and entered the mountains, turning from an operetta into an opera.' Two stages later the race climbed the Col de Laffrey and the Col de Bayard, two outlier passes of the Alps, and public interest for that stage was even more intense.

It started in Grenoble and the climbs were both on the Route Napoléon, now the N85, the main link between Grenoble and Gap. The most common way to make the 105-kilometre journey in 1905 was by stagecoach, which took twelve hours, the coach being pulled by six horses, with four more added for each of the two climbs. The leading Tour riders, Julien Maitron and Hyppolite Aucouturier, covered that part of the stage in four hours, and then they carried on for another 243 kilometres to Toulon, where Aucouturier won.

The Alps had lots of history, lots of mythology, and now here were men, skinny men in knitted shorts and baggy jerseys, riding funny little bicycles where Hannibal marched his elephants, where Romans came to conquer. What's more, the skinny men were three times faster than a coach and six horses. By taming the mountains, cyclists became heroes. And Louis Trousselier proved to be the biggest hero of all when he ran out the winner of the 1905 Tour de France.

The Tour visited the Ballon d'Alsace again the following year, when René Pottier was once more first to the top, but this time he didn't pay for his efforts with the tendon injury that forced him to quit on stage three in 1905.

Instead he pressed on to win the race. The climb became a regular feature, with Gustave Garrigou storming up it in 1908 in a reported time of 32 minutes, a fantastic record that stood for years.

The Tour de France was a success. It massively boosted the circulation of *L'Auto*, which quickly outstripped its rival, *Le Vélo*. News of *L'Auto*'s success, and the reasons for it, spread through Europe, and in Italy two newspapers were having a similar battle for circulation to the one between *L'Auto* and *Le Vélo*. They were *Il Corriere della Sera* and *La Gazzetta dello Sport*. *La Gazzetta* had the cycling pedigree, having promoted the first editions of the Giro di Lombardia, now called Il Lombardia, in 1905, and the first Milan–San Remo in 1907. Both races were thought up by a *Gazzetta* journalist called Tullo Morgagni, who lived in Milan.

The first edition of the Giro di Lombardia was actually called Milan–Milan and billed as a revenge match between Milanese cyclist Pierino Albini and Giovanni Cuniolo. The 'revenge' coming from the fact that Cuniolo had beaten Albini in a short-lived but once important race called the Italian King's Cup. Milan–Milan went north and along the fringes of the Italian lake district, in which the race is run today, then returned to Milan. The route was mainly flat but the road surfaces were appalling. They were so bad in places that where there were railway lines running alongside the roads, riders stopped, lifted their bikes onto the bed between rail-tracks and continued riding there because it was smoother.

Marginal gains is a phrase bandied about in cycling now to describe the search for advantages, no matter how slight. Well, the winner of the first Giro di Lombardia, Giovanni Gerbi, was a 'marginal gains' guy, although back then it was just called being crafty. He went round the route in the week before the race, building little earth ramps next to the rails where there was a really bad stretch of road, and in the race he used the mounds, which only he knew about, to cross over the rails and ride on the rail bed without dismounting.

The first ever Milan–San Remo more or less followed the route of a race between the two places in 1906. That was a two-day stage race for amateurs only, but buoyed by the success of Milan–Milan, which attracted enormous crowds, Tullo Morgagni negotiated with the San Remo Cycling Club, and *La Gazzetta dello Sport* took over running the race in 1907, making it a single-day race for professionals.

Thirty-three riders, all men, set off from Milan at 5.18 a.m. on 14 April 1907. The distance was 288 kilometres, not long compared with other races of the same period, but Milan–San Remo is now the longest single-day race in the men's World Tour. It rained throughout. The best riders took over 11 hours to reach San Remo on a course that crossed the plains south of Milan, climbed the Turchino Pass then descended towards the Mediterranean. When the riders hit the coast, they turned right and headed west along the water's edge and over the headlands: the Capo Mele, Capo Cervo and Capo Berta.

The field included Carlo Galetti, Luigi Ganna, Giovanni Gerbi, Gustave Garrigou. The race finished on the Corso Cavallotti in San Remo, where Lucien Petit-Breton won by 35 seconds from Garrigou and Gerbi. Only fourteen riders got through to the end, with last man Luigi Rota finishing over three and a half hours behind Petit-Breton.

Through Morgagni and the success of his races, *La Gazzetta dello Sport* planted its flag firmly on early twentieth-century Italian cycling, but then in 1908 word got round that *Corriere della Sera* were planning a Tour of Italy, a big stage race like the Tour de France. That could have blown *La Gazzetta*'s lead in Italian cycling, so Morgagni convinced the paper's owner, Emilio Costamagna, and its editor, Armando Cougnet, to use the experience and goodwill gained from Milan–San Remo and Giro di Lombardia to organise a Tour of Italy as soon as possible.

On 7 August 1908, *La Gazzetta* announced that the first Tour of Italy, known nowadays almost universally by its Italian title, Giro d'Italia, would run in 1909. It would start in Milan on 13 May with a 397-kilometre stage to Bologna, and end on 30 May with a 206-kilometre stage from Turin to Milan. There were six stages in between: the shortest being 228 kilometres and the longest 378 kilometres.

The first Giro avoided the high mountains, but still included some stiff climbs, like the ascents to Roccaraso, Rionero-Sannitico and Macerone on stage three between Naples and Chieti. The steep Passo Bracco featured on stage six from Florence to Genoa, and the Colle di Nava was a stiff test on stage seven from Genoa to Turin. As well as top Italian racers, other competitors included the French rider Lucien Petit-Breton and the Belgian Cyriel Van Hauwaert, so the first Giro d'Italia was an international race.

Rome was the southern extent, and the riders covered a total distance of 2,448 kilometres over a period of eighteen days; 127 riders started, but only forty-nine made it to the final finish line. The winner was decided on points awarded according to the finish order of each stage. But the problem with awarding the overall victory on points is that the winner might not have completed the course in the fastest time.

That was certainly the case in 1909. Luigi Ganna won the Giro, but he wasn't the quickest over its entire route. That was the third-placed rider, Giovanni Rossignoli. If the first Giro had been decided on time, Rossignoli would have won by quite a large margin, and deciding the race on points didn't prevent cheating. Three riders were disqualified before the start of stage three because there was no record of them passing through all the control points on the previous stage. It was later discovered that they had covered quite a large section of the stage by train.

But, like the early Tours de France, the public weren't put off by such infractions. They probably added spice and intrigue to the race anyway. And going forwards, spice and intrigue created by all sorts of unfair play, scandals and downright cheating became a big part of road racing. And it still doesn't put too many off the sport.

The first Giro certainly created lots of interest in Italy. An estimated thirty thousand people watched the finish in Milan, and Ganna was a worthy winner. He'd already won Milan–San Remo that year, and he was fifth in the 1908 Tour de France. His prize money helped him set up a bicycle factory in 1912. He also came up with one of the greatest winner's quotes of all time. At the finish, when asked how he felt now the race was over, Ganna replied, 'My backside is on fire.'

Second overall, Carlo Galetti raced on a Rudge-Whitworth bike made in the British Midlands. He won the next two editions of the Giro d'Italia, but after his initial second place Galetti switched to Atala, then the Bianchi team, so raced on their brands when he won. The 1912 Giro d'Italia team race was won by Atala. The last Giro decided on points was won by Carlo Oriana in

1913. Then Alfonso Clazolari won on time in 1914, before the race was halted by the First World War.

It resumed again in 1919 when Costante Giradengo won, and from then until after the Second World War the Giro was dominated by Italians. Other nationalities competed, but they found it hard to race against the Italians, who would unite to see an Italian winner, no matter what part of the country he came from, or what team he rode for.

The Giro was suspended again during most of the Second World War, with no race from 1941 to 1945. Straight after the war Italians continued winning through Gino Bartali, Fausto Coppi and Fiorenzo Magni. Coppi's 1947 win was particularly remarkable since he'd had to build himself back up after being a prisoner of war. It also came at the expense of his arch rival, Gino Bartali.

Coppi and Bartali – they are never introduced the other way around despite Bartali being older and ahead of Coppi in the alphabet – were almost at war themselves at the time. The pious Bartali represented the ideals of old Italy, whereas Coppi was seen as a more modern man. Bartali was the hero of the rural and older Italians. Coppi's fans were younger city dwellers and business people. Before the start of the 1947 Giro, Bartali declared with typical Italian passion that to win the race, 'Coppi will have to cross my dead body.' Italy was a froth of widely differing views and passions by the time Coppi won.

The Italian stranglehold was finally broken in 1950 by a Swiss rider, Hugo Koblet. Nicknamed Le Pédaleur de Charme because of his impeccable riding style and appearance, Koblet kept a comb and a sponge soaked in eau de cologne in his racing jersey, so that he could freshen up towards the end of a race and wouldn't appear in next day's newspapers covered in mud and sweat.

But Koblet was more than a cycling dandy, he had immense class, as he proved by winning the 1950 Giro, then the Tour de France in 1951, almost entirely without team support in either race. Koblet later suffered from an illness involving his kidneys, from which he never really recovered. He stopped racing in 1958, and six years later he died in a car crash, which some say was suicide. Koblet was travelling at great speed between Zurich and Esslingen when his Alfa Romeo piled into a tree. The road was straight, weather conditions were good and it was daylight, but witnesses said that the driver made no effort to deviate from his course, or to slow down. He just piled straight into the tree.

With Koblet's victory the Giro's profile began to grow internationally. Another Swiss rider, Carlo Clerici, won in 1954, then the Luxembourger Charly Gaul won in 1956. And he did it with his trademark devastation of a Grand Tour in one stage in terrible weather. Gaul was a beautiful climber, called the Angel of the Mountains by the press, but he was also incredibly tough, which made him doubly dangerous when bad weather hit the mountains. Cold didn't seem to affect him, or maybe he could just suffer and push himself more than others.

The final mountain stage of the 1956 Giro d'Italia was cold and wet, with lying snow banked at the sides of the roads on the mountain passes. Perfect for Gaul. He was lying 24th overall, 16 minutes behind the race leader, but with 242 kilometres and several high passes, he still thought he could win. Gaul attacked halfway through the stage and danced away, impervious to anything but gaining time. The others could do nothing about it, and Gaul wiped out his deficit and then gained enough time to win overall. He couldn't even walk by the end of the stage, which finished on top of Monte Bondone and took him nine hours to complete. Only forty-nine of the morning's eighty-nine starters made it to the finish.

By 1957 another star of men's road racing had emerged, Jacques Anquetil of France. Anquetil won his first Tour de France that year, but he wasn't good enough yet to take on Charly Gaul at full force in conditions that suited the Luxembourger. Gaul crushed Anquetil and everybody else in one horrible wet stage in the Chartreuse mountains to win the 1958 Tour. Then Gaul repeated his defeat of Anquetil in the 1959 Giro d'Italia.

Anquetil was leading the race by four minutes at the start of the twenty-first stage out of twenty-two, but that stage from Aosta to Courmayeur was 296 kilometres long, and included the Col de Petit St Bernard. When Gaul hit it he went into overdrive, holding close to 30 kilometres per hour for the entire length of the climb. That was Gaul's climbing strength; he hit a high pace revving a low gear and held it there. Rivals thought they could stay with him, so they followed him, and they could stay at first. However, Gaul always rode half a kilometre per hour faster than his rivals could sustain. They hung on and hung on, in a way goaded by Gaul's pace to do so, but while he could handle it they were slowly going deeper into the red. By the time they realised what was happening they were so deep they cracked, often losing minutes. It was an infuriating way to lose.

That's exactly what happened to Jacques Anquetil on the Petit St Bernard in 1959. He followed Gaul, and because Anquetil could suffer like no other he held him until three kilometres from the summit, then he cracked – really cracked. By the summit Anquetil had lost seven minutes to Gaul, and he was ten behind at the finish in Courmayeur in the Val d'Aosta. Gaul had won another Grand Tour in one incredible day.

But that was the end of the Angel's days of cycling grace. Anquetil won the 1960 Giro d'Italia, the first Frenchman to do so, and then he won the 1961 Tour de France. He won the Tour again in 1962 and 1963, then in 1964 Anquetil won the Giro again, the first part of a Giro d'Italia/Tour de France double that year. That made him the first rider in history to repeat Fausto Coppi's 1949 and 1952 Giro/Tour doubles, and the first to win five Tours de France.

Anquetil also helped boost the international profile of the Giro d'Italia, and Eddy Merckx took the first of his five Giro victories in 1968. Then a Swede, Gosta Petterson, won in 1971. The Giro d'Italia was a truly international race now, and one that every big star wanted to win. What's more, doing the double by winning the Giro d'Italia and Tour de France in the same year became a mark of greatness.

Coppi did the double, as did Anquetil and Merckx, then Bernard Hinault; and in time Miguel Indurain and Marco Pantani would do it too. But road racing's triple crown is winning the Giro d'Italia, the Tour de France and the world road race championships all in the same year. Up until the start of 1987 only Eddy Merckx had done that; then came Ireland's Stephen Roche.

Roche's career by then could be summed up as periods of bike racing genius interrupted by accidents, injuries and slumps. He fought back from a serious knee problem in 1986, which saw him thinking he would have to give up cycling altogether, but then everything just clicked into place, literally.

Roche was sure he could win the 1987 Giro, but his team-mate, the 1986 winner Roberto Visentini, was in the way. Their Carrera team, which was Italian, had told Roche that Visentini would support Roche in that year's Tour de France, but Roche knew Visentini had no intentions of even riding the race, so he had no choice but to attack. With Visentini leading, Roche attacked and took the pink jersey from him: a move that left the Irishman isolated within his team and the subject of a hate campaign by the Italian supporters, who wanted their countryman Visentini to win, and saw Roche's attack as treason.

Roche's only allies in the race were his Belgian domestique, Eddy Schepers, and the British climbing star Robert Millar, who rode either side of Roche for as long as possible to protect him from the fans. They were his only help in controlling the revenge attacks launched by Visentini and a number of other Italians.

Roche won in Milan, the first English speaker to win the Giro d'Italia, and Robert Millar took the climber's jersey, as well as second place overall. The first jewel in the triple crown was in place. Then Roche went on to win the Tour de France and the world championships, making 1987 his golden year. Still, thirty years later, only Eddy Merckx and Stephen Roche have ever done that.

The 1988 Giro was every bit as dramatic as 1987, and its winner, the American Andy Hampsten, just as groundbreaking. Victory was founded with a display of courage and endurance on a day when it snowed on the Passo di Gavia, one of the legendary climbs of the Giro d'Italia. The stage is still referred to as the day grown men cried.

Hampsten was warned well before the start that terrible

conditions awaited the race on the Gavia, and he and his 7-Eleven team prepared accordingly. They all packed bags with warm clothing in them to be handed to them before things got too bad on the climb. But, as he recalls, they didn't know how bad it would get.

I began to realise what was in store when I descended the Aprica that day. It was pouring with rain and my clothes were soaked. In the valley I changed as much as I could, but I kept my neoprene gloves on, which were keeping my hands warm. There's no point in swapping wet neoprene gloves for a dry pair. Your body has already warmed the layer of water that neoprene lets in, that's how it works. If I'd taken them off and let my hands get cold, then I wouldn't have been able to function at all. The climb was still a dirt road from the side we climbed in 1988, and so was the first bit of the descent. As we reached the first 16 per cent uphill section I attacked. The others knew I was going to do it, but I wanted to go early and demoralise them.

Hampsten has recounted that story so many times, but says it still gives him a little shudder when he does so.

The Dutch rider Eric Breukink was the only one not broken by Hampsten's attack. He was distanced by the American but chased hard on the descent, catching and passing Hampsten to win the stage. But even the descent was factored in to Hampsten's plan. 'I took my time putting on the hat and wet-weather clothes I'd arranged to be handed to me before the top of the climb. I also worked out from the wind direction that things were going to be much worse on the descent, so I saved some energy. Breukink descended quicker than me because he had no rain jacket on, but there was no way I was taking mine off,' Hampsten says.

He made the right choice. Being conservative not only gave Hampsten the pink jersey, but it preserved his strength to defend it, and so he became the first, and only rider so far from the USA, to win the Giro d'Italia, the number two Grand Tour behind the Tour de France.

4

Racing Into the Sky

The year of the first Giro d'Italia saw the Tour de France take a big jump of its own. The start list grew from 109 riders in 1908 to 195 in 1909. The majority were French, but the numbers of Swiss, Italian, German and Belgian entrants all increased. Under pressure from team sponsors, all of them bike manufacturers because interests from outside cycling weren't allowed to sponsor riders, Desgrange allowed them to list their men together. They weren't teams as such, because riders weren't permitted to support each other or engage in any kind of teamwork we would recognise today.

There were twelve pro 'squads', ranging from Legnano and Alcyon, with six sponsored riders each, to Le Globe with one. There were also 154 'Isolés' – independent riders from France, Switzerland, Italy and Belgium, who looked after themselves, booking their own hotels, and so on, for the entire race.

The first stage produced the first ever Belgian Tour de France stage winner. His name was Cyrille Van Hauwaert and he was the first Lion of Flanders, a title bike fans in the Flanders region of Belgium bestow on the very best of their riders. However, back in 1909 they were given a much less flattering name by French fans and the press. It was a name that stuck for a good few years after that as well. Riders like Van Hauwaert were called *flahutes*, the word given to long cloth bags in which labourers carried the food they ate at work. The bags were secured on their backs by two shoulder loops, a bit like a rucksack. Many Belgian labourers were employed on a day-to-day basis, and they rode old bikes or tramped around Flanders and northern France looking for their next job, with just a baguette and maybe a bottle of cold coffee in their *flahute* bags to sustain them. They were a tough breed.

Van Hauwaert was among the first of a long line of cycling champions from Flanders, a small region with a huge impact on road racing. He grew up in Moorslede in West Flanders, the son of a brick-maker, and like so many Flemish kids he came to cycling by chance. An old bike, which he found in a farmyard, gave Van Hauwaert the freedom to explore, and later to race. He became a tough competitor, but he had the soul of a poet as well. So many cyclists have – inside Kevlar body armour maybe, but it's there nonetheless.

Van Hauwaert wrote an autobiography after he stopped racing, and this passage from it will resonate with anybody who as a kid discovered the joy and freedom of exploring the countryside by bike. He recalls setting off one day in his mid-teens to visit the nearby town of Turnhout. But once there Van Hauwaert saw it was the same distance again to Bruges, so he pressed on. Then, after enjoying beautiful Bruges, a city sometimes called the Venice of the north because of its extensive canal network, he carried on west into an area he didn't know. He describes what he saw like this:

> The road climbed, and on top of a small hill I saw ahead of me the vast green plain of the sea, which merges far in the distance into the blurred line of the horizon. Neighbours told me about the sea when they returned from excursions to it by rail, but I was so proud that my little bike had carried me to see this magical sight.

Van Hauwaert didn't win the 1909 Tour. Instead it was won by the heaviest man ever to win a Tour de France. Road racers, even big road racers, aren't big by general standards: 82, maybe 85 kilograms are what the heaviest Tour de France riders weigh. And those are the bigger sprinters and time triallists, or some big strong team workers. François Faber was massive by comparison, weighing 92 kilograms.

His mother was French and his father came from Luxembourg, so although he was born in France and regarded himself as French, Faber held dual French-Luxembourger nationality, so was technically the first foreign winner of the Tour de France. He is listed in the Tour's *Encyclopédie*, the official book of Tour de France results, as being from Luxembourg.

The Vosges were included in the 1909 race, as were the edges of the Alps, which Faber could handle, although others handled these climbs better. What played into his hands was the weather. It was very bad; cold and wet through the entire race. Those conditions generally favour big riders over smaller ones. The bigger a person is for a given height, the less surface area of skin they have in proportion to body volume, which helps them preserve body heat. Faber, whose nickname was the Giant of Colombes and who had worked as a furniture remover and a docker before becoming a pro cyclist, won three out of the 14 stages.

It was a fine achievement, but 1909 was the end for big riders like François Faber, as far as winning the Tour de France was concerned. Next year the race went into the mountains, big mountains with passes of over 2,000 metres. The Tour de France began to take the shape it has today.

Alphonse Steinès had heard of the majesty of the Pyrenees, of names like Tourmalet, Aspin and Peyresourde. He'd seen their pale grey, snowcapped silhouettes shimmering distantly in the sun when the Tour passed through the southwest. He'd read about the Pyrenees too. Maybe he'd also heard that some intrepid touring cyclists had ridden, or more likely pushed, their way over some of the highest Pyrenean passes, as the London Bicycle Club had done in 1879.

But still, only locals really knew the Pyrenees, a place where wild and mysterious legends grew. The passes were far in excess of anything tackled in competition. Steinès wanted to send the Tour over those passes, so he brought the subject up with his boss, and quickly found out that Desgrange knew little more about the Pyrenees than the same distant profile Steinès had seen.

So Desgrange let Steinès write something in *L'Auto* about the possibility of racing in the Pyrenees, just to see if any readers responded with informed opinions. They did; people who knew the mountains said that sending racing cyclists over their high passes was crazy. The mountain roads were blocked with snow for most of the year, and when it melted they were revealed to be little more than cattle and sheep tracks.

But Desgrange was more intrigued than put off. He told Steinès to go to the Pyrenees and check out a route – and what an assignment that turned out to be. Steinès drove his car from Paris to Pau, one of the gateway towns to the Pyrenees, and when he told some locals why he was there they laughed. They told Steinès about a Mercedes racing car someone had tried to test by driving it over the Col du Tourmalet, one of the high Pyrenean passes, and one that Steinès wanted to include in his Tour de France stage. Not far up the climb the Mercedes was flipped over by the rough surface.

Locals told Steinès that they were used to outsiders coming to pit their strength against the mountains, but the mountains always won. So Steinès went elsewhere for guidance. He spoke to the superintendent of roads for the region, a man called Blanchet, only to find that he also thought the idea of sending cyclists over the high passes was mad.

Steinès wanted to follow an already defined way, a trail known to drovers, transporters of goods and itinerant workers. The way is the D616 and D918 today and crosses the Col de Peyresourde, Col d'Aspin, Col du Tourmalet and Col d'Aubisque. The stage Steinès wanted would start in Bagnères-de-Luchon, at the foot of the Peyresourde, and cross all those climbs but then continue on through the foothills and the flats to Bayonne, a total distance of 326 kilometres.

Undeterred by the stories he heard, Steinès hired a local guide who agreed to help him, and set off from Bagnères-de-Luchon early one morning in his car. They crossed the Col de Peyresourde and the Aspin without too much trouble, but the Tourmalet nearly killed Steinès. They slipped and slid up the first six kilometres of the pass, then the car got stuck in a snowdrift and the guide, who was driving, wanted to turn back. It was six o'clock, getting dark and it was a long way to the summit. It was even further down the other side to Barèges, the next place of habitation. The guide told Steinès about the local bear population, before leaving him to his own devices.

True Pyrenean bears are thought to have died out now, but in the Seventies the population was augmented by Slovenian bears of the same breed, and about twenty of these Slovenian-Pyrenean hybrid bears exist today. But there were quite a few of the original bears at the turn of the twentieth century. They were a common sheep killer, and a possible threat to anyone wandering alone who might disturb one and be perceived as a threat.

With night falling around him, Steinès abandoned his car, but luckily he soon met a local shepherd, who led him on foot to the top of the pass. But then the shepherd had to turn for home, and we are talking big distances: the two main places of habitation on either side of the Tourmalet, Ste Marie-de-Campan and Barèges, are 36 kilometres apart. So at the summit the shepherd pointed Steinès in the direction of Barèges at the foot of the Tourmalet's west side, and told him to walk next to the Bastan stream. That would have taken him where he needed to go, where he had told people he would be arriving that day. Unfortunately Steinès lost his way, stumbled and was swept off course by a small avalanche.

He was discovered hours later, half-dead, by locals who started a search party when he failed to arrive in Barèges.

Even while he was having that misadventure, Steinès knew that the road over the Aubisque was nowhere near as good as the one over the Tourmalet, but he had a plan. Once recovered from his night out on the mountain, Steinès is said to have sent a telegram to Desgrange, which read, 'No trouble crossing the Tourmalet. Roads satisfactory. No problem for cyclists. Steinès.'

Then he asked Desgrange for 5,000 francs to make some road improvements he'd noted were necessary along the route. In fact he needed most of the money to help pay for a better road over the Aubisque, which was a chewed-up goat track. Steinès had previously agreed a price of 3,000 francs with Blanchet, the superintendent of roads, but he asked Desgrange for more because he knew his boss would try to knock him down. He did. Desgrange offered 3,000 francs, which Steinès accepted. He could pay Blanchet and his stage would go ahead.

With the road improvements agreed, Desgrange announced in *L'Auto* that a stage of the 1910 Tour de France would cross the Col de Peyresourde, the Col d'Aspin, the Col du Tourmalet and the Col d'Aubisque. Interest was huge. Blanchet mended the roads and built a new one over the Aubisque, while Steinès kept the secret of his night on the Tourmalet to himself.

Desgrange was still worried. He realised that the riders would be out on those high wild roads for a long time. The Tour was a race for heroes, but they needed some support. To do otherwise would be inhumane, so Desgrange introduced the Voiture Balai, the broom-wagon, a truck that would be the last vehicle on the road, there to sweep up any stragglers. And the practice has stuck. Almost every road race has at least a token broom-wagon, a last vehicle behind the race, which can pick up stragglers who can't carry on, or who don't want to.

The Tour de France broom-wagon has a symbolic role today. The last vehicle in the convoy following the race still has a broom strapped to its back doors, but modern Tour racers who drop out of the race, and it's not something anybody does lightly, are whisked off to the finish in air-conditioned team vehicles. Or in an ambulance if they have sustained injuries.

That's a fairly recent phenomenon, though; the broom-wagon served its practical purpose well into the Nineties. Photographers and, later, TV cameras would crowd around it to capture the end of a rider's race, the ritual removal of his numbers by the broom-wagon driver, and the exhausted last step into its dark insides.

Stage ten of the 1910 Tour de France got under way at 3.30 a.m. to avoid riders being out on the mountains after dark, because the big climbs were all in the first half of the stage. It would only just be getting light as the riders tackled the first, the Col de Peyresourde, but even the slowest of them should cross them all by night-fall. Steinès briefed the riders, telling them not to take risks. He also told them that the time limit would be suspended for the day. It had been introduced to keep the race more compact by disqualifying riders who finished outside a certain percentage of the stage winner's time, the percentage being calculated according to the conditions and terrain of each stage.

As the stage progressed, Octave Lapize and his team-mate Gustave Garrigou steadily drew ahead of the rest, Garrigou winning a special 100-franc prize for riding all the way up the Col du Tourmalet without once getting off to walk. The two were well ahead by the summit. Alphonse Steinès and Victor Breyer, a colleague from the organisation, then went ahead to the next and final climb, the Col d'Aubisque, and waited at the summit. They thought they'd see Lapize and Garrigou still in the lead, but an almost unknown rider, François Lafoucarde, got there first. He was riding very slowly and Breyer asked Lafoucarde what had happened. Where were the others? But he didn't reply and just plodded past, staring straight ahead.

A quarter of an hour later Lapize emerged. He was exhausted, half stumbling, half pushing his bike. He looked at Steinès and Breyer and is alleged to have spat out the single word 'Assassins'. Lapize then caught Lafoucarde, went straight past him and won the stage, but Faber did well too. He was the race leader, and had been since stage two. Lapize was second overall, but the stage that suited him far more than Faber only brought him three points closer to the giant rider. Faber finished ten minutes after Lapize, but still came in third. It took Lapize another three stages to dislodge Faber and finally win the Tour in Paris by four points.

The Pyrenees were judged a success, so the following year the Tour visited the high Alps as well. Stage four went from Belfort to Chamonix, right into the heart of the mountains. Next day the riders climbed the Col d'Aravis, the Col du Télégraphe, and then the giant Col du Galibier. When Henri Desgrange encountered the Galibier it was love at first sight. This is what he wrote about his favourite mountain climb in 1934: 'Oh Laffrey! Oh Bayard! Oh Tourmalet! I would be failing in my duty not to proclaim that next to the Galibier you are pale cheap wine. In front of this giant I can do nothing more than raise my hat and salute.'

From 1911 on, Desgrange waited at the summit every year the race climbed the Galibier to time the riders through. Near the top of the south side there's a huge memorial to Desgrange, and whenever the Galibier is in the Tour a special 'Souvenir Desgrange' prize is given to the first rider to the top.

The riders climbed the Galibier's north side in 1911, the hardest side. It starts in St Michel-de-Maurienne with the ascent of the Col du Télégraphe, a step to the start of the Galibier. Linked like Siamese twins, together they provide 34 kilometres of climbing, with a short 4.7-kilometre descent into the ski town of Valloire in between.

There's a steep upwards ramp coming out of Valloire, then about 4 kilometres of false flat, giving space to consider the massive change of scenery. This is another world. Gone are the Télégraphe's lovely tree-lined hairpins, and the pleasant summit café with its twee little garden. This is a huge landscape, a deep U-shaped valley, bare of trees and edged by enormous scree slopes, and snowcapped mountains beyond. The road barely twists, but it slowly racks up in gradient towards what looks like an impenetrable wall.

Even the great Eddy Merckx found this part of Galibier daunting. 'The long straight section through the valley is difficult to deal with tactically,' he says. 'Attacks have to be timed well before it, or after it. Because if you attack on that section it is impossible to get out of sight. You just hang out in front of the chasers, providing a target for them to aim at.'

Further and further up this section there doesn't seem any way out of the valley. Then, suddenly, at a place called Plan Lachat, the road veers sharp right and the final fierce phase of the Galibier begins. Hairpin follows hairpin for 7 kilometres of 8 per cent climbing. Until 1978 all traffic on the Galibier, including the Tour de France, passed through the oak-doored summit tunnel. But then the tunnel was shut for repair, and an extra piece of road was built over the top, where the old pre-tunnel Galibier pass went, the pass used by muleteers to get from the Maurienne valley to the villages of the Guisanne and Romanche valleys before 1891.

Emile Georget was the first rider to the top of the Galibier in 1911, and he went on to win the stage from Chamonix to Grenoble. But Gustave Garrigou extended his overall advantage on the big climb, widening the gap on his nearest rival, François Faber, from one point to ten. Faber won the next stage to Nice, with Garrigou second, but then dropped to third overall by the end of stage eight. A new challenger emerged, the stage eight winner Paul Duboc. He closed the gap further by winning stage nine as well.

The race was now in Bagnères-de-Luchon, and the next stage was a repeat of the Pyrenean epic of the previous year to Bayonne. Duboc led over the Tourmalet and looked strong, but then the story goes that he accepted a drink from a spectator, and after taking a sip he became ill. He could hardly ride and limped the rest of the way to the finish, where he arrived in twenty-first place, 3 hours and 17 minutes behind second-placed Garrigou. Within hours Garrigou was receiving death threats from Duboc's fans, and the threats increased as the race approached Duboc's home region of Normandy. His fans were convinced that Duboc had been poisoned, and that Garrigou was behind it.

Duboc recovered to win stage 11, then Garrigou won stage 13 to Cherbourg. The next stage passed through Rouen, Duboc's home city, and Garrigou was terrified of being attacked there by Duboc's fans. He even talked about giving up the Tour de France. Desgrange had to step in. He confronted Garrigou, convinced that in his worried state he wouldn't dare lie to him, and asked him outright, was he involved in the alleged poisoning of Duboc? Garrigou said no, and Desgrange took him at his word.

Next day Desgrange got a make-up artist to prepare Garrigou. He fitted a false moustache, a big hat, and gave him sun goggles to wear. He was allowed to change his racing colours, and his bike. Garrigou was unrecognisable, but just to ensure his safety in case he was recognised, Desgrange asked the riders to stay together until after Rouen, where a huge angry mob had assembled. Luckily, though, the disguise and bike riders' solidarity confounded them. The fans couldn't pick out Garrigou in the middle of the fast-moving bunch, and once safely through Rouen, Garrigou removed his disguise and pedalled on.

Duboc won the stage, then finished second, one place ahead of Garrigou, on the final stage to Paris. But Garrigou won the Tour by 18 points to Duboc, who lost 19 points on the Luchon to Bayonne stage where he fell ill. A lot of bad feeling still went Garrigou's way, especially from Normandy.

In 1912 the tenth Tour de France saw its first true foreign winner, a Belgian called Odile Defraye. He was sponsored by Alcyon, which was also Garrigou's sponsor and had signed Paul Duboc for the Tour as well. There were two other Belgians in Alcyon's 1912 five-man line-up.

A Frenchman, Charles Crupelandt, won the first stage. Crupelandt, incidentally, is the only man from the Roubaix area ever to win Paris–Roubaix. The last stretch of cobblestones in the race, a ceremonial one, is on the Avenue Charles Crupelandt, which was named in his honour. Defraye won the next stage, then took over the race lead after stage three. Octave Lapize and Eugène Christophe of France fought Defraye hard and got closer to him, but Lapize abandoned on stage nine.

Teamwork wasn't allowed in the early Tours, but collusion between different teams is harder to prove, and reports of the 1912 Tour contain more than a suspicion that the Belgian riders in the race colluded to help their countryman win. If one of Defraye's rivals attacked, the Belgians would work hard to catch him. Or they would work with Defraye but not with his French rivals. Eventually the Belgian drew 59 points clear of Christophe to win in Paris.

A Belgian victory was a step up in the international reputation of the Tour de France, but it saw the end of a points system to decide the overall classification. A rider could finish an hour in front of the next man on a stage, but still only gain one point in the overall standings, and that wasn't fair. Defraye was a consistent rider, but not the best in the 1912 Tour in athletic terms. You can't say for certain, but if the 1912 Tour had been decided on time there's a strong argument that Defraye wouldn't have won. Eugène Christophe led the race on time at the start of the final stage, but as he was already 48 points behind Defraye he didn't follow the Belgian when he moved ahead with a breakaway, and lost his theoretical time lead.

So Desgrange changed the rules. Total time to cover

the whole course would decide the 1913 Tour de France, but the change still produced a Belgian winner, when the very popular Eugène Christophe lost tons of time in the Pyrenees, through no fault of his own.

It was the first ever anticlockwise Tour de France, so the Pyrenees were before the Alps. That suited Christophe, because going anticlockwise meant that the key Pyrenean stage, Bayonne to Bagnères-de-Luchon, had its big climbs in the second half, and Christophe was an excellent climber. Previously there was plenty of distance between the last climb, Col d'Aubisque, and Bayonne, making it possible for riders to catch an attacking climber on the flat roads between the Aubisque and the finish. Now the Aubisque was the first climb, and it was followed by the brutal sequence of the Tourmalet, Aspin and Peyresourde before a short descent to the finish at Bagnères-de-Luchon.

Defraye took the race lead on stage three, with Christophe in second place. As expected, Christophe made an early move on stage six, Bayonne to Bagnères-de-Luchon. Seven riders went with him, but Defraye crashed and ended up so far behind when the Tourmalet was reached that he gave up and dropped out of the race. Christophe led with two Belgians, Philippe Thys and Marcel Buysse, after the Aubisque, which was in a terrible condition following bad weather. Several times they were forced to dismount and push their bikes through ankle-deep mud.

Buysse was quickly dropped on the Tourmalet, where Thys later left Christophe to cross the summit alone. There wasn't much in it, so Christophe descended as fast as he dared. It must have been terrifying on those old bikes. Mountain descents are so steep that nowadays, riders can reach speeds of 70 to 80 kilometres per hour without trying. Bikes in 1913 were nowhere near as aerodynamic as they are now; neither were their riders and kit. There would have been more friction in a 1913 bike too. But still, they would have descended quickly, and slowing them from any sort of speed with flimsy brakes was no joke. Christophe must have been terrified when 10 kilometres down the east side of the Tourmalet the forks on his bike broke.

He couldn't swap anything. The only way to continue in the race was to repair the fork. Christophe had learned some blacksmith's skills when he was younger, but the nearest forge was at the bottom of the climb in the village of Ste Marie-de-Campan. So Christophe picked up his bike and began to jog down the mountain. *L'Auto* said he ran for 14 kilometres to the village, although that wasn't held to be anything extraordinary, just typical of the many mishaps that befell riders in early road races. The legend of this stage grew after 1919, when Christophe lost another Tour de France due to a similar incident. And it continued growing because Christophe never did win the Tour de France. He is one of the best riders never to have done so.

Once at the blacksmith's, Christophe stoked up the forge, took some metal tubing from the smith, and made a new fork blade. It was a difficult job and Christophe needed both hands for the repair, but a forge needs regular blasts of air to keep the fire hot enough to work the metal. Legend has it that Christophe asked the boy who worked in the forge to operate the bellows for him, and doing so was noted by the officials who had stopped to see that he did the repair himself, as the Tour de France rules said he must.

With the repair done, Christophe was ready to complete

the stage, but he knew he'd broken race rules by having the blacksmith's lad help him. He knew the officials who'd watched could penalise him. The story goes that when one of them said he was going out to the village to get some food because he was starving, Christophe growled, 'Stay there and eat coal. While you are watching me I am your prisoner and you are my jailer.'

Work in the forge took Christophe three hours, after which he set off to climb the Aspin and the Peyresourde, eventually arriving in Luchon 3 hours and 50 minutes behind the stage winner, Philippe Thys. He'd taken nearly 18 hours to complete the 326 kilometres. There's a plaque commemorating Christophe's epic day in the village centre of Ste Marie-de-Campin today.

Thys took over the race lead, lost it next day to Marcel Buysse, but took it back after Buysse crashed and had to run to a village to make repairs of his own on stage nine. Then Thys began to pull ahead with consistent rather than flashy riding through the Alps, and won his first Tour de France.

Thys won again the following year in a race that was contested under the gathering threat of the First World War. Archduke Franz Ferdinand was assassinated in Sarajevo on the day the Tour started, and when the race ended on 26 July, Europe was eight days from war. On 3 August the German army invaded Belgium and many of the men who had raced in the Tour were drafted into their national armies. Not all of them survived.

5

Growing the Roots
of Tradition

By the second decade of the twentieth century cycling
had two of its three Grand Tours, and four of the
single-day races known as the monuments. Road racing
was taking root. It would have to wait until 1935 for the
third Grand Tour, the Vuelta a España, but the fifth
monument was born in 1913.

The Tour of Flanders, or De Ronde van Vlaanderen in
Flemish, was another product of a newspaper trying to
establish itself, but with some extra inspiration. The race
had, and still has, a lot to do with Flemish regional identity.

Flemish cycling, like Flanders itself, suffered during the
early part of the twentieth century. While a few road
races had been held in the region towards the end of the

previous century, interest was mainly focused on the track. But now, even the velodromes were closing.

There weren't many Belgian road racing teams, so the best Flemish road racers, like Cyril Van Hauwaert, had to ride for foreign teams to make a reasonable living. Also, there was a growing feeling in Flanders that it was Belgium's underdog; that the region of Flanders had got the bad end of the deal ever since Belgium was formed in 1830.

Language was a big source of discontent. People from Flanders speak a variation of Dutch we call Flemish but they call Vlaams-Nederlands. It's an old language with a history and a literature of its own, but in early twentieth-century Flanders, French was the language of officialdom, used for legal documents. It was taught in schools and spoken in the up-market shops of Flanders. French was also used by army officers to give orders, which caused big problems and even deaths during the First World War, so there was even greater discontent in Flanders after it.

But one very good thing happened in 1912, and it has a direct link with why excellence in cycling, and road racing in particular, is part of Flemish heritage and identity today. As we have seen, a Belgian, Odile Defraye, won the 1912 Tour de France, the first truly foreign winner. Defraye was born in Rumbeke, in West Flanders, so he was Flemish to his very core.

Defraye's victory gave cycling in Flanders a much-needed boost. A boost noted by two directors of the press group Société Belge d'Imprimerie. They were August De Maeght and Leon Van Den Haute, both of them Flemish, and they decided it might be a good time to launch a new Flemish sports newspaper.

It was called *Sportwereld*, and the first edition was

published on 12 September 1912, a few days before the Championship of Flanders, which is one of the oldest road races in the region. It dates back to 1908 and is still held every September in the West Flanders town of Koolskamp. Like Count De Dion before them, De Maeght and Van den Haute wanted an enthusiastic young cyclist to write about the sport for their new publication. They found him in Karel Van Wijnendaele.

Van Wijnendaele was fiercely Flemish, so fierce that when he began writing he changed his Latin-sounding Christian names, Carolus and Ludovicius, to Karel, the Flemish version of Carolus. He also dumped his family name Steyaert in favour of Wijnendaele, the old Flemish spelling of his village, Wijnendaele. Many family names in Flanders were derived from the places people came from. Now nobody could be mistaken that Karel Van Wijnendaele was Karel from the small village in West Flanders called Wijnendaele.

Van Wijnendaele was one of fifteen children. He left school at 14, worked for a baker and then went into service, employed by rich French-speaking families in Brussels and Ostend. He was treated very badly there, and the experience stuck with him for life. But instead of putting up with it, which was what most young Flemish people did in those days, Van Wijnendaele returned home and decided to try his luck as a professional cyclist.

He did okay, he won some money, although nothing big, but while he raced Van Wijnendaele developed a profound understanding of the sport. He really understood cycling, and he understood what it took to make a good bike racer. Years later he wrote, 'If you grow up with no frills and you know what hunger is, you grow up hard enough to withstand bike racing.'

Van Wijnendaele didn't have much schooling, but he was intelligent. He could read, so he could find out what he needed to know, and more importantly he could write. He started supplementing his bike-racing income by reporting on races in his region for a local newspaper in Izegem, then became the West Flanders correspondent for a sports newspaper in Antwerp.

By January 1913 Van Wijnendaele was the editor of *Sportwereld*, and he was working hard with Leon van den Haute at organising the first ever Tour of Flanders. The race would be run 'only on Flemish soil, and visiting all the Flemish cities', Van Wijnendaele wrote when he introduced the idea to *Sportwereld*'s readers. He wanted a Tour of the 'true' Flanders, the land at the core of the old County of Flanders, which once extended north into Holland and south into France, but not as far east as Antwerp or Brussels. The core of the County of Flanders is where East and West Flanders are today.

The first Tour of Flanders was held on 25 May 1913. It started in the Korenmarkt (corn market) square in Ghent at 6 a.m. and covered 330 kilometres of cobbled roads, with a few cinder paths thrown in. The course went northeast to Sint Niklaas, then south to Aalst, then to Oudenaarde, then west to Kortrijk, then Veurne where it met the sand dunes of the North Sea coast. There the riders turned right and went along the coast road to Ostend, where they turned inland and headed to the finish in Mariakerke, a separate town in those days but now a suburb of Ghent.

Five riders came to the finish together, where they completed four laps of a big wooden outdoor track. Paul Deman, a West Flandrian, won the sprint ahead of a Frenchman, Joseph Van Daele. Flemish riders occupied the next seven places, and even Van Daele was Flemish in a sense. He was born in Watterlos, which is almost on the Belgian border and now part of the Lille conurbation, but was once a town in the County of Flanders.

The race was a success for Deman, for *Sportwereld* and Van Wijnendaele, and for Flemish cycling. The field grew from 37 to 47 riders in 1914, but it was still a struggle to put such a big race on. *Sportwereld* wasn't yet two years old, and starting any new business eats cash even without the distraction and demands of putting on a big new bike race covering lots of country. An additional problem was the major French teams forbidding their Belgian riders from taking part.

They did so again in 1914, and most of the top Belgians obeyed their teams and stayed away from the Tour of Flanders, but one Flemish rider took no notice of his team. He was Marcel Buysse, Flemish through and through and a supporter of the growing Flemish national movement. He defied his French team, Alcyon, and not only took part but became the second winner of the Tour of Flanders. Buysse never raced for a French team again. When he resumed racing after the First World War, he rode for Bianchi-Pirelli for three years, then did the next four years for his own team, M. Buysse Cycles-Colonial.

There was no Tour of Flanders in 1915, and the race didn't run again until 1919, after the First World War ended. The already ropy roads of Flanders were now shattered by bomb blasts. Hasty repairs were made, but the race distance was reduced to 203 kilometres because some of the roads that had been used didn't exist any more.

A new route was found for 1920, and the race went back up to 250 kilometres, with Jules Vanhevel the winner. The Tour of Flanders was growing in stature, with an increasing number of non-Belgians taking part, and in 1923 it had its first foreign winner, a brilliant Swiss racer called Heiri Suter. One week later Suter achieved the first ever cobbled classics double, when he won Paris–Roubaix.

Suter was the first of a new type of road racer, a classics specialist. He excelled at single-day races, winning 58 big ones during his career. They included five Swiss road race titles; the Grand Prix Wolber twice, a race once regarded as an unofficial world road race championships; the Züri-Metzgete, Switzerland's classic, six times; Paris–Tours twice; and Bordeaux–Paris once. Suter never took part in a Grand Tour, and extended his racing career from 1931 until 1946 by focusing on motor-paced racing on the track. He was 47 years old when he stopped.

By the mid-Twenties the Tour of Flanders was by far the biggest race in its region, which led to problems because hundreds of people were following it in motor cars. That was solved by an appeal to fans in *Sportwereld*, thanking them for their support and encouraging them to continue being involved in the race, but only in a responsible manner. Later, after the Second World War, the race would face a much bigger problem, or rather its organisers would.

During the occupation the German authorities allowed several things to happen in Flanders, providing the locals didn't cause them trouble, which they didn't allow in the rest of Belgium, and in many other areas of occupied Europe. One of those things was cycle racing in general, and the Tour of Flanders in particular.

The race was shorter during the war, but it had top-quality winners; Achiel Buysse in 1940, 1941 and

1943, Briek Schotte in 1942 and Rik Van Steenbergen in 1944. Schotte was a remarkable racer with a remarkable Tour of Flanders record. He took part an incredible twenty times during his racing career, winning it twice (the other occasion was 1948), and he racked up a total of eight appearances on the podium. Then, after he stopped racing, Schotte presided over five Tour of Flanders victories and eleven podium places in the teams he managed.

Paris–Roubaix was created to publicise a new velodrome in Roubaix, and it's the only big race to finish in a velodrome today. That wasn't so in the early days of road racing, when lots of races finished in velodromes. Liège–Bastogne–Liège finished at Rocourt for many years. The Tour of Lombardy, Il Lombardia, has finished in the Velodromo Vigorelli in Milan, and on a track in Como. Grand Tours stages often had velodrome finishes. The Tour of Flanders is no exception.

Its first editions finished on an open-air track in Mariakerke, but a couple of times the race finished on the indoor track located in the Sportspaleis in Ghent's Citadel Park. That track is known as the Kuipke because it's so small and steeply banked it resembles a bowl, *kuipke* being Flemish for a small bowl.

Briek Schotte's first Flanders victory was on the Kuipke, and shortly before he died in 2004 he described the 1942 race finish to me:

Part of the banking near the big doors to the Sportspaleis, where the track was housed, was removed. We rode through the doors, then up onto the track on some loose planks that were put there for the race. It was a really tricky finish, because as well as the loose planks you had to turn sharp right to get into the Sportspaleis, then sharp right again once inside to get on the track. There was never a sprint inside, the first man through those doors always won.

The Tour of Flanders continuation through the Second World War came back to haunt its organisers when the hostilities ended. Many Flemish nationalists were accused of collaborating with the Germans, and *Sportwereld* was one of several newspapers that became controlled by the Belgian government. Several journalists, most of them not sports writers, were convicted of collaboration with the Germans. Karel Van Wijnendaele wasn't convicted of any offence, but he was banned from ever working as a journalist again.

But Van Wijnendaele was no collaborator. It was love of cycling, and love of the race he'd grown from seed, that led him to continue running the Tour of Flanders during the war, not sympathy for fascism. In fact Van Wijnendaele had secretly worked for the Allies by hiding downed British pilots in his house. In response to being banned from doing the job he loved, he sought support from the British authorities, and received it in the form of a letter from General Montgomery that verified Van Wijnendaele's heroic acts. As a result he was back in the game, but straight into another fight.

Before the war *Sportwereld* and the Tour of Flanders had been taken over by the newspaper that runs the race today, *Het Nieuwsblad*. And, once the war-dust settled, Van Wijnendaele was employed by *Het Nieuwsblad* to write about cycling, and to run the race. But by then *Het Nieuwsblad* had a growing rival in Flanders called *Het Volk*, which is Flemish for The People, and it was politically left leaning, where *Het Nieuwsblad* was centrist. *Het Volk* started their own new bike race in 1945, and called it the Omloop van Vlaanderen.

Omloop and *ronde* have similar meanings in Flemish, so *Het Nieuwsblad* protested to the Belgian Cycling Federation, which insisted that *Het Volk* change the name of its race to Omloop Het Volk. So another famous Flemish race was born, although *Het Nieuwsblad* and *Het Volk* merged in 2009, and what was Omloop Het Volk is now Omloop Het Nieuwsblad. However, it still marks the opening of the Belgian racing season on the last Saturday in February each year.

So with the Ronde cracking on into the Fifties, and a new big Flemish race established, we turn to an older French race, once highly regarded but, sadly, less important in cycling today. Paris–Tours is one of the oldest races on the calendar, and until quite recently was regarded as a classic. It was first held in 1896, when it was for amateurs only, and became a pro race in 1901. After that it only missed three editions through two world wars. Like most early races it was long, sometimes as much as 350 kilometres, and in early editions it was how well riders coped with the distance and rough roads that decided the winner.

Then in 1911 Paris–Tours was switched from September to the spring, when it was billed as the revenge race for Paris–Roubaix, which at the time was always held on Easter Sunday, giving rise to another name, La Pascale, for Paris–Roubaix. So if Easter was early, difficult weather could hit Paris–Tours. The worst conditions were in 1921 when the riders had to battle through freezing cold and snow. Only eight made it to Tours, with Francis Pelissier the winner. But gradually road conditions improved, the race distance was cut and, since the direct route to Tours is flat, Paris–Tours came to be known as the sprinters' classic.

In 1951 the race moved to early October, so that it coincides with the start of the French hunting season. That's when the obligatory Paris–Tours photographs first appeared, with the peloton cruising across the treeless Plaine de la Beauce, cheered on by groups of heavily armed men with hungry-looking dogs.

Paris–Tours settled nicely into its autumn slot, and the fact that a sprinter won most years didn't upset anybody very much, apart from cycling journalists and the race organisers. Sprinters got a bad deal in the Fifties and Sixties, when they were regarded as a lower form of cycling life by the press. It was as if they thought sprinters won because they had been sneaky and duplicitous.

Happily, things have changed, and sprinting is seen in its true light today as one of the arts of cycling. Sprinters are admired for their speed, skill, race-craft, bravery and raw power. But back in more unenlightened times, a series of experiments began in 1959 designed to thwart sprinters and produce more 'worthy' winners of Paris–Tours. The organisers tried to change the race, to break it up and make it more difficult, which they thought would make it more interesting. But the changes either didn't thwart the sprinters, or they were so big they altered the whole character of the race, so it wasn't Paris–Tours any more. The event has gone back to its roots now, but with a few twists to ensure that the sprinters, if they win, don't get the race handed to them on a plate.

Tours straddles the River Loire, and the northern approach to the city, the way you arrive direct from Paris, is flat. However, just south of the Loire there are lots of short sharp hills, so for the last edition of the race in the Fifties the organisers sent the riders through Tours, across the Loire, to complete four laps of a circuit in the suburb of Joue-les-Tours, which included the Côte de l'Alouette. The race finished at the top of this stiff little hill. In a wonderful irony the winner, Rik Van Looy, was one of the fastest sprinters of his time – and he dropped the field on the final climb. But he was a sprinter with a difference; he could do other things as well. More of Van Looy later.

So even with the Alouette climb near the end, more often than not Paris–Tours was still won by sprinters. Félix Lévitan, the race organiser and joint Tour de France director at the time, seemed to take this as a personal affront. So in 1965 he tried running Paris–Tours without the riders using derailleur gears. It threw the race back to the early days, when riders had a choice of gear ratios on their bikes but had to dismount to change them. Lévitan thought that would somehow change the outcome of Paris–Tours. It didn't, not really.

That year a Dutchman, Gerben Karstens, won the fastest Paris–Tours to that date, clocking 45.029 kilometres per hour for 246.8 kilometres. Britain's Barry Hoban rode that race, and he remembers how Karstens won:

We were allowed three sprockets on a free-wheel, and to change gear you had to stop, get off your bike and swap the chain by hand. That involved loosening the rear wheel. It was quite a long process and not one you wanted to do often in a fast race. If you did you'd end up chasing all the time, and get knackered well before the finish.

I chose 51 x 15 as the gear to start with, and I was going to swap to something a bit higher later on, but the race was so fast I didn't dare stop at all. About 20 kilometres from the finish Karstens and his whole team stopped together and swapped their chains onto the 13 sprocket, and that's how he won. By all stopping at the same time his team were able to pace him back up to the bunch. Then, because they had higher gears going into the finale, we were just revved out by them, and nobody could get around Karstens in the sprint.

The funniest thing that day was Jacques Anquetil. He thought the whole idea of not using derailleurs was ridiculous, and he didn't like Félix Lévitan very much anyway. So he tried to ride all the way in 53 x 13. His team complained like mad because there were some hills in the Chevreuse Valley just after the start, and Jacques made them drop back and push him up them.

The equipment manufacturers disliked the no-derailleur rule even more than Anquetil, so it was abandoned after 1966, when a sprinter called Guido Reybrouck won anyway. But that only renewed Lévitan's crusade to thwart the sprinters. In 1974 he switched the route around, so Paris–Tours became Tours–Versailles, then Blois–Chaville, and later Blois–Montlhéry, then Creteil–Chaville, all done in an effort to toughen up the race. Eventually its identity got so lost that the race was called the GP de l'Automne. It was a debacle really; it was always meant to be the sprinters' classic, the perfect race for awarding the Ruban Jaune.

The Ruban Jaune, or yellow ribbon, was created in 1936, and is still awarded to the rider who wins a road race of 200 kilometres or more with the fastest average speed to date. Gustaf Daneels was the first holder of the Ruban Jaune when he won Paris–Tours in 1936 at an average speed of 41.45 kph. It set a precedent.

Of the twelve times the Ruban Jaune has been awarded, Paris–Tours was the race where the speed record was set on nine occasions. Amazingly, Paris–Roubaix has held it twice, and another old race once regarded as a classic, Paris–Brussels, had it once. The current Ruban Jaune was set in 2015 when Matteo Trentin won Paris–Tours at the cracking pace of 49.641 kph.

At times Paris–Tours has been a long way shy of the fastest 200-kilometre-plus road race in the world. In 1988, when it made its comeback as Paris–Tours after being routed all over the place, the riders faced a howling headwind and torrential rain that pinned them down to a 34 kph average. It was almost dark when the bunch sprinted it out on the Avenue de Grammont. The Dutch rider Peter Pieters was the winner of that slow-motion Paris–Tours; the sprinters' classic.

So far I've not written anything about road racing in Spain, because the sport was a little slower to take hold there than in most major European countries. But there were races early on in Spain, some of which are going strong today. The oldest is the Volta a Catalunya, which dates back to 1911 and is the fourth-oldest stage race behind the Tour de France, the Tour of Belgium and the Giro d'Italia.

It was another race created by a newspaper, this time the Barcelona-based *El Mundo Deportivo* working with the then president of the Spanish Cycling Union, Narcisse Masferrer. The first Volta a Catalunya was very different to the first Tour de France or Giro d'Italia; it was held in early January, was only three stages long, and totalled just 363 kilometres. The modest length and distance probably reflected the factor that held Spanish road racing back for a while: a lack of usable roads. Even as late as the Sixties, stages held to publicise the embryonic Spanish seaside resorts saw riders bussed in over rough gravel roads to ride circuits of the only tarmac strips in town.

The first three editions of the Volta a Catalunya were domestic affairs with all-Spanish podiums. The next two editions in 1920 and 1923 were won by a Frenchman, José Pelletier and Maurice Ville. After that the Volta a Catalunya has run every year, except at the height of the Spanish Civil War in 1937

Spanish racers were insular for a long time. The first Spaniard to take part in the Tour de France, Salvador Cardona, didn't do so until 1928, when by coincidence, and incredibly considering the journey they had to take in order to get there, the first Australians took part. Cardona, who won the Volta a Catalunya in 1931, was the first Spanish racer to win a stage in the Tour de France in 1929. But even Cardona didn't ride many races outside Spain, and he certainly didn't win another big one. He was content to be one of the best in late Twenties and early Thirties Spanish bike racing.

Mariano Carnado was another star of that era. He won the Volta a Catalunya a record seven times, and in 1930 won Spain's other big race, the Tour of the Basque Country, which started in 1924 and so also has a longer history, albeit interrupted, than the Spanish Grand Tour, the Vuelta a España. Frenchman Francis Pélissier won the first Tour of the Basque Country. It's a rugged race over tough terrain, and it doesn't always get the best of weather. The Basque region is close to the Atlantic coast and gets plenty of weather systems in spring. Carnado's 1930 victory was the first by a Spaniard, and the last for a while.

But that wasn't due to lack of Spanish contenders. It was simply because there was no Tour of the Basque Country from 1931 until 1935, when Gino Bartali of Italy won. Then the Spanish Civil War intervened, and scuppered the race for a long time. It wasn't resurrected until 1969, when the five-time Tour de France winner Jacques Anquetil won, but it has grown in stature since. The Tour of the Basque Country is still a very tough race, and as well as being held in high esteem it's also perfect preparation for Liège–Bastogne–Liège, and another big race in the French-speaking part of Belgium, La Flèche Wallonne.

The first La Flèche Wallonne, or the Walloon Arrow (several Belgian races have the word 'arrow' in their titles) was held in 1936. It's not as big as Liège–Bastogne–Liège is now, but at one time they were seen as being on a par: especially when both races were held over one weekend, called Weekend Ardennais.

Once they were separated, La Flèche Wallonne's profile suffered a dip because it didn't have a defined route. Where Liège–Bastogne–Liège had its set-piece climbs, and Paris–Roubaix its cobbled roads, passages of the races that fans look forward to and talk about and compare performances on, for a while La Flèche Wallonne was just a race around the hills between Liège and Charleroi. Sometimes it went east to west, sometimes west to east. It was always hard, though, and always prized among knowledgeable fans and by those who won it. It also satisfied a thirst for bike racing among the huge Italian community working in the steel mills and mines of the surrounding Meuse area. But it had no defining shape. That changed once the Mur de Huy was included in the race route.

Today, La Flèche Wallonne starts in Charleroi and heads

east on a big loop north of the Meuse, before plunging down into Huy for the first time. The race then builds in a crescendo, with three ascents of the Mur de Huy in quickening succession on the way to the finish at the top of the final ascent.

But back to Spain and the birth of cycling's third Grand Tour, the Vuelta a España. When the Tour of the Basque Country was resurrected in 1969, it was done by a cycling club from the Basque city of Eibar, a club with a history of successful race organization. The club's first promotion was in April 1932 with a race created to celebrate Spain's first birthday as a republic, called Grand Premio Republica. It was a five-stage race from Eibar to Madrid and back, and is seen in Spain as the template for the Vuelta a España.

According to Lucy Fallon and Adrian Bell in their book *Viva la Vuelta* (Mousehold Press, 2005), the idea for a Tour of Spain came from a former racer called Clemente López Doriga. He saw the press as the most likely promoters, so he lobbied them tirelessly because he felt passionately that it was time Spain had its own national Tour.

Several things were against him. Spain had terrible roads, which weren't even a fully joined-up network in the Thirties. The cost would be high and the country was poor. Finally, there was a severe lack of accommodation, especially away from the coast. There just weren't the hotels in Spain there are now, and for years accommodation for riders on the Vuelta a España was basic to say the least.

Still, López Doriga persevered and eventually attracted interest from Juan Pujol, a director of the Madrid daily newspaper *Informaciones*. Pujol was an idealist who wrote when announcing the first ever Vuelta in 1935 that it would be 'an incarnation of patriotic exaltation'. Spain was in turmoil and just over a year away from civil war, but Pujol was undeterred.

On Monday, 29 April 1935, fifty riders lined up at one of the Madrid gates to start the first Vuelta a España. It was a good field, but not the best in the world because the 14-stage race finished in Madrid only three days before the Giro d'Italia started in Milan. For a long time its location in the calendar stifled the Vuelta as a truly international race. An April start and May finish meant it was crammed between the northern classics and the start of the Giro d'Italia. So the Vuelta, while always important to Spanish teams, was less so for other nations.

It became a race that the great riders of each generation would do during their careers, and try to win, but unless they were Spanish it wasn't one they did every year. Even some Spaniards didn't do it every year. The five-time Spanish Tour de France winner Miguel Indurain started the Vuelta nine times during his thirteen-year career, but only finished four, with a best placing of second overall in 1991.

Things began to change after 1995, when the Vuelta was swapped to late August/early September. Then, when the UCI World Tour was formed, it included the Vuelta as one of the three Grand Tours. All World Tour teams must take part in all World Tour races. So now, although it's still the third Grand Tour in status behind the Tour de France and Giro d'Italia, the Vuelta a España is a great race, often a very interesting one, and it's on the rise.

But going back to its origins, of the fifty riders that started the first Vuelta, thirty-two were Spanish, six were Belgians, four were Italians, plus two each from France, Austria, Switzerland and Holland. Mariano Carnado carried the home nation's hopes. He was a strong, powerfully built rider from Navarra.

The other top Spaniard in 1935 was very different to Carnado, but far more typical of the best Spanish road racers. Spain is famous for producing tiny climbers, who sprout wings when the road goes uphill. However, at 1.57 metres tall and weighing just 50 kilograms, Vicente Trueba was so tiny he was nicknamed the Torrelavega Flea. He was already more famous outside Spain than Carnado, because in 1933 Trueba became the first ever King of the Mountains in the Tour de France. There had been a mountains prize before, but this was the first year it was given a title.

There were other good Spaniards in the race too, but it was a Belgian, Antoon Digneff, who won the first stage of the first Vuelta, and another, Gustaaf Deloor, who won overall. He was impressive too, winning a really tough stage through the Cantabrian Mountains that went from Santander to Bilbao. Carnado was his closest rival, while the rest of the Spaniards were burned up by the strength of the Belgians.

The weather was a factor that year. It was cold in the mountains of the north, which is to be expected in April, but it even rained on stage 10 in Andalucia, when the Austrian rider Max Bulla won a stage to Granada. Carnado kept fighting but he seemed to have terrible luck, crashing several times on the terrible Spanish roads, as well as having plenty of mechanical problems.

Even the final stage through the Sierra de Guardarrama to Madrid was hit by drizzle, making it really cold high up. Carnado attacked once more, but took Deloor and Bulla with him. Deloor won the stage, which finished on the velodrome in Madrid's Casa de Campo, the city's largest park. His brave efforts throughout, and especially on the final stage, saw Carnado finish second overall to Deloor, with Antoon Dignef third.

The second Vuelta a España saw big changes. The average length of the stages was reduced from 245 kilometres to 207, but the number of stages increased from fourteen to twenty-one, making it a three-week race. Growing unrest in Spain saw only eight foreign entries, four Italians and four Belgians, and the weather was bad again. Gustaaf Deloor took his second overall victory, with his brother Alfons in second place. And that was it for la Vuelta, because six weeks after the 1936 race a coup d'état brought about the start of the Spanish Civil War. The next Vuclta a España was held in 1941.

The country was now under the dictatorship of General Franco, which lasted until his death in 1975, and it affected all walks of life in Spain, including cycling and the Vuelta a España. It saw a lot more Spanish winners, but not just because Spanish cyclists were improving; foreign riders were less keen on racing in Spain because of the conditions there.

It struggled through the Forties, and by 1950 only forty-two riders entered, with five Belgians and three Italians the only foreigners. There were twenty-four stages, but the racing was so dull that the few sponsors supporting it pulled out. There wouldn't be another Vuelta a España until 1955, when there was a landmark edition.

For a start the field was 100 riders for the first time in the race's history. There were sixty-two Spanish, twelve French, twelve Italian, six Swiss, two German, and six British riders. That was a big breakthrough because proper road racing had only just become established in the UK –

but more about the reasons why that was so in a later chapter.

By 1955 Spain had enough riders to field three complete teams, and their A-team was formidable. It was headed by two men, Jesus Lorono and Federico Bahamontes, Tour de France Kings of the Mountains in 1953 and 1954 respectively. They were both terrific climbers, and Bahamontes was one of the best of all time, but they were very different personalities, and that led to a stinging rivalry. Lorono was Basque; quiet, dignified and stoical. Bahamontes was from Toledo; hot-blooded, volatile and sometimes fragile.

The very fast and talented Miguel Poblet was also in the Spanish A-team. He was a rare thing in Spain in that he was a fast sprinter who excelled in single-day races, but he was still capable of winning the Vuelta, if the dice fell in his favour. There were two support riders, Francisco Massip and Bernardo Ruiz, as well as the very experienced Julian Berrendero, the Vuelta winner in 1941 and 1942.

Despite all that Spanish firepower, however, stage one was won by Gilbert Bauvin of France. Stage two broke with tradition and finished outside Spain for the first time. Bahamontes and Lorono launched a two-pronged attack on the Jaizkibel climb, famous now for the part it plays in Spain's biggest single-day race, the San Sebastian Classic. Bauvin went with them and won his second consecutive stage on home turf in Bayonne, France, but his glory was short-lived.

Lorono took over the race lead the next day, but the French hit back on stage four, a relatively easy one from Zaragoza to Lerida. They attacked from the start and kept on attacking, while the Spanish had nothing but mechanical problems. Afterwards the recriminations started, with the Spaniards blaming each other for the lack of joined-up team thinking. Raphael Geminiani of France now led the race. The Spanish had more bad luck, while the lead passed within the French team from Geminiani to Jean Dotto, who ended up the first foreign winner of the Vuelta a España.

A new Spanish team manager, Luis Puig, was appointed, but at first he wasn't any more effective at getting the Spanish national team to work together. An Italian, Angelo Conterno, won the 1956 Vuelta, and then Jesus Lorono won for Spain in 1957, after which the Vuelta went through a transition in the late Fifties and early Sixties, from a national/trade-team mix to being contested by all trade-sponsored teams. Contrarily, it was when trade teams took over that the Spaniards often acted as one if they were threatened by a common rival. The man who suffered most at the hands of this occasional cross-team loyalty was Britain's Robert Millar, as we will see shortly.

By 1964 the Vuelta was much more international, and well established, although conditions were still primitive when Barry Hoban became Britain's first stage winner in the Vuelta. These are his reflections from his 2015 autobiography, *Vas-y-Barry*:

The 1964 Tour of Spain started in Benidorm. It took several train changes to get there, but what a difference Benidorm was then to what it is now. There was just a fishing village and the bay, which now has rows and rows of high-rise hotels. There was nothing like that then. I think the hotel we stayed in was three or four storeys high, and that was the biggest building in Benidorm.

The first stage was a 42-kilometre criterium followed by an 11-kilometre time trial, both run on the one and only road in Benidorm. It was a promotional event really. They had plans for Benidorm, so having the first stage there was an early part of those plans. There wasn't even a proper road into and out of town. The main road was eight kilometres away, with no link road, so for the first stage proper we all got into the team cars and we were driven out of Benidorm, to start 10 kilometres away where the main road began.

It was my first Grand Tour, which is enough to take on, but Spain was a very different place in 1964. The country was still a dictatorship and full of policemen and priests. They used to tell a joke that when the Americans first got to the moon they found a Spanish priest. The Americans asked the priest how he got there, because Spain doesn't have any rockets. He said: 'We don't need rockets, we got a policeman and a priest, a policeman and a priest, a policeman and a priest, one on top of the other's shoulders, until we reached the moon.' You'd go mile after mile in the race and the road was lined with policemen either side. And if any of the crowd tried to push through, they just took their batons out and whacked them one.

Franco's Spain was pre-package tour Spain, there were no hotels of much significance, especially away from the coast. The interior of Spain was actually a bit daunting. We finished one stage in the centre of Spain's coal mining area, and the town looked like going into Blaenau Ffestiniog in a thunder storm in the middle of the night; it was horrendous. We stayed in this apartment block with dingy, badly lit corridors. It was basic, like you'd find in the Eastern bloc countries. Nothing like you get in Spain today. The food was particularly bad, not that it was all that good anywhere else back then.

Diet never came into our lives very much, you ate

what you got, and we ate a lot of carbohydrates. We ate lots of rice, and sometimes the meat was a bit suspicious, so I just had a plate full of rice, and I'd get some eggs, soft boil them, take them all out of the shell, chop them up and grate some cheese on top, and that would be my meal. I also carried these big bags of muesli around with me. I've ridden a stage race on muesli and yoghurt after seeing what came out of the kitchen. It certainly wasn't anything like it is today; it was very, very basic.

Robert Millar was the first British rider to win a major Tour de France classification, the 1984 King of the Mountains. He also finished fourth overall in that Tour, which made him the highest ever British Tour de France finisher until Bradley Wiggins equalled it in 2009. Wiggins was later promoted to third when Lance Armstrong was stripped of his 2009 third place, as well as almost everything else he'd won. But that point became less relevant when Wiggins won the 2012 Tour de France, the first ever British winner.

Millar wasn't just the best British Grand Tour rider of his generation, he was one of the best in the world. He really should have won the 1985 Vuelta a España, but didn't because of Spanish inter-team collusion. Millar had worked his way into the race lead by stage ten. It was never a big lead; he was just 10 seconds clear of Spain's Francisco Rodriguez, and 1 minute and 15 seconds ahead of Pello-Ruiz Cabestany. But he looked in good shape, because neither rider was a good enough climber to distance Millar in normal circumstances. Rodriguez tried, but he couldn't drop the Scot.

Then on the penultimate stage Millar punctured at the foot of a climb. Not a problem in itself, but when he caught the group of riders he'd been with, some in it congratulated him and acknowledged that he would be the overall winner. What nobody told Millar was that two riders had attacked and left the group. What's more, they were well ahead and quickly gaining time.

The escape wasn't announced on race radio either, and it wasn't on any of the marshal's blackboards that informed the different groups on the road where everybody was, back in the days before race radios. Neither did Millar's team manager Roland Berland, who was following the Millar group in the Peugeot team car, know about the attack.

The attackers were two Spaniards, José Recio and Pedro Delgado. The stage covered some of Delgado's home roads, and he was sixth overall, six minutes behind Millar, so was dangerous. Delgado gained most of that time back before Millar and Berland found out what was going on. Millar began to chase, but nobody in the group would help him, while up front Recio was really helping Delgado, despite them being in different teams. Delgado rewarded his compatriot with the stage win, because they gained enough time for Delgado to take the Vuelta lead by 36 seconds. Robert Millar fell to second, and that is how it stayed through the final stage.

Millar was disgusted with the way the Spanish riders combined to make him lose, and with his entire reception in Spain. 'The crowds throw things at you and spit at you because they want a Spaniard to win,' he told *Winning Magazine*:

> But I don't let them affect me, I still get on with the race. The other night, though, at the hotel in Albacete I blew my top. We had been waiting an hour for dinner, and

when it came it was food you wouldn't give your dog. The other riders and staff there couldn't believe it when I stormed out. I went down to the cake shop and stuffed myself with cakes.

Then next day the whole Fagor team attacked with Delgado at the first feed because they thought I was hungry. I had planned for our team to ride through both feeds to make the others hungry, but the guys said they were hot and hungry, and they wanted their feeds. The Fagor riders also rode against me on the stage to Tremp. If they hadn't done that, we would have finished two or three minutes ahead.

The other riders combining together lost the race for me. But I'll get my own back on them. In the criteriums there are those who like to win their local race. As a named rider on the publicity posters for races like that, I am expected to show myself at the front, riding ahead for a few laps. The others in the race will expect me to do that and not chase me, but when I can I will just carry on riding hard and lap the field; that will show them.

Millar was also very upset with Roland Berland, criticising him for not offering to pay some non-Spanish riders in the group to help him chase Delgado and Recio. That often happened in similar situations in those days. It happens less now, so we are told. And there was the feeling that Peugeot hadn't really backed Millar right from the start of the Vuelta. They had to fly a special time-trial bike out to Spain for him when he was defending the leader's jersey. If they had believed in Millar's chances, they would have taken a time-trial bike with them. Millar's contract with Peugeot was up at the end of 1985, so he signed for Peter Post's Panasonic team for 1986.

Then, despite saying he would never race in Spain again, Millar lined up for the 1986 Vuelta, bent on revenge. He won the sixth stage to the mountain-top Lagos de Covadonga and took over the race lead, but then he lost it to Alvaro Pino in an uphill time trial. Millar wasn't too worried, as he planned to attack on stage 17, which finished on the Sierrra Nevada climb at over 2,500 metres.

He went early on the day because he needed to gain as much time as possible, and Pino cracked, leaving Millar to forge on alone for 18 kilometres. But behind him the Spanish collusion started again. A concerted effort by a number of different Spanish teams, most notably from Marino Lejarreta and his team, who were Pino's rivals, worked steadily but efficiently to pace Pino back up to Millar with six kilometres to the finish. With his attack nullified, Millar finished second overall in the Vuelta for the second year in a row.

Millar's experience in the Vuelta a España was far from unique. The history of road racing is littered with examples of teams from home nations combining against foreign riders, and of nationalist fans giving foreigners a rough time while physically helping their own. Thankfully it is something that disappeared soon after the abolition of a rule about the national make-up of teams. The rule said that teams had to take the majority of their riders from the nation the team was based in. Today's top-level teams are multinational, and this vastly reduces collusion between them.

6

The Freelancers

It's easy to hang the story of road racing on the shoulders of the great riders, and in the end that is probably the best way to tell it, but before I go on I want to write about some unsung heroes who have played an important part. They were called *isolés* or *touriste-routiers,* and although they flourished mainly in the Tours de France before the Second World War, hence their French name, their freelance spirit continued for a long time through a tradition called racing *à la musette.* Don't worry, I'll explain the terms as we go.

First off, *touriste-routier* is a misleading term. *Touriste* in the cycling sense means someone who cycles for adventure, to explore and to enjoy the countryside, someone who is in no hurry and will stop wherever and whenever he or she pleases. And *routier* means 'man of the road'; lorry drivers are often called *routiers* in France today.

But in cycling touriste-routiers were men who took part in the Tour de France but were totally self-supporting. Their heyday was the Twenties, and although some weren't up to much in performance terms, others were, and they were almost always what you might call characters. They had to be characters to spend their holidays racing around France with nobody to rely on but themselves.

Some were young riders trying to break into a team. Some were older and had been good enough once to be in sponsored teams, but they couldn't quite kick their fix of bike racing yet. And a few preferred to race solo, which meant that any money they won was theirs and theirs alone. In teams the prize money is shared. This chapter is their story.

The first Tours de France accepted entries from anyone who wanted to ride. Some were full-time professionals with sponsors, but most weren't. The Tour was particularly attractive to adventurous young bike-shop owners, who would take part on a make and model they sold in their shops. If they got through they put the bike they rode on display in their shops so people could marvel at how durable it was, and hopefully buy one for themselves. The bikes would be on show for months, sometimes years, still carrying the mud and dust from the last stage into Paris.

Some entered the Tour just for the hell of it, for the adventure, or just to see how far they could go. Henri Pépin was such a character, although a little out of the ordinary. His airs and graces, and the fact that he employed an experienced racer, Jean Dargassies, to accompany him in the 1907 Tour, led the press to think he was aristocracy, and without much fact checking they gave him the title Baron Henri Pépin de Gontaud.

It was a good story rather than a true one, but good stories sell papers. Pépin was fairly well off, but he wasn't a baron. His possessions were labelled with the very baronial title of Pépin de Gontaud, and that was enough to give the impression of nobility. In fact he just lived in Gontaud, where he owned a big house. He didn't get too far in the 1907 Tour de France either, dropping out with Dargassies on stage five.

When Henri Desgrange allowed sponsors to list their riders in groups in 1909, not teams because teamwork wasn't allowed, he still took entries from individual riders and listed them on the start sheet under the title of 'Isolés'. Then after the First World War, when the Tour de France resumed in 1919, riders were split into A and B categories, with no sponsors listed. The following year they were split into 1st and 2nd class. In both years the B and 2nd class entries were the freelancers.

In the Twenties the number of individuals who just wanted to have a go in the Tour grew, so in 1923 Desgrange created the touriste-routier class and, according to the French journalist René de Latour, gave them this message: 'There are special prizes for you. You are welcome to come and get them if you have the courage, but apart from being in the race on the road, I don't want to know you exist.'

There was no limit on the number of individual entries. 'The more the better,' Desgrange said. He liked to see them on the road lending extra colour and numbers to the race, but once the finish line was crossed, the race organisation had no responsibility for them until the start of the next stage.

The professionals had hotels booked for them. They

had support from the race organisation and from their sponsors. They were cared for between the stages, them and their bikes. Touriste-routiers got very little from the organisation. Some race food maybe, yet every kilometre was as long for them as it was for the professionals; the sun just as hot and the rain just as wet.

And their troubles continued when a stage ended. Showers were usually available at local schools or similar institutions. Then the touriste-routiers had to retrieve their luggage from the baggage van, which according to reports broke down a lot, then balance their suitcases on their handlebars and ride around town searching for a place to stay.

The more experienced riders booked hotel rooms in advance by post, but the majority trusted to luck, probably not wanting to commit to booking in advance, fearing they might not get all the way round the race, and so lose their deposits. Sometimes it was hours before they found a meal and a bed, and in between the two they had to clean, check and make any necessary repairs to their bikes.

It didn't put people off, though, and for the 1924 Tour there were 124 *touriste-routier* entries. They came from France, Belgium, Germany, Switzerland and Italy. There was even one entry from Monaco. Some of them were good riders, but just lacked the extra bit that would land them a pro contract. They came from all walks of life and all ranks of society too.

Léopold Gelot was a policeman from Paris. Journalists loved him, as he was a natural storyteller, and they called him Le Flic Volant, the flying cop. Another popular character was a schoolteacher from Perpignan, to whom the press gave the nickname Bobo. His humorous adventures regularly filled a paragraph or two, as did his frequent crashes – *bobo* is a French word for bruise or hurt.

Ambitious young racers often took part in the Tour as touriste-routiers, trying to attract a sponsor. And others couldn't stop riding after their pro career was over, like Paul Duboc who was second overall in 1911. He carried on racing after his final sponsorship ended with Peugeot in 1919, riding the 1923 and 1926 Tours de France as a touriste-routier. He started the 1927 race on the same footing, when he was 43 years old, but that was a Tour that did no favours for individual entries.

Ever the re-inventor, Henri Desgrange introduced separate starts on stages one to nine, then again on stage 14 and stages 18 to 23. On all those stages the professional riders started with their individual teams, and the teams started the stages at different times. The teams rode together, as they would in a team time trial today, but at any point a rider could go ahead of his team and set a quicker time for the stage. The individual times of the riders counted, so somebody with a strong team could benefit from them all working together while he sheltered, then make a big individual effort to go ahead near the end of a stage.

It was very complicated, and it unfairly favoured the larger teams like Dilecta-Wolber with eight riders and J. B. Louvet with eleven. The practice only lasted for three years. In 1927 Duboc started the first stage with a group of fellow touriste-routiers, lost time throughout and failed to finish it. The attrition rate for touriste-routiers was always high.

The 1928 Tour was particularly tough on them. Of the 121 who started, only eleven survived through to the finish in Paris. Many retirements came in the mountains;

others left the race when their money ran out and they could no longer meet hotel bills. But leaving the race wasn't a decision to be taken lightly, as many touriste-routiers had no other transport than their bikes, so they had to cycle home.

Touriste-routiers were a picturesque addition to the Tour de France, courageous and enterprising men who not only padded out the field but added to the Tour de France story. But as the race grew in stature and sophistication, they were increasingly outclassed. The professionals weren't just stronger, fitter and classier than these individuals; they had help and support behind them. Occasionally, though, a touriste-routier made headlines for performance, rather than as a human interest side-bar. Giovanni-Michele Gordini is a prime example.

Bayonne to Luchon was the first mountain stage of the 1927 Tour. It was the classic Pyrenean stage that had been in the race since 1910, in one direction or the other, but always linking the two towns through the same incredible route over the Aubisque, Tourmalet, Aspin and Peyresourde mountain passes. In 1927 this stage started at midnight in a gale-force wind and heavy rain.

Conditions were diabolical, and the rough weather and early darkness made it difficult for the organisers to keep track of the race. The crowds still turned out, and after a few hours of slow progress along the route Henri Desgrange, who was in a car just in front of the race, or so he thought, started to pick up a vibe from them that something extraordinary was happening.

Desgrange kept hearing people by the roadside shouting things like 'He's got fifty minutes' and 'They will never catch the breakaway.' Puzzled, Desgrange stopped and asked some spectators what they were talking about.

They told him that a rider – 'A giant of a racer,' Desgrange later wrote in *L'Auto* – had ridden past them almost an hour before the rest.

At first Desgrange didn't believe it was one of his competitors. It must be some local rider wanting to get to the first mountain pass to see the Tour go by. But the crowd told him the rider had a number, number 244. He was definitely a Tour de France rider.

Giovanni-Michele Gordini was number 244. The Italian had used confusion at the start caused by the weather to ride away, and was now an hour ahead of the rest. They had no clue he'd escaped, and were riding steadily to save themselves for the mountains, which were all in the second half of the stage. Gordini was now close to leading the Tour de France overall.

When Desgrange relayed the true race situation to the promenading peloton, the pace was upped as the top riders set off in pursuit. It would have been great if Gordini could have held on for a famous victory, but a series of punctures and problems with his drive chain steadily reduced his lead. Eventually he was caught by Nicolas Frantz, who won the stage (and ultimately the 1927 Tour de France) for Luxembourg, then by three others, all of them top riders. Gordini finished fifth on the stage, and his ambitious exploit helped him take a worthy 24th overall in Paris. He was also first overall in the mountains classification, but six years before the King of the Mountains title was coined. In the end, though, Gordini's big day was a one-off for him. The best ever touriste-routier, a man dubbed the King of the Touriste-Routiers, was Benoît Faure.

In 1930 the Tour de France changed its rider format again, inviting the cycling federations of Belgium, Italy,

Spain, Germany and France to pick their eight best riders and send them to the Tour. No trade-sponsored teams were invited, and all the selected riders had to wear national team jerseys and ride unbranded identical yellow bikes, which were supplied by the Tour.

But having just one team from each of the established road racing nations would mean only forty riders taking part. It wasn't enough to create a spectacle, or to provide lots of human interest angles to hang newspaper stories on, so the touriste-routier category was preserved. Eighty-five of them entered the race, bringing the total number of competitors up to a more satisfactory 125. One of those touriste-routier entries was Benoît Faure.

Faure was tiny his other nickname was Le Souris, the Mouse, and he was a marvellous climber. In 1929 he won the Cannes to Nice stage of the Tour, and finished 15th overall. He did even better in 1930 and took eighth overall in Paris. That brought Faure the offer of a place in the French national team for the 1931 Tour. He accepted, finishing 13th overall, but he can't have liked the experience. Maybe he didn't like sharing any money he won with team-mates either, which had already become the practice in professional road racing by then.

Faure never raced for the French national team again, although he rode other races for trade-sponsored teams, like Génial-Lucifer-Hutchinson and Mercier-Hutchinson. He did the 1932 Tour as a touriste-routier and finished 12th overall. Only two French riders finished ahead of him; the winner André Leducq, and tenth overall George Speicher, and they were in the French national team. Faure also placed third in the 1932 French national road race championships. He was a natural-born freelancer, taking another 12th overall in the 1935 Tour as a *touriste-routier*, but he wasn't the only freelancer to perform well in the Tour.

I've already introduced Vicente Trueba of Spain, the first official King of the Mountains, when he won that title in 1933, but what I didn't mention was that he did it as a touriste-routier. Gustaaf Deloor, winner of the first two editions of the Vuelta a España, rode the 1937 Tour de France in the touriste-routier category too.

So some good riders raced as touriste-routiers, although more were colourful adventurers like Jules Deloffre. He was a fair cyclist and a good acrobat. After each stage, Deloffre would prop his bike up somewhere and do acrobatic tricks such as somersaults and walking on his hands. Then he'd get up, hold out his racing cap, and the crowd would give him enough small change to pay for his meals and lodgings.

It sounds romantic, but in reality it wasn't. Consider the effects of limited resources on a touriste-routier's personal hygiene, for example. Giovanni Rossignoli was first of the touriste-routiers to finish the 1926 Tour, although over seven hours behind the overall winner, Lucien Buysse of Belgium. But Rossignoli had been so poor when he rode his first Tour de France in 1923, he only had one pair of shorts. They were at least new, but the Tour lasted a month then, and some stages were 480 kilometres long. After a fortnight his fellow riders started complaining. It seems that Rossignoli was either ignorant about, or didn't believe in, washing his shorts between stages. 'The greasier they are the better,' he told his rivals. 'Anyway,' he added, 'if you don't like the smell, let me break away.'

Touriste-routiers added to the race in many ways, but as the Tour de France developed and became more professional there was less space for them. The touriste-routier category disappeared after 1937, but freelancing continued in another way, with a practice called racing *à la musette*.

Nowadays a professional cyclist signs a contract with a team for an agreed salary and benefits, and for an agreed length of time. Contracts run up until the end of each year, so even though a rider might be leaving a team, having signed a contract with another, they will be paid by their old team up to a certain date, usually 31 December. The rider cannot be seen in his or her new team's kit, or do any kind of advertising or promotion for that team, until after that date. This wasn't always so.

Even as recently as the Eighties a twelve-month contract from a team was by no means a given. There was no minimum wage either, and some riders, even ones good enough to ride the Tour de France, weren't paid at all. They got expenses, free kit, maybe some bonuses and a share of the prize money their team won. But racing *à la musette* was even less secure and still common in the Fifties and Sixties. Those guys had no contract and no regular team, but hired themselves out on a per-race basis. They might end up riding for three or four teams in the same year.

For some it was a way of life, but for others it was a way into a big team. Brian Robinson, Britain's first ever Tour de France stage winner, and the first rider from his country to get a regular and reasonably well-paid place in a big team, got there by racing *à la musette*.

In 1955 Robinson and Tony Hoar were the first British riders to finish the Tour de France. They were part of the first all-British team to ride the race. Robinson was 29th overall in Paris, a good performance which got him invitations to do other races, but no permanent place in a European pro team. He had to wait another year and put up some fine performances before that happened. This is Robinson describing the early days of his European pro career:

I didn't have anywhere I could call a home after the start of the 1955 Tour, I was living out of my suitcase basically. Once the racing ended in 1955 I came home to Yorkshire and took up my old job as a builder, but I was determined to go back to France the following year.

Raymond Louviot was an ex-rider who wanted to become a directeur sportif, so in 1956 he put together a group of guys who would ride for any team in any race. It was quite a common practice in those days, and some riders liked it because it let them pick and choose the races that suited them, or those quite local to them. Anyway, Louviot asked me to join his, so I agreed.

I had a tough start to the year, because the weather was awful when we were supposed to do some pre-season training in the South of France in January. Bernard Pusey and I rented a bungalow for a month, but it snowed, even on the beaches. It hadn't snowed for more than thirty years. All the early-season races were cancelled, we couldn't even train, so I came home to sit it out.

I kept training because I was determined to go back, and eventually Louviot got me in some races, enough to have another go. They went well and Louviot was able to get a place for me in the Tour of Spain as part of Hugo Koblet's Cilo team. Koblet didn't finish the race, but I was eighth overall. I rode for Koblet's team again in the Tour of Switzerland, and did well enough there to get a full contract with a big French team, St Raphael. That was it, I was in.

But even then, Robinson was contracted only for each racing season, so from February to the end of October. Very few riders were paid through November, December and January. During those months they either survived on savings, or they rode a few six-day races on indoor velodromes, if they were good enough to get invited, or they did cyclo-cross races. But a lot took jobs, sometimes doing what they did before they were pro racers.

The Breton rider, André Le Dissez, was a famous example. He was a pro from 1957 until 1965, and ended his career with the Mercier-BP team. He rode some big races, and he won some too, including a stage of the 1959 Tour de France. But every winter Le Dissez worked as a postman in his home town of Plougonven. Word got around and soon Le Dissez was known to riders and fans as 'Le Facteur', the French for postman.

Finally, there were a few pro racers who never really gave up their original career. One was a French farmer called André Foucher. He started racing at 15, then as he progressed he took out an independent licence, which meant he could race against professionals in some races, and earn cash prizes if he did well. He did road races in the summer and cyclo-cross in the winter, but he kept his racing fairly local to Brittany and Normandy, where there were plenty of races he could ride.

Cycling became a nice way to earn some extra cash for Foucher, but when he won the 1958 French national road race title for independents, his supporters wanted him to turn pro. So did a number of pro teams, but Foucher was reluctant. 'I have my work, I have my farm. Cycling isn't a job, it's a recreation,' he said. He carried on racing as an independent, but because he also carried on winning, the pro teams kept upping their offers.

Eventually Foucher relented. He turned professional for Pelforth-Sauvage-Lejeune, but with a provision written into his contract. 'They agreed to let me start my season a little later than the rest of the team, because I couldn't do many races until we'd made the hay in late spring,' he says. He was still good. Foucher rode his first Tour de France in 1961 at the age of 28. He went on to win the Midi Libre stage race in 1964, and he finished sixth overall in the 1964 Tour de France. Foucher always got stronger towards the end of each season, when he wasn't so busy on the farm.

Foucher ended his pro cycling career in 1967, but he carried on racing until 1999, when he was 67 years old. 'At first I raced with a category in France called Hors Catégorie, which was for ex-professionals and riders who were formerly independents. Then I raced with the amateurs. I even trained with the Madiot brothers, Marc and Yvon, who come from the Mayenne, when I was in my fifties,' he told me when we met at a cycling function in Brittany.

There are stories similar to Foucher's all over Europe, members of farming families who were pro racers in the summer and worked on the family farm in the winter. But the most famous of them all was Portugal's Joachim Agostinho. He was a very successful rider, and he also invested a lot of the money into a farm, which he ran while he raced. Things didn't always go smoothly.

One year, shortly before the Tour de France started, thieves tried to steal some of Agostinho's cattle, which were scattered far and wide around the hills of Torres Verdes. Agostinho had to get them back, so he got some help and went after them. Instead of tapering his training for the Tour, Agostinho spent long days on foot slogging through tough terrain, looking for his cattle and bringing them back home. He didn't have his best ever start to that Tour.

But perhaps the most interesting alternative job ever held by a pro, a true winter job too, was Robert Poulot's. Poulot, who comes from Arrens in the Midi-Pyrénées, was a pro for three years and he won only one race, the 1964 Tour des Combrailles. So, not a glittering pro career, but Poulot was an excellent skier – good that he was recruited by the ski section of the Douane, France's customs service, and spent every winter patrolling the high Pyrenees looking for smugglers. It was years before the Schengen agreement created a borderless Europe, and long before the single currency, so the cost of goods, especially luxury goods, varied between countries. Smuggling stuff to avoid tax, and benefit from favourable exchange rates, was a very lucrative business back then. Poulot became a full-time customs officer when his pro career ended.

In today's men's World Tour riders don't need to work at anything other than cycling. There's a big funding disparity between the men's and women's World Tour, and work needs doing to close that gap, but the men earn well. There is a minimum salary for riders, which is reasonable, and pay grades increase exponentially with performance. The top riders are on very good salaries.

It could be better. There are still rumours about riders with individual sponsors buying places in teams. And for the dedication, hard work and sheer risk involved, all professional cyclists, men and women from the top to the bottom of the sport, are worth more. But overall the situation for men is satisfactory, although it's only been consistently so since 1990, and it's because of reforms created by the American triple Tour de France winner, Greg LeMond.

LeMond won the 1989 Tour de France, making an amazing comeback from life-threatening injuries sustained when he was accidentally shot in 1987. It was his second Tour de France win, achieved even though his moderate showing since his accident meant LeMond was in an under-funded team, with a deal that was far from satisfactory. But winning the 1989 Tour and the world road race title put LeMond in the best negotiating position in the sport, and he used it not only for his benefit, but for others as well.

In September 1989 it was announced that LeMond had signed a three-year deal worth 5.5 million dollars with a children's clothing company called Z to lead its team. LeMond, with the help of his lawyers, negotiated victory bonuses for his team-mates, and he had the whole deal underpinned by a bank guarantee from Z. Soon all teams had to do the same, and bank guarantees instantly made everyone's position in a team more secure. All top-level professional cycling teams must be financed like that now.

But right up until LeMond kicked off reform, pro cycling was a free-for-all. Some riders got rich but many more got nothing. Teams sometimes folded mid-season, or the money would dry up and the riders carried on racing for prize money. As late as the 1980s there were two years when unemployed riders banded together to form teams without any fixed sponsorship. They were Les Amis du Tour (Friends of the Tour) in 1980, and the Zero Boys in 1988. Les Amis du Tour even rode the Tour de France; well, they sort of rode it.

Pro cycling went through a downturn in 1980. An article in the French magazine *Miroir du Cyclisme* entitled

'One Franc per Kilometre' included an interview with a mid-level 26-year-old pro from a big team. The magazine called him Jean-Claude, which wasn't his name, but they wanted him to talk frankly about his life.

Jean-Claude earned about £225 a month all told. He had a share of the prize money the team won, but his team wasn't winning much. His income could only be boosted by riding a good Tour de France to attract contracts for the post-Tour criteriums held in towns all over France, at around £100 to £120 each. Up until the changes LeMond made, pro road racers depended on start money from criteriums and other exhibition races to boost their income. It put a world of pressure on them to perform during the Tour, and even more to show in the criteriums after it if they got contracts.

When it was all totted up, and his money divided between the kilometres he raced and trained, Jean-Claude was earning one franc per kilometre. Tough conditions, but thousands were willing and able to take Jean-Claude's place. They wanted to ride the big pro races, especially the Tour de France. They wanted to live the dream, and it was to help those doing so to live it a little longer that the Amis du Tour team was formed in 1980.

It gave unemployed riders a chance to race, but there was no sponsor, only the state benefits that French riders were entitled to as unemployed workmen. But they did get a ride in the Tour de France, which theoretically gave them a window to perform and perhaps get some criterium contracts and a place in a proper team. But even outside of the Amis du Tour, the French benefits system gave pro racers who had lost their place in a team the chance to try again. It was also why French amateur races were so hard at the time.

When a French pro racer couldn't get a place in a team, the state paid a percentage of what his last team paid him for one year, so the rider had a year of racing with the amateurs, then had to get other work. Because of their experience, and the strength they'd gained from riding at a higher level, these new ex-pros hammered their amateur opposition, and with regular income from the state added to their winnings they often earned more than they had as a pro. A few made it back to the pro ranks, which was the idea of the scheme, but not many.

But back to 1980 and Les Amis du Tour. At the last minute the Tour organisers decided the team wasn't strong enough as a whole to take part, so they persuaded the Boston team, a relatively week Belgian outfit that also wanted to ride the Tour, to merge their strongest riders with the strongest from Amis du Tour and make a composite team. They still didn't fare very well. Only four riders from Boston/Amis du Tour finished, with Patrice Thevenard their best in 55th place overall.

Zero Boys was formed along the same lines as Les Amis du Tour. It was 1988, and again the pro cycling market was in a downward spin. The traditional pathway for an unemployed Dutch professional rider in those days was to get a place on one of the Flemish teams that took part in what amounted to an alternative world of pro racing, the kermesses. There was a full calendar of these round-the-houses races for professionals, each associated with a town or village festival. They were restricted to Flanders, and were pretty tough, with betting and plenty of skul-duggery. Most riders survived on the prize money they could win, and/or deals they could do to see others win. There's more about kermesses in Chapter 15.

So in 1988 a group of enterprising Dutch riders who

didn't have contracts came up with the idea of renting their jersey space to sponsors on a race-by-race basis. They called themselves the Zero Boys, and they wore black shorts and a plain white top to give maximum room for any sponsors who might want to dip a toe into cycling.

Zero Boys thought that maybe they would be better doing big races as freelancers than they would in Belgian kermesse teams. They didn't, but at least they kept one rider going who would eventually become part of the famous ONCE team, Australia's Neil Stephens.

In the late winter of 1987 Stephens travelled to Europe from Australia on the promise of a place in a team that was going to pay him well, but while Stephens was mid-flight the team folded. He was now in Europe, and it was the middle of March, so he had little choice but to join the Zero Boys. He didn't earn much money but he managed to win one race, and just when he was on the point of being totally broke, Stephens got a contract with top Spanish team Caja Rural. He thrived and went on to make his name as one of the best domestiques in the business, and eventually to win a stage in the Tour de France.

So that was the rough old world of the European freelance professional road racer, a world that British riders only discovered in the second half of the twentieth century. In Chapter 10 I'll go into why they were late-comers to the professional road racing party, but the next thing I want to talk about is what puts so much colour into road racing, the humble yet in many cases iconic cycling jersey.

7

Rainbow, Yellow, Pink and Polka-dot

Cycling jerseys play a big part in the story of road racing. Competitors' teams or nationalities can be identified by the jerseys they wear. Jerseys can also indicate the titles riders have won, or the classifications they lead in stage races. They also add their own layer to the aesthetic of road racing

The first competitors wore their own day clothes for competition, but soon after the start of the twentieth century, with trade sponsorship coming into cycling, competitors started wearing jerseys in the colours of their sponsors.

Soon riders were allowed to carry their sponsors' names and logos on their jerseys. They still had to race as individuals, even if they had the same sponsors, but slowly rules about that were relaxed and teams formed. They were allowed to help each other, but strict rules about who could sponsor a professional cycling team lasted until the early Sixties.

When the first professional teams formed they were always sponsored by bicycle companies. In fact, as professional cycling grew in stature it became enshrined in the rules that the headline sponsor, the most prominent name on the jersey, must be a bicycle manufacturer. Two other sponsors were allowed on a team's jerseys. One, called a co-sponsor, had to be a tyre manufacturer, and the other could be a company from outside cycling. They were called *extra-sportif* sponsors in the language of cycling.

So by 1954 you had teams like Mercier-BP-Hutchinson. Mercier was a bike manufacturer based in St Etienne in France, Hutchinson was a French tyre manufacturer, and BP was BP, a massive petrochemicals business, but as far as cycling was concerned it was an extra-sportif sponsor. Extra-sportif sponsors were also allowed to support other teams, so during some of Mercier-Hutchinson-BP's existence there was another French team, Peugeot-Michelin-BP.

There were also rules about the size of lettering on clothing. From 1954 the maximum height for a headline sponsor's name was eight centimetres, while the co-sponsor's name could only be three centimetres high, and had to be below the headline sponsor. Only two lines of letters were allowed, and they could only be on the front and rear of each jersey. The extra-sportif sponsor's name or logo also had a size limit, and it had to be on the sleeves, or in certain cases on the chest. No other lettering was allowed, nothing on the sides or shoulders, and writing on shorts had to go around the legs not up them.

The rules were relaxed over the years, but only very slowly. It was the late Eighties before jerseys looked anything like they do today, with lettering on side panels, shoulders and many more places. And the changes came mostly by teams pushing the limits of the rules, rather than initiatives from the authorities.

The push started in Italy, where after the Second World War a rebirth of the Italian engineering industry took hold and the country entered a more modern age. People wanted cars and scooters, not bikes, and the Italian cycle industry was hit by dwindling sales. Sponsoring a cycling team slowly became a big drain on the bottom line of a company's profits. People still loved watching big races, but they weren't buying bikes, so company accountants started questioning team sponsorship as a way to advertise something fewer people were buying. A crisis loomed.

People still watched bike racing, and idolised its best performers, but the performers were getting paid less because the bike manufacturers had less money. So in 1954 one of the stars of Italian cycling, Fiorenzo Magni, asked a personal sponsor to take over his team. The sponsor, Nivea, agreed, made a deal with the Swiss bike manufacturer Fuchs, and the age of the extra-sportif headline sponsor began. It was against the rules, but the Italian Cycling Federation turned a blind eye.

Another extra-sportif sponsor, Carpano, launched a team in Italy in 1956. Carpano was created by Antonio Benedetto Carpano in Turin in 1786. It's the original vermouth, made from white wine, over thirty different herbs, and a dash of spirits for sweetness. The team jersey was based on Turin's Juventus football team strip, because the man who created the team and got Carpano to sponsor it, Vincenzo Giacotto, was a huge Juventus fan.

Carpano wasn't the only beverage company involved in team sponsorship. St Raphael, a French aperitif that contained quinine, sponsored a team from 1954, and got around the headline sponsorship rules with the help of one of its riders. The official name for the 1954 team was St Raphael-Raphael Geminiani – Raphael Geminiani being the team's best rider. He had just launched a brand of bike with his name on, and, if asked, he would claim that the St Raphael referred to him. In other countries the team competed as St Raphael-Quinquina, which was the full name of the aperitif, so they weren't hiding the fact that St Raphael was the headline sponsor. Only in France was the Quinquina reference dropped and Geminiani had to use his 'saint' excuse.

Wine-based drinks flavoured with quinine, plus other aromatics, were very popular in Europe at the time. They were collectively called Quinquina. Officials in the other European countries had no problem with the team competing with St Raphael-Quinquina on its jerseys; it was only in France where the riders had to wear St Raphael-Raphael Geminiani jerseys. But French officials must have willingly suspended disbelief to have believed Geminiani's self-canonisation story. Or, more likely, they accepted extra-sportif sponsors taking over as headline sponsors as inevitable because the teams and the sport needed more money.

Unfortunately these officials were prodded into action in 1962, when the Tour de France changed to a trade team formula. Geminiani had stopped racing by then, and was the team's manager. For 1962 he signed the 1957 and 1961 Tour de France winner, Jacques Anquetil, and needed more money to pay for him, so he sold his team to St Raphael, and St Raphael wanted its proper brand name printed as the headline sponsor on the team jerseys in all countries.

However, the Tour de France directors at the time, Félix Lévitan and Jacques Goddet, were against extra-sportif companies being headline sponsors. They feared big commercial interests could undermine their power base. Lévitan and Goddet not only ran the Tour de France like a private dictatorship, they tried to pull strings in the wider cycling world, and they certainly pulled them in France.

Lévitan and Goddet were behind the wrangles Geminiani had with cycling's international governing body, the UCI, over the registration of the St Raphael-Hclyctt-Hutchinson team during the winter of 1961/62. The UCI had never looked at the team's name so closely before, and initially the body told Geminiani he couldn't have St Raphael as his team's headline sponsor.

Things weren't resolved at the start of Milan–San Remo on 19 March 1962, when Geminiani told his riders to go to the start line wearing their St Raphael jerseys under another unmarked top, and to remove that extra top as soon as the flag dropped. Presented with a fait accompli the UCI backed down, and St Raphael, with various co-sponsors, went on to be one of the best teams ever. It also opened the door for other extra-sportif sponsors to take over teams, and a lot more money to come into the sport. The soft drinks company Kas in Spain, Pelforth beer and Bic pens in France, Salvarani kitchens and Faema coffee machines in Italy, Solo margarine in Belgium and Willem II cigars in the Netherlands were all headline team sponsors from the early Sixties onwards.

And so the pattern for modern team sponsorship was set. It paid companies, who sold to the demographic that supported cycling, to sponsor teams. So, manufacturers of household goods, motor cars, insurance companies and banks have all sponsored teams. The only change has been the recent return of bike manufacturers as headline sponsors, which was brought about by the increased popularity of cycling, meaning increased bike sales, which in turn means it makes financial sense again for bike manufacturers to sponsor top-level professional cycling teams.

But professional teams are only part of the jersey story. Cycling jerseys show the titles that riders hold, and they are used to, identify who is leading a stage race, as well as its subsidiary competitions and classifications. The most famous jersey in cycling comes from a stage race, and that's the yellow jersey of the Tour de France.

There was no yellow jersey in the early Tours. The overall leaders wore green armbands up until 1919, when it's generally accepted that the yellow jersey was born. However, the idea of having a yellow jersey may have been discussed earlier.

In 1956, when he was 67, the 1913, 1914 and 1920 Tour de France winner Philippe Thys told a Belgian magazine, *Champions et Vedettes*, that Henri Desgrange approached him when he was leading the 1913 Tour, and asked him to wear a distinctive yellow jersey so people could identify him. Thys claimed that at first he refused because it would make him more obvious to his competitors, and therefore easier to mark, but later in the race he relented, after his manager Alphonse Baugé told him that wearing a distinctive jersey might be good publicity for his sponsor, Peugeot. Thys said that Baugé's argument persuaded him and he agreed, so a yellow jersey was bought for him and he wore it in the race.

The thing is, no mentions of a yellow jersey in any newspapers or other records of the 1913 Tour de France have come to light, although admittedly loads of records were destroyed in the two World Wars. Thys certainly wore the yellow jersey when he became the first triple Tour de France winner in 1920, because there are plenty of references to the leader's yellow jersey in reports of that Tour. So now it's generally accepted that the yellow jersey was introduced during the 1919 Tour de France.

The first man to wear the Tour de France yellow jersey was probably Eugène Christophe in 1919, and another thing that makes Thys's recollections look sketchy is that it wasn't awarded until the tenth stage of the 1919 Tour. But that in itself adds fuel to the fire of another debate: why was yellow the chosen colour?

The official story which has been widely accepted for years now is that the yellow jersey is yellow because the pages of *L'Auto* were yellow. However, there is an alternative story that says Desgrange took so long to make up his mind about awarding a leader's jersey, because the idea was unpopular with the riders, that when he finally did so the only colour he could get in the numbers and sizes he needed for the rest of the 1919 Tour was yellow.

This could be true, as yellow had certainly been an unpopular colour in Europe. It was the colour of Judas Iscariot, the colour of the capes that the Spanish Inquisition made heretics wear, and the colour of money lenders. That was all a long time ago, and yellow was used extensively in late nineteenth-century art, in particular in the work of Vincent Van Gogh, but beliefs about colours can last a long time. Still, the colour of the pages of *L'Auto* is a more logical explanation, and there is no doubt about the version Henri Desgrange wanted to promote.

On the morning of the tenth stage of the 1919 Tour,

Desgrange wrote in *L'Auto*: 'This morning I gave the valiant Christophe a superb yellow jersey. You already know that our director decided that the man leading the race should wear a jersey in the colours of *L'Auto*. The battle to wear this jersey is going to be passionate.' Classic Desgrange, and the initials HD on today's yellow jersey are there in Henri Desgrange's memory.

Eugène Christophe might have gone down in history as the first man in the yellow jersey, but he didn't like it. He thought it was his wearing yellow that gave rise to the nickname, Cri-Cri, which he was given. It's a word French people used as baby-talk when referring to birds, and Christophe thought it came from the canary yellow of that first yellow jersey.

Christophe kept the jersey for the next two stages, extending his lead over Firmin Lambot of Belgium to 28 minutes, but on the penultimate stage 14, disaster struck Christophe again. It was a massive stage, 468 kilometres from Metz right across the north of France to Dunkirk: a route that had been the front line in the First World War. The landscape was wrecked and the roads were terrible. The area is still famous for its cobblestone tracks, but this was awful.

On the bomb-cratered cobbled roads Christophe's forks broke again. This time he found a bicycle factory, not a blacksmith's, and used its forge to repair his bike, but he lost nearly two and a half hours doing it. Christophe dropped to third overall and Firmin Lambot won the 1919 Tour de France, and so became the first cyclist ever to win the yellow jersey outright. Lambot was born in Florennes in French-speaking Belgium. He won the Tour again in 1922, while in 1921 it had been won by Léon Scieur, who was from the same small town. With three

Tour de France victories, and a population of only ten thousand today, Florennes is very proud of its cyclists.

Wearing the yellow jersey hasn't always brought riders good luck. A number have dropped out of the race while in yellow. The 1936 Tour winner, Sylvère Maes of Belgium, left the race when he was leading the following year because, he claimed, French fans were giving undue help to their countryman, Roger Lapébie. Maes reckoned that fans pushed Lapébie all the way up some hills. The race judges saw it and didn't do anything about it, which caused Maes to announce: 'I'm not going to continue while being steadily robbed of my lead.' And with that, he returned home to Gistel in West Flanders, where he owned a bar.

Others crashed out in yellow, like Luis Ocana in 1971, Rolf Sorenson in 1991, David Zabriskie in 2005 and Tony Martin in 2015. When that happens it's traditional for the rider who takes over the lead not to wear the yellow jersey during the following stage. Eddy Merckx didn't wear it when Ocana crashed out in 1971, leaving a full day without a yellow jersey in the peloton, although he still led the race. There have been plenty more. Ferdi Kübler refused to wear yellow on the stage after Fiorenzi Magni left the 1950 Tour. Magni was leading, but supported a decision to withdraw from the race made by his Italian team when its captain, Gino Bartali, was threatened by spectators.

One rider, Louison Bobet once even refused to wear the yellow jersey on taking the lead because he didn't like the material it was made from. That year the yellow jersey had synthetic yarn mixed with the traditional wool. The synthetic yarn was made by a company called Sofil, which was one of the Tour's sponsors that year, but Bobet claimed he'd ridden in a similar mix and it made him sweat too much. The organisers had to get some pure-wool yellow jerseys quickly, just for Bobet.

Then there were two Tours de France with more than one yellow jersey. In 1929 Nicolas Frantz of Luxembourg and Frenchmen André Leducq and Victor Fontan couldn't be separated on time at the end of stage seven, so all three wore yellow jerseys on the next stage. Luckily, Gaston Rebry of Belgium gained time on that stage, so he took sole occupation of the jersey and Frantz, Leducq and Fontan dropped down to equal second. The other Tour with shared leadership was in 1931, when Charles Pelissier and Raphaele Di Paco led at the end of stage six. Eight riders shared third place overall that day, with twelve in second place the day before.

The man with the most yellow jerseys to his name is Eddy Merckx, who wore it 96 times between 1969 and 1975, winning five Tours de France along the way. Another five-time winner, Bernard Hinault of France, is second to Merckx with seventy-three days in yellow. Not surprisingly, the next two places are also filled by five-time winners: Miguel Indurain of Spain and another Frenchman, Jacques Anquetil, with sixty and fifty days in yellow respectively. At the end of the 2017 Tour, Britain's Chris Froome was one day behind Indurain. Only four men have worn the yellow jersey every day from the start to the finish of the Tour de France: Ottavio Bottecchia of Italy in 1924, the Luxembourg rider Nicolas Frantz in 1928, Roman Maes of Belgium in 1935, and Jacques Anquetil in 1961.

The yellow jersey might be the most famous in cycling, but it's not the oldest winner's jersey. That honour falls to Belgium and its national champion's jersey, which is the same design as the Belgian flag, and has never changed. It was first used in 1903, when the Belgian road race champion for that year, Arthur Vanderstuyft, wore a black yellow and red jersey in races. It was quickly followed by France, with a national champion's jersey in 1911 based on the French *tricolore*, and the Italian national champion's jersey was first seen two years later. All three jerseys were originally based on the colours of their country's flag, and Belgium and France remain true to that design today. Some recent Italian national champions have made personal interpretations of their national champion's jersey.

The most famous jersey after the yellow jersey is the rainbow jersey awarded to world champions. Rainbow jerseys are white with equal-width blue, red, black, yellow and green bands around the chest. The colours were adopted by the sport's current governing body, Union Cyclisme International (UCI), and they were taken from the five Olympic rings. The Olympic flag, the five coloured rings on a white background, is made up of the colours of all the countries that competed in the 1912 Olympic Games, which is when the Olympic rings first appeared. The creator of the modern games, Baron Pierre de Coubertin, said of the flag: 'The six colours [he was including the flag's white background] combined in this way reproduce the colours of every country without exception. The blue and yellow of Sweden, the blue and white of Greece, the tri-colours of France, England and America, Germany, Belgium, Italy, Hungary, and the yellow and red of Spain next to the novelties of Brazil and Australia, with old Japan, and new China.'

The rainbow jersey was created by the UCI in 1927 to make the reigning world champions more obvious to spectators in races. There had been world track and road race championships before that date, but 1927 was the inaugural world professional road race championships, and the men's pro road race rainbow jersey has become the best known. It inspired the story of 'the curse of the rainbow jersey', which refers to the bad luck, even tragedy, that has befallen some winners of the world pro road race title, which is now called the elite road race title, in the year they wore the rainbow jersey.

Tom Simpson was the first British winner of the world pro road race title in 1965, then broke his leg in a skiing accident early in 1966 and never got back to full form that year. He even crashed out of the 1966 Tour de France while wearing the rainbow jersey. Things were far worse in 1971 when the 1970 World Champion, Jean-Pierre Monseré, was killed while wearing the rainbow jersey in a small race in Belgium. His compatriot Freddy Maertens had a terrible year after taking his second world title in 1981. Having previously won around fifty races a year, in 1982 Maertens won two. Then there was Stephen Roche, who not only won the 1987 world pro road race title but also the Giro d'Italia and Tour de France in the same year, but then an old knee injury flared up and Roche's next season was a wipe-out. And the list goes on; eleven World Champions since Simpson have had bad years while wearing the rainbow jersey. On the other hand, as of 2017, forty winners haven't suffered in the following year.

The very first world road race championships were run in Copenhagen in 1921. It was a time trial of 190 kilometres, only open to amateurs, and Jean Aerts of Belgium won. The title moved to Liverpool the following year and British riders, who had a fine pedigree in time trials, filled all the podium places. Dave Marsh was first, with William Burkhill second and Charles Davy third. The race was based on an established course, using roads where the Anfield Cycling Club ran its 100-mile time trial.

After 1922 the amateur world road race title was decided in a bunched road race. It returned to a time trial format for one year in 1931, but from 1923 there wasn't another British men's medallist for over forty years. British road racers were strong, they could ride hard at one pace all day, but they weren't adept at riding in a bunch because until the Forties almost all British road races were time trials. The reasons why will be covered later.

The first rainbow jersey went to the winner of the first professional world road race championships, which was held in 1927. Alfredo Binda of Italy was the winner. The jersey he was presented with and entitled to wear in road races had significantly wider bands of colour than those that decorate the rainbow jersey today.

The jersey remained similar to the first one until the introduction of shirt-style buttoned collars on cycling jerseys in the Forties. And those collars stayed part of the ceremonial rainbow jersey awarded on the podium long after zipped collars were in general use, and well into the Seventies. Since then, road race rainbow jerseys have remained pretty true to the original design.

Rainbow jerseys are also awarded to the world champions of each discipline in track cycling, and to world time trial champions, as well as the champions of BMX, the various off-road disciplines and artistic cycling. The designs of all these rainbow jerseys refer to the discipline in which they were won. World champions are only allowed to wear their rainbow jersey in the discipline in which they are world champion, so the time trial world champion cannot wear his or her rainbow jersey in a bunched road race, and vice versa.

You might see that rule being broken in photos from some professional criterium races from years gone by. In those days decisions about who wore what in criteriums were left to individual race promoters. Criteriums are show races, and to put on a good show promoters would have the Tour de France winner wearing a yellow jersey, and if the world road race champion wasn't in the field, then the world pursuit champion might be asked to show the rainbow colours.

In some cases riders rode criteriums in jerseys they had specially made, such as the rainbow jersey worn by Eddy Merckx for a series of criteriums in 1968. Here the white background of the standard rainbow jersey was pink, to show that he was the reigning world road race champion, and that he'd just won his first-ever Grand Tour, the 1968 Giro d'Italia.

Which brings us nicely on to the pink jersey worn by the leader of the Giro d'Italia, which first appeared in the 1931 edition of the race. There is no doubt about why pink was chosen; the pages of its creator, the sports newspaper *La Gazzetta dello Sport*, are pink, and there are no counter-stories. Like the yellow jersey, its colour has never changed, although its design has, especially in recent years.

The first pink jersey, won by the Italian racer Francesco Camusso, had a roll-neck collar and front pockets for food. A grey shield was sewn on to the middle of the chest, bearing the symbol of the Italian fascists, the ruling Fascist Party having decreed that it should be put there. The jersey remained solid pink for the rest of the twentieth century, but since 2000 there have been slight shifts in design. The 2006 jersey had a bike motif picked out in darker pink. Then in 2009, to celebrate the Giro's centenary, the jersey's collar and side panels were edged with the green, white and red colours of the Italian flag.

That jersey was designed by Dolce & Gabbana, and the

trend for guest fashion designers continued with Paul Smith designing the 2013 pink jersey. He called his creation the Maglia Rosa Passione. Then in 2014, when the race started in Belfast, all the Giro d'Italia classification jerseys were created by the Irish designer Fergus Niland on behalf of the Italian cycling clothing company Santini. The pink jersey featured stylised shamrock and tweed motifs, and bore the legend 'Giro fights for Oxfam', as well as the name of the jersey sponsor, Balocco.

Eddy Merckx, the holder of so many cycling records, won the Giro five times, amassing a total of seventy-seven days in the pink jersey. Nearest to him is Alfredo Binda with sixty-five days in the lead, also for five victories. However, Binda's victories span the period from 1925 to 1933, so he didn't wear pink every day he led. If anything though, Binda was more of a dominant figure than Merckx in the Giro d'Italia. In 1927 Binda won twelve of the fifteen stages making up the race, and in 1929 he won eight stages in a row. But this was an age when heroism and long lone breakaways were the thing fans admired in cycling, and Binda was an excellent tactical rider who never wasted effort. His way of winning became so ruthlessly efficient that the Giro organisers thought he was making the race boring. So in 1930 they paid him 22,000 lire not to ride it.

Only one man has won all three main leader's jerseys in the Giro d'Italia, and you won't be surprised to find it was Eddy Merckx. He won the overall, points and mountains classifications in the 1968 Giro. However, the following year Merckx was thrown off the race while in the pink jersey again, due to a positive dope test. He protested his innocence, claiming his sample had been tampered with. He went to great lengths to prove it too, and the suspension he was likely to serve, which would have prevented him riding the 1969 Tour de France, was lifted on a balance of probabilities basis. Merckx rode the Tour and won it, taking the three main classifications along the way – the only time that has ever happened in the Tour.

Tracing the story of the pink jersey shows how clothing developed in road racing. The first Giro d'Italia's pink jerseys were made from Merino wool by the pioneer of Italian cycling clothing, Vittore Gianni. He was a tailor who founded his business in Milan in 1896, with AC Milan, Juventus and the Milan Ballet among his regular customers. He started making cycling clothing in 1910, and in time made clothing for Alfredo Binda and other champions.

In 1935 Armando Castelli started working for Gianni, and Castelli bought the business from him in 1939, keeping the Vittore Gianni name. Castelli continued making jerseys and shorts out of fine Merino wool for the likes of Fausto Coppi, Gino Bartali and Rik Van Looy, as well as supplying twelve professional teams.

Armando's son Maurizio took over the business in 1974 and changed its name to Castelli, and Castelli took over making the pink jersey for the Giro d'Italia. The leader's jerseys have recently been supplied by another Italian manufacturer, Santini, but Castelli will be supplying them until at least 2021.

Today many road racers ride in skinsuits, for reasons of improved aerodynamics. Once the skinsuit was developed in the late Seventies they were readily adopted for use in time trials, which is the event for which they were originally designed. But it wasn't long before some road racers saw the advantage of using a skinsuit in shorter races. Stephen Roche famously won a short, almost all uphill stage of the 1985 Tour de France dressed in a skinsuit.

But skinsuits weren't widely used in the longest road races and stages until the whole Great Britain team wore them in the 2011 men's elite world road race championships, when Mark Cavendish became the second Brit to take the title. The decision was made by team coach Rod Ellingworth, and it was made to suit the tactics he believed would give Team GB the best chance of victory, as he told me during an interview I did for *Cycle Sport* magazine shortly after the race:

> It involved the team controlling the whole race to ensure a bunch sprint. That meant the team being on the front and riding at 45 to 48 kilometres an hour for a very long time, which is why I insisted that they all raced in skinsuits. Some of them didn't like it, but I made them do it. Some also used aerodynamic helmets with filled - in vents. There's a watts saving from doing this, and that saving was crucial considering our tactics.

He told me he didn't know how many watts, but said that Chris Boardman, who was working as a technical advisor for the British Cycling performance programme at the time, had tested it all. 'They keep the results to themselves, but I know there is a definite advantage.'

Another BC source calculated that the skinsuit and Cav's helmet combination provided an energy saving of four watts. That figure was bandied around, and some analysts at the time said that, considering Cavendish's winning margin was just three hundredths of a second, so around 0.001 per cent of the whole race time, those four watts could have clinched it.

But Ellingworth felt they missed the point, because the Copenhagen sprint was much slower than a typical Tour de France sprint. The average speed for the final kilometre of the 2011 worlds was 56 kph, and for the final 400 metres was 51.5 kph, whereas a typical Tour de France sprint will have a 60 kph final kilometre, with riders hitting 66 and more in the final 400 metres. The aerodynamic advantage of Cavendish's skinsuit and aero helmet was more about saving him energy throughout the race than on increasing his sprint speed. A four-watt saving sounds small, but it is very significant in a six-hour race. That's why a lot of road racers use a skinsuit and aero helmet combination today.

As well as taking the rainbow jersey in 2011, Mark Cavendish also won the green jersey given to the rider who scores the most points awarded on all the stages of the Tour de France. Some early Tours were decided on points, not overall time, but once it was decided that time was the best way to decide the overall outcome of a stage race, the door was open for a subsidiary points competition that would give a different kind of rider something to go for over the three weeks of the Tour de France. So a competition based on points, separate from the overall standings, was introduced to the Tour de France in 1953, which was the Tour's fiftieth anniversary. It was called the Grand Prix Cinquantenaire, and the first winner was a Swiss rider, Fritz Schaer.

A green jersey was awarded to the leader, the colour chosen by the first sponsor, a lawnmower company called La Belle Jardinière. The jersey has been green ever since, with one exception. That was in 1968, when the points competition sponsor, Sodas Sic, insisted on the jersey being red.

The first rider to wear the green jersey was Wout Wagtmans of Holland. Schaer won the first stage of the 1953 Tour, so he led the Tour and wore the yellow jersey next day, with Wagtmans second. That always happens when a rider has the yellow jersey plus another. The yellow jersey takes precedence, and the second rider in the other classification wears that classification's leader's jersey, which was Wagtmans.

Erik Zabel of Germany has the most victories, winning the green jersey for six consecutive years from 1996 to 2001. Next is Peter Sagan with five victories, but since they are also consecutive, 2012 to 2016, and at the time of writing he is only 27, the Slovak rider looks very capable of beating Zabel's total and setting a record that will be very hard to equal. Sean Kelly of Ireland is third in the all-time green jersey standings, with four victories: 1982, 1983, 1985 and 1989.

The leader of the King of the Mountains competition in the Tour de France wears a white jersey with red polka-dots, known as the polka-dot jersey. However, although the first King of the Mountains award was made in 1933, a leadership jersey wasn't designated for the competition until 1975, and there is some debate about its origins.

The usual explanation is that the company sponsoring the King of the Mountains competition in 1975, the French chocolate producer Chocolat Poulain, produced a bar that had a white wrapper with red dots on it. But there is very little except word of mouth to back this up. There is certainly no reference to red-spotted wrappings on the company's extensive website, which has pictures of wrappers going back many years.

The first man ever to wear the polka-dot jersey was a Dutchman, Joop Zoetemelk, and the first rider to win it was Lucien Van Impe, who went on to take six Tour de France King of the Mountains titles. Van Impe is equal second in the Tour's mountain classification victory standings with Spain's Federico Bahamontes. Richard Virenque of France is first, with eight victories.

The polka-dot jersey's design has hardly changed since 1975. The only addition is that some riders opt to wear red or even polka-dot patterned shorts to match it. The current jersey sponsor, as of 2017, is the supermarket chain Carrefour. Points for the King of the Mountains competition are awarded at the top of all climbs in the Tour de France that are categorised by the race organisers. The climbs range from fourth category, which could be a steep hill or a short mountain climb with a relatively low gradient, to first category, which are real passes.

There is a category above first, and that is *hors catégorie*, which is French for beyond categorisation. Hors catégorie is reserved for the most famous mountain climbs of the Tour de France; the likes of Col du Galibier, Alpe d'Huez, Col du Tourmalet and Mont Ventoux are all hors catégorie climbs.

In the 2013 Tour de France riders were awarded twenty-five King of the Mountains points for leading over a hors catégorie climb, dropping down to two points for tenth. First-category climbs attract ten points for first and one for sixth, and so on down to one point for the first rider over a fourth-category climb.

A mountains classification was introduced to the Giro d'Italia in 1933, although there was no leader's jersey until 1974. Plain green was the chosen colour, and this served until 2012, when a new sponsor of the mountains classification, Banca Mediolanum, wanted a blue jersey for the term of their sponsorship. The points leader in the Giro d'Italia wears a mauve jersey, the Maglia Ciclamino. The first Giro points jersey in 1967 was red. That lasted until 1969, when the Ciclamino was introduced. In 2010 the Giro points jersey was red again, but the mauve Maglia Ciclamino returned in 2017.

The Vuelta a España has had a number of mountains leader's jerseys. For many years it was green, but in 1986 there was a red jersey with white polka-dots, and in 1989, when the mountains classification was sponsored by Café de Colombia, the leader's jersey was white with a brown coffee bean pattern. More recently, the Vuelta's best climber's jersey has been white with large blue polka-dots.

The Vuelta a España has always been a bit free and easy with its jersey designs. The overall leader's jersey was orange until 1941, when it changed to white. It was orange again in 1942, then from 1945 until 1950 it was white with a horizontal red stripe. There was no Vuelta from 1951 to 1954. In 1955, when the race was resurrected, the leader's jersey was yellow, and except for 1977, when it was orange again, yellow stayed until 1992, when the colour deepened to gold. Red was the colour chosen for the Vuelta leader's jersey in 2010, and red it has stayed since.

All very colourful, but the most garish Vuelta jersey was one given in an intermediate sprint competition, which from 2004 until 2006 was sponsored by the Spanish fishing industry – it was light blue with little yellow fishes.

And finally we'll talk collars and cuffs. Former national champions are allowed to carry a reference to their title on the collars and cuffs of their registered team jerseys for the rest of their careers. So you get former Belgian champions with black, yellow and red banded cuffs, Italians with green, white and red, and so on. Some recent British national champions have gone for an elongated version of the union flag on their collars and cuffs. Former world champions can use the rainbow bands for theirs.

8

Women's Road Racing

Women have had a bad deal in sport, and there are generations who never got the chance to fully explore and exploit their talent. Even now there is disparity between the coverage and reward men and women get in many sports. And cycling has been one of the worst offenders.

It's almost unbelievable, but there were no official women's world titles at all until 1958, and when they were introduced it was just a road race, a track sprint and an individual pursuit. It took until 2017 for women to get full world championship parity with men, when the Madison was added to the women's track programme. And the Olympic Games was even worse.

Women weren't included in the Olympic cycling programme at all until 1984, when in Los Angeles there was one event, a road race. The first women's Olympic cycling gold was won by Connie Carpenter of the USA, the mother of current pro Taylor Phinney. More events were added over the years, but only slowly. It was 2012 before women had medal parity in cycling with men, and it happened partly because men lost events to make way for more races for women. Contrast that with swimming and athletics, where Olympic parity between sexes was achieved much earlier and without any loss of races. But the loss of events is an aside; the main thing is that hundreds of talented cyclists were deprived of a shot at Olympic glory, glory that was seen as a right in other sports. It's a very strange state of affairs when you consider that a woman took part in the first ever proper road race.

She was the mysterious 'Miss America', one of the thirty-four riders who battled through to the end of Paris–Rouen in November 1869 within the 24-hour time limit. She was 29th, 12 hours and 10 minutes behind race winner James Moore, but equal on time with two other men, Turner and Taboureau (sorry, race results weren't very hot on Christian names back then), 25 minutes ahead of Ch. Chatelain (whatever Ch. stands for, possibly Charles), and 2 hours and 20 minutes ahead of the last two finishers, E. Fortin and Prosper Martin (they obviously felt Prosper was a name worth preserving for posterity, and they were right).

Little else is known about Miss America, except that she was most likely English, and obviously entered under a pseudonym, probably so as not to cause outrage among those, mostly male, who still believed that women endangered themselves by taking part in sports, or even by being adventurous at all. Still, many women were determined to push at the boundaries society had created for them.

Miss America was a pioneer, and so was Paris–Rouen. As cycling became established as a sport, track racing was more popular to begin with, so the first women cyclists to achieve fame were track racers; women like Lottie Stanley, who started winning long-distance track races in America in 1888. She raced in women-only events and against men, and as her fame spread she raced in other countries too. In May 1890, for example, she won a handicap one-mile race against professional male riders at the Molyneux Grounds in Wolverhampton. Her handicap allowance over the mile was 355 yards, and her winning time was 2 minutes and 37.75 seconds. She also won several women's six-day races on the track, and some races that were even longer.

Other pioneering women raced on the track, but as women's bike racing grew as a sport, so did reaction to it in the press. Bicycle racing wasn't a seemly pastime for women, or so late nineteenth and early twentieth-century opinion held. This opinion led, mostly by newspapers, to inventions like 'the hygiene saddle' for women, which it was claimed was designed to avoid erotic friction while cycling. Perhaps here was a clue as to why some men felt threatened by women taking up cycling.

Luckily such beliefs and opinions didn't prevent women from cycling, or from racing and putting up some incredible performances. The Belgian Hélène Dutrieu, later a pioneer aeroplane pilot, raced as a professional in the 1890s, setting a motor-paced women's hour record of over 40 kilometres in 1893. A few years later there was Marie Marvignat in France. She entered the Tour de France in 1908, but the organisers refused to let her ride, so she rode the whole route anyway, provoking early calls for a women's Tour de France – something that's still not part of cycling, and should be, despite several attempts at making it happen.

The French cycling authority, the Union Vélocipédique de France, was particularly backward in its attitude towards women's racing. It was simple discouragement at first, and when that didn't work, in 1912 the governing body directed its membership to stop organising races for women.

Luckily for the sport and its development, the attitude was very different in neighbouring Italy. Women racers were encouraged, and one in particular became a star and a national hero. She was Alfonsina Strada, and during her long cycling career she rode two of Italy's biggest professional road races: the Giro di Lombardia and Giro d'Italia. The press and fans of all sports in those days loved giving their favourites nicknames, and one of those favourites when Alfonsina started racing was Giovanni Gerbi, who was also known as the Red Devil. So Alfonsina Strada became the Devil in a Dress.

She was born Alfonsina Morini in Castelfranco Emilia, near Modena, in 1891, and learned to ride her father's bike at the age of 10. She quickly discovered racing, and by 1907 she was Italian national champion. In 1911, still as Alfonsina Morini – she didn't marry Luigi Strada until 1915 – she set a new women's world hour record of 37.192 kilometres, but it was never ratified, for reasons which vary according to what source you read.

The most likely is that cycling's governing body, the UCI, didn't ratify an official women's hour until 1955. And when they did, the new record of 38.473 kilometres by the Russian, Tamara Novikova, was only 1.28 kilometres further than Strada's. By 1955 the men's hour record was 4.33 kilometres further than the men's hour in 1911. So, an increase of just 1.28 kilometres in forty-four years is a measure of how good Alfonsina Strada was. Good enough to race against the best male professionals of her day, in fact.

In 1917 Strada was invited by *La Gazzetta dello Sport* to ride the Giro di Lombardia, where she lined up with male racers like Henri Pélissier of France; Phillipe Thys of Belgium, the 1913 and 1914 Tour de France winner, who would win again in 1920; and the young Italian star Costante Giradengo, already twice Italian road race champion and a future double winner of the Giro d'Italia and six editions of Milan–San Remo, as well as many other good pro riders.

Philippe Thys won the race from Henri Pélissier, covering 204 kilometres at an average speed of 29.28 kilometres per hour. Fifty-four riders started but only thirty-one finished, and Strada was one of them. She was 1 hour and 34 minutes behind Thys, but still in the company of two male riders. She was placed 31st, but shortly after the race two other riders who finished quite a bit ahead of her were disqualified, so she ended up in 29th place.

Strada rode the Giro di Lombardia again the following year, in what was a shorter version of the race. The field was smaller than normal because the First World War had taken so many cyclists away to fight or do other vital work. The race was more tactical than in 1917, with the riders sticking together until quite late on. Strada finished 21st with a group of seven men 23 minutes behind the winner, Gaetano Belloni, and ahead of one man.

During the war the few riders who continued competing and were in the forces did so by the grace of the commanding officers. Many couldn't race at all, and in

1919, with hostilities over, it became clear why the organisers had wanted Strada in their race in 1917 and 1918. When there was a big entry for the 1919 Giro di Lombardia, she wasn't invited. She'd been a useful sideshow to attract publicity, but now the main show was back, and the organisers felt she was no longer needed.

However, Strada continued racing in women's and men's races, and she continued winning. During her long career she won a total of twenty-six races against male opposition, and she proved useful again to a professional race promoter in 1924. It was the year when Giro d'Italia organiser *La Gazzetta dello Sport* was in dispute with the professional teams who usually took part.

The reason was that a few top Italian riders wanted to miss the Giro that year so they could have a good go at the Tour de France. One of them, Ottavio Bottecchia, who was the revelation of both the 1923 Giro and the 1923 Tour de France, was riding for a French team, Automoto, by then, so the Tour de France came first. He went on to win the 1924 Tour, becoming the first Italian to do so.

So the Giro d'Italia organisers decided to do without the big names and opened the race to freelancers, called *isolati* in Italy. Some top pros were prepared to go freelance for the race and entered anyway, but that still left too few riders to provide a spectacle worthy of the event. So to attract entries *La Gazzetta dello Sport* published details of how much free food any rider would be given if they raced. That might not sound like much now, but money was scarce in Italy in the Twenties and the promise of free food, and plenty of it, was enticing. They also invited Alfonsina Strada to take part, and her presence helped make the race.

She was listed as Alfonsin Strada, which renders her gender less obvious, but *La Gazzetta* made no secret of it once the race was under way. With the stars absent, some of its references to Strada, for example 'riding happily along in the shortest of shorts', ensured a massive male turnout on the race route. She was always at or near the back of the field, but she kept going while many men dropped out, and the stages were incredibly long.

The total race distance was 3,613 kilometres, but done in just twelve stages, with a day between each one. Even the shortest, 230 kilometres between Taranto and Foggia, was about as long as the longest stage in a modern Giro d'Italia. And the longest stage, Bologna to Fiume, which was then part of Italy but is now in Croatia, was 415 kilometres long.

Strada managed the first six stages fine, but the seventh was the second day in the Apennine Mountains. The roads were bad, the hills were long and hard, and the weather was awful. Strada crashed, and as well as sustaining some bad bruises and grazes, the handlebars on her bike were broken in two. A spectator ran the short distance to his house and returned with a broom. With his help Strada made a makeshift set of handlebars from the broom's handle, and she was off again. But the delay proved too much, she finished the stage outside of the time limit, and that was her Giro d'Italia over. Well, it was according to the race officials.

Strada being in the race had sold a lot of extra copies of *La Gazzetta dello Sport*, and now she was out those sales could be lost. The race was directed by Emilio Colombo for *La Gazzetta dello Sport*, so Colombo made a deal with Strada. If she continued riding the stages unofficially, *La Gazzetta* would pay her, and pay her well. She agreed to do it, and the race continued as before. Officially she received 50,000 lire, but some say that by the end Strada made more money from the 1924 Giro d'Italia than the winner did. She was certainly very popular in Italy, and quite well known in the wider world.

She raced until 1938, when she was 47 years old, travelling to Russia, France, Spain and Luxembourg. Her husband Luigi Strada died in 1946 after spending years institutionalised through poor mental health. She remarried and ran a bike shop in Milan, buying a motorbike when she no longer had the energy and strength to cycle long distances. Alfonsina Strada died in 1959, after suffering a heart attack on returning home from a long motorbike ride to watch a pro road race in Varese. She is remembered very fondly in Italy.

Strada's bikes have been saved for posterity, along with those belonging to many other great champions, in the chapel of the Madonna del Ghisallo high above the picture-postcard Italian lakes of Como and Lecco. The Madonna del Ghisallo is the patroness of cyclists, declared so by Pope Pious XII during the 1949 Giro d'Italia, and her chapel is dedicated to cycling and to cyclists.

Inside the chapel an eternal flame burns in memory of every cyclist who has died on the road. Visitors come to remember lost friends, or maybe reflect on the champions, like Alfonsina Strada, who have donated their bikes and jerseys. They line the walls, motionless, some of them fading now, but so redolent of the grace, beauty and passion of cycling.

Then, for one day in October each year, the Madonna del Ghisallo changes. The Passo del Ghisallo wasn't on the Giro di Lombardia route when Strada rode it, but once the race found its home in the heart of the Italian

Lake District it became an important place, for many years the last climb before the finish in Milan. Moving the finish to Como in 1961 put the Passo del Ghisallo closer to the end, making it crucial. It's still part of Il Lombardia, the race's new name, but other climbs follow the Ghisallo now. Its summit is also home to a museum of Italian racing, turning the chapel site into a veritable cathedral of cycling.

As befits a nation that has always had bikes at the heart of its transport system, the Netherlands has produced some great cyclists, men and women, although as elsewhere it took a while for women who wanted to race bikes, rather than just ride them, to gain acceptance. One early Dutch champion was Mien Van Bree. She started the first Dutch cycling club for women in 1929 when she was 16 years old, but she had to move to Belgium to race, because were no women's road races in her own country. In 1937 she won a race billed as the world road race championships for women. So she is regarded as her country's first female world cycling champion, although it wasn't an official title.

The story of women's cycling is punctuated by races like the unofficial world championships Van Bree won, brave attempts to gain parity with men's sport. In most cases, they were created by ambitious, fair-minded people who saw no reason why there couldn't be world titles, classics and even a Tour de France for women. One such person was the Frenchman, Jean Leulliot. His story will be told in greater detail later, because he had a big role in men's road racing as well, but I mention him now because in 1955 Jean Leulliot created a Tour de France for women. It was called La Grande Boucle Féminine Internationale.

One of the meanings of the French word *boucle* is loop, and the Tour de France is often called La Grande Boucle, meaning The Big Loop. So to avoid copyright conflicts with the then Tour organisers, *L'Equipe*, whom Leulliot didn't get on with anyway, he called his race the Grande Boucle Féminine instead of the Tour de France Féminine. He had big plans for it, and many years later the idea was resurrected and for a while it flourished. Unfortunately, Leulliot died before he could see it.

The first Grande Boucle Féminine Internationale of 1955 was restricted to Normandy and it was dominated by a Great Britain team. June Thackeray won stage two, but the race remained close until Millie Robinson, who was from the Isle of Man, won stage four on her own. That put her in the race lead, and Robinson won the final time trial to become the first British winner of a Tour de France. Only Nicole Cooke (twice) and Emma Pooley have won the equivalent of the Grande Boucle Féminine for Britain since. They won a new version, which we'll visit later in this chapter.

Meanwhile, two stars of women's road racing started their careers in the Fifties; one was Belgian and the other British. The Belgian was Yvonne Reynders, from the Antwerp region, who was the 1955 and 1956 Belgian junior discus champion. She had wanted to be a runner, to emulate her hero, Fanny Blankers-Koen, the Dutch golden girl of the 1948 Olympic Games in London. Blankers-Koen won four gold medals at the London Games, in the 100 metres, 200 metres, 80 metres hurdles and the 4 x 100 metres relay. However, when Reynders took up athletics at school, her sports teacher decided she'd be better at the field events. She was right, sort of: Reynders was good, but she hated throwing the discus, and shortly after she left school she decided to try bike racing.

She already had some cycling-specific strength, because when she left school her father bought the 16-year-old a three-wheeled carrier bike and helped her set up a coal delivery round. She kept her carrier bike in Antwerp, and each day she bought coal wholesale from a merchant, loaded as many ten-kilogram sacks onto her carrier as she could, and pedalled through the streets of Antwerp, delivering to customers and collecting money as she went.

But hauling coal on a bike isn't flying on a bike, it isn't racing, and despite some promise in early races Reynders knew she had to lose weight before she could hope for the success she wanted. 'I weighed 74 kilograms when I was a discus thrower, and I am not tall,' she told the Belgian journalist Jos Van Landeghem. 'Some of my friends laughed when I said I wanted to become a racing cyclist. They told me I was too fat,' she added. It sounds brutal, but Reynders' friends were trying to help her, and they were right.

So she set about losing weight. She lived 40 kilometres east of Antwerp in the beautiful Kempen area, and each day she rode those 40 kilometres into Antwerp on her race bike. Then she did her coal round, 8 to 16 kilometres every day on a heavy bike with a heavier load. In the afternoons she switched back to the race bike and rode 100 to 140 kilometres along the Schelde valley, eventually returning home. Reynders did that every weekday, plus more training at the weekends, for six months. It was a gruelling schedule, and at the end of it she weighed 59.5 kilograms. Now she could fly. She won ten out of fourteen races entered in her first full year, and gained selection for the Belgian national team.

The next two years weren't so good because she was plagued with leg pain. She visited lots of doctors, without finding a solution. Finally a pro racer from Antwerp called Frans Aerenhouts, one of the top men of his day, arranged for Reynders to see his masseur, and he diagnosed a problem with her back. It was probably caused by lifting those heavy coal sacks. Some physio, a bit of treatment, and Reynders was winning again.

In 1959 she won her first world road race title. Reynders eventually won four road and three pursuit world titles, as well taking several silver medals and one bronze in the world championships. Her last medal came in 1976, in the road race, when she was 39.

Another star of women's cycling in the Fifties, Sixties and Seventies is among the all-time greats of all women's sport, the British rider Beryl Burton. She was born Beryl Charnock in Leeds, and grew up and lived in Morley for the majority of her life. She had rheumatic fever as a child and was warned against doing any form of exercise, but her determination knew no bounds. She knew what was best for her, despite what the doctors said, and she achieved some amazing feats of speed and endurance despite having a heart arrhythmia all her life.

Burton got into cycling in 1953 after being introduced to it by her husband Charlie, and she joined his club, the Morley Cycling Club. 'She was handy from the start,' Charlie told me in 2014, 'but not that competent on a bike. We had to push her on club runs sometimes, guide her a bit, but slowly she got better. By her second year of riding, she could keep up with any of us, and by the third year she was going out in front and leading us all. I dabbled a bit at time trialling back then, so in 1956 Beryl decided to have a go.'

In 1957 Beryl won her first national title, in the 100-mile time trial. Charlie then stopped racing, and the couple became a two-person race team. Beryl competed and Charlie did everything else. They travelled to Amsterdam in 1959 for the world championships, and Beryl won her first world title in the track pursuit.

The following year they ventured behind the Iron Curtain to Leipzig – a real experience – and they did it with little or no help from cycling's governing body in the UK, the British Cycling Federation. But the Burtons were used to that; they took it in their stride and Beryl won the road race and track pursuit world titles in East Germany. She won the pursuit title three more times in 1962, 1963 and 1966, and took silver medals in 1961, 1964 and 1965, as well as four bronze medals between 1967 and 1973. Burton's career continued from strength to strength, becoming more remarkable as it progressed.

By 1967 she was a class above any other female road racer in the world. In the world championships that year in Holland she was beaten in the pursuit by Ludmila Zadorozhnaya, but Burton proved unstoppable in the road race. She raced as if nobody else was there, surging away from the peloton until she broke it and only Zadorozhnaya could follow her. But then she carried on; she didn't even ask the Russian to share the pace setting, but rode harder and harder until her rival had to let go, leaving Burton to do what she did best and time trial to the finish. She won by 1 minute and 47 seconds from Zadorozhnaya, and was nearly six minutes ahead of the third-placed rider.

But women's road racing, as it was then, didn't really stretch Beryl Burton. There was not much of an international calendar, and the races there were, even the world championships, were relatively short, 60 to 70 kilometres. Burton's week-in-week-out diet was British time trialling, and in 1967 and she did something that surpassed all of her world road race titles really. She set a record for the 12-hour time trial that has only been bettered by one woman, Alice Lethbridge, and that was as recently as 2017, when Lethbridge benefited from several big aerodynamic developments that were nowhere near available to Burton, and aerodynamic advantages make a huge difference in time trial performance.

The length of time her 12-hour record stood is amazing in itself, and it speaks volumes for Beryl Burton's talent; but what says more is the fact that Mike McNamara set a new men's record in the same 12-hour race as Burton in 1967, but Burton rode further than him – she beat him. Perversely, though, it was McNamara's distance, not Burton's, that stood as the British 12-hour record, because the rules were worded in such a way that the British 12-hour record was a men's only record.

It's hard to find a sport in which strength and endurance are the keys to success, where a woman is faster than the best men. It happens in ultra-endurance events, races that take days of non-stop effort to complete. But a 12-hour cycling time trial isn't an ultra-endurance race. Yes, it's a long bike ride, but it requires skill and speed and not simply the ability to keep going and going, then going some more. What makes this story even better is that Burton caught McNamara early in the race – time triallists set off at one-minute intervals in UK races – and offered him a licorice allsorts sweet as she passed him, which he accepted.

Burton was Yorkshire, really Yorkshire; down to earth, straight talking and fiercely competitive. It might not seem like it, hearing stories of her chomping licorice allsorts while setting records, or if you'd seen her getting her knitting out to relax after races. She couldn't abide people making excuses when they didn't do well, or wasting her or their time, and there was one occasion when the high standards she set for herself got the better of her.

It was 1976, and after Beryl's daughter Denise outsprinted her to win the British road race championships, Beryl refused to shake hands with Denise on the podium. She was in her forties then, so well towards the end of her racing career, and Denise Burton was getting to the peak of hers. It sounds like terrible sour grapes, but Beryl was cross with herself for losing. She was also cross that her daughter hadn't worked as hard as she had in their successful breakaway. She would have been angry with any rival who'd done that. So it wasn't a family thing, a mother-daughter jealousy thing; it was a bike racing thing.

Burton's training was a diet of hard miles squeezed in between housework, being a mother and working on a farm owned by Nim Carline, an excellent long-distance time trialist with national titles of his own. Burton was awarded an MBE in 1964 and an OBE in 1968, and carried on riding her bike all her life. She died in 1996 at the age of 58, while out on her bike delivering invitations to her 59th birthday party. The cause of her death was heart failure, and maybe the arrhythmia finally caught up with her, but her daughter Denise thinks, 'Her competitiveness and relentless drive eventually wore her body out.'

Apart from the world championships, Burton had few opportunities to perform on the world stage in her sport.

There wasn't the programme of big international road races there is for women now, and there wasn't a women's Tour de France, which was only revived in 1984 after Jean Leulliot's earlier efforts. It was called Le Tour Cycliste Féminine, and the number of stages varied through its history. Initially it was run at the same time as the men's Tour de France, finishing in Paris when the men did. The men and women shared the final victory podium and it worked, it looked good, and it was the right thing to do.

The first winner of Le Tour Cycliste Féminine was Marianne Martin of the USA, then the race quickly evolved into a thrilling annual battle between the two best women's road racers of their generation. One was a pure climber, Maria Canins of Italy, the other a more all-round rider, Jeannie Longo of France. Canins won Le Tour in 1985 and 1986, with Longo second. Then Longo won from 1987 to 1989 with Canins second.

Longo has an incredible record, although it was slightly tarnished in 2011 when *L'Equipe* reported that her husband, Patrice Ciprelli, had purchased a quantity of the performance-enhancing drug EPO from China. In a subsequent enquiry Ciprelli stated that it was for his own use, and there is no evidence that Longo ever used the drug. Longo won major international titles from 1985 until 2001, and in her final Olympic Games in 2008 she took fourth place in the time trial, two seconds off the bronze medal position. Before that she won five world road race titles, four time trial titles and was the 1996 Olympic road race champion.

Le Tour Cycliste Féminine was a very good race, but it was difficult for the organisers to get sponsorship for it. They were forced to depend on the towns, cities or regions that wanted the race, and would pay to host it.

Consequently Le Tour, which was fifteen stages long at its height, was a logistical headache. It was also a problem for the riders, because they faced long transfers between stages that were often spread far apart.

There was no Le Tour Cycliste Féminine in 1990 or 1991, but it returned in 1992, and was won for the next two years by the new star of women's cycling, Leontien Van Moorsel of the Netherlands, who could win anything. Van Moorsel was world road race champion in 1991 and 1993, but stopped racing in 1994 when it was revealed that she had developed an eating disorder. Her comeback at the 2000 Olympics in Sydney was amazing. She won the individual pursuit gold medal on the track, setting a new world record for the 3,000 metres pursuit distance that women raced, and took the silver medal in the points race. After that she did the golden double on the road, winning the road race and the time trial.

Fabiana Luperini was the next big star of the race, and of women's road racing. She was an out-and-out climber, like her compatriot Canins, and she looked incredible as she danced up the slopes of the famous Tour de France climbs. She also achieved a breakthrough for women's cycling by being the first to the top of a new major mountain climb that has since become a legend in the sport.

The climb is Monte Zoncolan, and it is located deep in the Carnic Alps in the northeastern corner of Italy, close to the Austrian border and not so far from Slovenia. Monte Zoncolan is so extreme that it can lay claim to the title of the toughest climb in cycling. Both sides are incredibly tough, east and west, but the west side is steeper for longer and it's only been possible to include it in road races since the advent of compact chainsets.

The first racing ascent of Monte Zoncolan was made during the 1997 Giro d'Italia Femminile, when Luperini conquered it with a virtuoso display of climbing.

She was born in Pontedera, where Vespa scooters are made, and she lives near the base of one of Tuscany's most famous climbs, Monte Serra. As well as winning stage races, Luperini won four Italian road titles and La Flèche Wallonne twice. She won her fifth Giro d'Italia Femminile (it's sometimes called the Giro Donne or Giro Femminile or the Giro Rosa but they still mean the women's Giro d'Italia) in 2008. That give her a thirteen-year spread of Grand Tour wins, another record. She was sixth overall in the 2009 race.

However, the true beauty of Luperini's cycling career lay not in statistics but in the way she won, and in particular the way she climbed. She was simply glorious to watch as she flew uphill with apparent ease. Then, no matter how tough the conditions were, no matter how wrecked the opposition, Luperini always looked as if she'd been out for a Sunday afternoon spin instead of a hard-fought brutal race.

Luperini won the Tour Cycliste Féminine in 1995, 1996 and 1997, after which the race ran into trouble when the Tour de France said it infringed their trademark. The name was changed in 1999 to La Grande Boucle Féminine Internationale, which solved that problem, but the ones caused by logistics and sponsorship proved insurmountable. There was no race in 2004, and when it returned in 2005, La Grande Boucle Féminine Internationale was much smaller.

Later editions had only five stages, and remained in one region. In 2008 there were seven stages in six days, but in 2009 it was down to four days, and only sixty-six riders took part. That was the last Grande Boucle Internationale Féminine, and its winner, the British rider Emma Pooley, the third British winner after Nicole Cooke in 2006 and 2007, said the race was 'more petite boucle than grande'.

Nicole Cooke was a force of nature in women's road racing from the moment she started. In 2002 she won the Commonwealth Games road race gold medal riding for Wales. She was only 19 years old, but she was already racing in Europe, winning big races in Italy and Holland, and she quickly became the new world number one.

Cooke won the UCI road race world cup in 2003, plus classics like the Amstel Gold Race and the GP Plouay, and she was third in the world championships in Hamilton. She won the Giro Femminale in 2004 and was fifth in the Olympic road race. She won the Flèche Wallonne three times, in 2005, 2006 and 2007. She was second in the world road race championships in 2005 and won the World Cup again in 2006. Cooke dominated the 2008 Olympic road race in Beijing, opening the flood gates on an unprecedented Olympics for Team GB cycling. For Cooke, her Olympic gold medal in Beijing was just one part of an incredible year, during which she won the British and the world championship road races.

Emma Pooley won the silver medal in the time trial at the Beijing Olympics, then went on to fulfil her potential. She was a runner and triathlete, a Cambridge University sporting blue at cross country, who started cycling when she got injured. She quickly made progress, and was selected for Great Britain for the 2005 world road race championships.

She graduated to the women's World Tour, winning six of its biggest single-day races, as well as seven international stage races. Pooley is now winning duathlons, triathlons and other endurance races, but is still a powerful advocate for women's cycling. She was instrumental in the birth of La Course by Le Tour de France, a race that could be the seed of a proper women's Tour de France.

Like the Tour itself, La Course is organised by ASO, and will be pushed by a group called www.letoureniter. com, formed by Pooley, Marianne Vos, Kathryn Bertine and four-time Ironman world champion Chrissie Wellington. The group's manifesto calls for 'a women's race at the Tour de France, supported by wider changes in the sport, to help harness the full potential of women's road cycling and develop the sport equitably and sustainably'.

Things are getting better for women's road racing, let's stress that. Women have a UCI World Tour now, which is slowly gaining more coverage and more races. However, where men's World Tour teams have annual total budgets in the tens of millions of euros, women's teams have more like half a million.

Some of the women's World Tour races tie in with the men's World Tour. The Tour of Flanders is a good example, and there was the first ever women's Liège–Bastogne–Liège in 2017. Some races, like the Tour de Yorkshire, run a race for women over the same course with the same prize money as for the men. That's a step forward, but in the case of the Tour de Yorkshire it's only one stage of the men's three. Moving to four stages for men and two for women happened in 2018, which is good news for both sexes, but women still lag behind. They don't deserve to, because their racing is every bit as exciting as the men's.

But coming back to the Tour de France, women's road

racing needs a local Grand Tour. It has a Giro d'Italia, the Giro d'Italia Femminile, but to have symmetry with men's cycling it needs a Tour de France as a focal point. It's hoped that La Course is bringing that focal point a little nearer.

The first three editions of La Course were held in Paris on the Champs-Elysées before the final stage of the men's Tour. The first in 2014 consisted of thirteen laps of the Tour de France finishing circuit, and 157 countries saw TV pictures of the race. The Dutch queen of women's cycling, Marianne Vos, won in a time of 2 hours and 41 seconds for 89 kilometres, raced at an average speed of 44.5 kph. There's one 180-degree turn on the Champs-Elysées circuit, two 45-degree turns and two right-angled turns; so 44.5 kph around that circuit is fast.

Vos is coming to the end of a long career, but what a career it is. The Dutch woman has won the UCI World Cup five times, with 17 individual wins in the races that comprise it. She is a triple world road race and world cyclo-cross champion, and in 2012 she won gold in the Olympic road race in London. Vos wins stage races too, and won the biggest in women's cycling now, the Giro d'Italia Femminile, in 2011, 2012 and 2014. She has been called the Eddy Merckx of women's cycling, and the comparison is valid. But at the same time it's hard on women like Beryl Burton, who had nowhere near the programme of races Vos has. (There is still work to do, though.)

Cycling as a whole needs La Course to grow. It quickly became part of the men's Tour de France final day, with another Dutch star, Anna van der Breggen, winning in 2015, and the Australian Chloe Hoskins in 2016. Then in

2017 La Course evolved a little when it moved into the mountains. It covered the final 66 kilometres of the eighteenth stage of the men's Tour de France to finish at the top of the Col d'Izoard. Annemiek Van Vleuten of the Netherlands, who had crashed badly while leading the 2016 Olympic road race, won from Lizzie Deignan, the current number one British road racer and world road race champion in 2015. The top finishers then rode a handicap road race, which the organisers called a chase, in the streets of Marseilles using the route of the Tour's time trial stage in the same city. All the riders set off with the time advantage they had at the end of the Izoard stage. So Van Vleuten started 43 seconds ahead of second-placed Lizzie Deignan and ended up extending her margin to win La Course 2017.

The most important fact from that race, though, wasn't the result. It was that Van Vleuten set the third-fastest time up the Izoard, as recorded on the sports app Strava that day. Only two men on their stage went faster. If any single fact shows that women's road racing should have closer parity with men's, it's that.

So that's where women's road racing is now, but how does it move forward? I asked somebody who is personally involved, Britain's most successful female Paralympian of all time and a multinational champion in able-bodied cycling, Dame Sarah Storey. She owns a UK-based women's road race team, so she's talking chiefly from a British perspective, but it reflects what's happening elsewhere. This is what she said:

> The number of women racing has increased, there is more motivation to ride, a better programme of races, and organisers have done a lot for equal prize money in some

races, but the level to which teams are funded hasn't changed for a while. In the UK you'll find none of the riders are paid, and most teams are run by volunteers. Even in the UCI World Tour there are probably lots of unpaid riders. There's no easy fix. The key is more TV coverage of women's racing, then companies would invest in teams to get their company logos and names on TV. But even the companies who are committed to covering women's racing, like Vox Women, need funds. They need funds from adverts so they can cover races, so they need the TV channels to give women's racing more air time.

Teams need TV coverage to increase the level of funding they get from sponsors, but TV companies need more funding to cover women's racing when it's separate from the men's. The short-term fix is to have more women's racing run alongside men's racing, but logistical problems can make that difficult. It seems like a vicious circle, until you look back to how it was in Beryl Burton's day. The changes and improvements made between then and now give plenty of hope for the future.

9

Behind the Iron Curtain

In 1945, in the aftermath of the Second World War, an Iron Curtain fell across Europe, splitting the Continent in two. The East was gathered together under communism as Soviet Russia tried to block off itself and its satellite states from the influence of the West. Countries east of the curtain were part of the Warsaw Pact, and those to the west part of NATO. The East was trapped under the influence of Russia, but one way its people could reach out, a way that was encouraged by governments but for propaganda reasons, was through sport.

The East, also referred to as the Communist, Soviet or Eastern bloc, was against professionalism, citing it as an example of Western decadence and corruption, so its athletes were all amateurs according to the international rules of sport. However, the best of them, those who were part of national teams, or on the verge of selection, were sponsored by the state. They were often recruited into their country's armed forces, and although it's commonly held that they trained for and competed in their sports instead of performing official duties, that's only true in the later years of Eastern bloc sport. Earlier generations had to fit in training around duties, although they were readily given leave when they needed to compete or attend specific training camps.

Under this system Eastern European athletes were very successful, and in the Fifties, Sixties and Seventies their cyclists were a major force in amateur track and road racing, winning many amateur world titles. Also, because Olympic Games were only open to amateurs then, they won many Olympic medals. The Eastern bloc even had its own great stage race, the Peace Race, which grew to two weeks in length at its height, and was often referred to as the Tour de France of the East.

The first Peace Race, held in 1948, consisted of seven stages and was 1,104 kilometres long. It started in Warsaw, capital of Poland, and finished in Prague, capital of the country known then as Czechoslovakia. By 1952 it had grown to twelve stages and 2,135 kilometres, linking Warsaw with Berlin as well as Prague. Sometimes those capital cities were linked in a different order, but that became the Peace Race default route. Change only came when the grip of communism relaxed in the Eastern bloc during the second half of the Eighties.

The Peace Race was created to ease tensions among Eastern and Central European countries that arose after the Second World War. And as the race grew it created its own legends: places like The Wall of Meraane, a 300-metre ramp of cobbles in the centre of Chemnitz;

the laser-straight roads with wicked surfaces spearing through vast birch-woods in Poland; and the snow-capped mountains of the Czech Republic. And then there was the Peace Race leader's jersey, which was yellow with a dove of peace symbol on it.

In common with communist ideology the Peace Race was open only to amateurs, and its reputation grew as its organisers reached out, inviting teams from many different nations. An Indian team rode in 1952, 1954 and 1955. And in 1952 a British rider, Ian Steel, won the race after a terrific struggle, with his Great Britain team backing him so well that against all odds they won the team prize as well.

The British team was there because of an organisation called the British League of Racing Cyclists (BLRC). There is a lot more about the BLRC later on in the book, but for now suffice to say the BLRC was responsible for a revival of road racing in the UK, and for the purposes of the Peace Race it had links to a communist sports organisation in France called the Federation Sportive et Gymnique du Travail (FSGT). The Peace Race organisers sent their first invitation in 1948 to the official body that governed cycling in the UK, the National Cycling Union, but the NCU turned it down. Someone in the BLRC heard about this and got in touch with the FSGT in France, and through its communist connections strings were pulled and the invitation was sent to the BLRC instead. They accepted and sent a team every year until the BLRC merged with the NCU in 1959 to form the British Cycling Federation (BCF). I'll go deeper into British road racing politics later in the book.

The Peace Race was an incredible experience in those days, especially for the Brits who didn't have a great tradition of racing in big bunches on open roads. And they certainly had never been watched by such large crowds as they met there. The Peace Race was massive, a real eye-opener. Vin Denson, who later rode the Tour de France several times, remembers the 1959 Peace Race: 'Most stages were a blur of cobbled city roads and tram lines, interspersed with bumpy highways and giant pot-holes. You bounced around, and jumped your bike up onto the smoother pavements, when the crowd allowed you to. Millions came out to watch us, they must have been starved of entertainment, and crashes were frequent. It was madness.'

The Peace Race was so tough that pro teams, especially French ones, set great store by it when dishing out contracts. Billy Bilsland, a Scot from Glasgow, raced successfully in France as an amateur in the late Sixties and was offered a place in the big French pro team, Peugeot-BP. He was only asked two questions at his inter-view. 'When I turned pro at the end of 1969 I'd won a lot of big amateur races in France that year and raced for the top club in Paris, but all Peugeot wanted to know was had I won a race in Belgium and had I won a stage in the Peace Race. I answered yes to both questions and that was it, I was in the team,' Bilsland remembers.

The race was a tough test for amateur riders in the West, but it was a source of great national pride in the East. And in the days of communism East European riders were mature, while most West European amateurs were young and inexperienced because the best turned professional once they'd proved themselves in the amateur ranks.

It meant that although Peugeot might have thought winning a Peace Race stage was a good qualification for becoming a pro, a lot of coaches in the West advised their best amateur charges to avoid it. Most notable in that category was Eddy Merckx, whose first coach Félicien Vervaecke found himself at loggerheads with the Belgian Cycling Federation when it wanted Merckx to ride the 1964 Peace Race. Vervaecke refused to let him. Merckx was strong that year, and later won the world amateur road race title in Sallanches, France, but he was still only 19 and far too young for a gruelling 14-stage race of 2,246 kilometres against very strong, very experienced opposition.

So the best East European stage race became the domain of the best East European road racers, men who were household names in their own countries and feared competitors in the West. Ryszard Szurkowski and Uwe Ampler won four Peace Races each for their respective countries, Poland and East Germany, although Ampler's final victory in 1998 was after the fall of the Berlin Wall, and he was a professional rider by then. Sergei Sukhoruchenkov, a Russian, won in 1979 and 1984, and was Olympic road race champion in 1980.

There were many more, but arguably the biggest name of the Peace Race, and of East European cycling, certainly the one who left the biggest impression in his country, was East Germany's Gustav-Adolf Schur. Schur won the 1955 and 1959 Peace Race, he was world amateur road race champion in 1958 and 1959, and he took a silver medal in the 1960 Olympic Games road race. But Schur was more than a big race winner; he was an intelligent racer, a charismatic person with an extremely generous nature. All of Schur's personality was underlined by a remarkable act of unselfishness at the 1960 world road race championships, held on the Sachsenring in East Germany, to which we will come shortly.

Schur was so popular in his country he was voted East German Sports Personality of the Year nine times in a row between 1953 and 1961. Then, on the eve of German reunification in 1989, a poll voted Schur the most popular East German sportsman ever.

Known as Täve to his millions of fans, he was a personality when the political ethos of communism, in which all are equal with no individual more important than the state, was policed hard in East Germany. He appealed to a collective feeling in the country, where many felt they were German first and East German second.

Schur would have been an outstanding professional road racer, able to win classics and Grand Tours, because his power and tactical awareness in races were up with the very best. His powers of recovery were terrific too. For years Schur was head and shoulders above his rivals, once lapping sixty of the world's best amateur road racers twice during a post-world championship revenge criterium.

He was born in Magdeburg, and his background and early life were working class. He left school with few qualifications and was given a labouring job with a building firm. However, it was soon obvious that Schur was more than labouring material, and he was taken into the company's drawing office and trained as a draughtsman.

With a better-paid job, Schur bought a second-hand racing bike and so enjoyed riding in the countryside that he joined Magdeburg's entry-level cycling club, the Green and Red Club, in 1949. East German sport was strictly tiered, with entry-level, mid-level and elite-level clubs in most sports covering the entire country. With the Green and Red, Schur began competing in tourist road races, the category created for novices who wanted to have a go at the sport.

Progress was slow at first. It was hard to get decent lightweight bike equipment in East Germany, but once he had his bike up to scratch Schur started winning, and he quickly climbed up to the next level and was recruited by the best cycling club in the wider Magdeburg area, a mid-level club called Aufbau Börde Magdeburg.

Now he had some back-up, a qualified coach and a bike with good-quality equipment bought by the club. Every worker in East Germany in those days contributed to a sports fund, and money from those funds was dished out to different sports clubs, who used it to buy equipment and pay for qualified coaches and for the services of sports doctors.

Schur was 21 when he moved up a level, but as he had only started racing at 19, he was still relatively inexperienced. The club management wanted him to develop slowly. Top-level road racing was fierce in East Germany because a lot of older riders had been successful professionals before the country was created in 1949. Those former pros were now state-supported amateurs, and Schur's club didn't want him to go up against them until he had more races in his legs, and experience in his head.

Towards the end of the 1951 racing season Schur was unbeatable in mid-level road races. It was time to move up, so his club selected him for the team they entered in the Rund Um Berlin, a 175-kilometre event that was not a circuit race as its name implies, but went from Berlin to Frankfurt an der Oder, near the Polish border, and back to Berlin.

The pace was hard from the start, but Schur was equal to it. A breakaway of twelve riders went clear, with Schur among them, virtually an unknown among the best riders in the country, and they ignored him. Showing real race gumption, Schur sat at the back of the group, and the others let him. They almost forgot he was there until he attacked 20 kilometres from the finish and flew away to victory.

At that time the Rund Um Berlin was a classic in amateur road racing, but was one of the oldest races in Europe, and had been a pro race for its first sixty years, with big prize money. Schur's victory was a surprise in itself, but the way he won made him a marked man at the top level in 1952. It didn't stop him having his most successful season, winning a number of races and taking tenth overall in his debut Peace Race. At the end of the year Schur received his first civil decoration, Verdienter Aktivist, a state award given to people who were outstanding in their field.

In 1953 Schur was offered a place at Leipzig University, where he studied to qualify as a Sports Leader and Instructor. At the same time he transferred to the famous Sports Club Wissenschaft in the city. Leipzig was also home to the German High School for Physical Culture, composed of instructors and students who were specialists at different sports.

Schur was now in the top tier of East German sport. He no longer had to worry about equipment, about getting to races and about finding the time to train. Under the professors at Leipzig he gained a qualification, and with the expert coaching there he polished his natural ability until it really shone.

He won everything he could win early in 1953, and although he wasn't selected for the East German national team for the Peace Race, Schur still finished third overall for his club team. Later in the year he won the Tour of East Germany, and in doing so captured the hearts of bike fans, who formed solid walls of people when the race went through towns and cities, all chanting 'Täve, Täve!' Schur was the new big star of East German cycling.

To keep fit in the winter he took up cyclo-cross and won his first national title. In 1954 he won the East German road race title for the first time. He would win five more national road race titles between 1955 and 1961, finishing second on the two other occasions within that period. He also won the Tour of East Germany four times during this period, taking seventeen stage wins in the process. And he won the Peace Race in 1955 and in 1959.

The other outstanding statistic of Schur's cycling career is his record in the world road race championships. He made his debut in the annual race for the rainbow jersey at the Klinger Ring at Solingen in Germany in 1954, riding for the United Team of Germany because East Germany was not yet affiliated to cycling's governing body, the UCI. Schur was later selected for the United Team of Germany in the 1956 Olympic Games road race in Melbourne, where he won the team bronze medal.

Just a word about the Olympic road race team competition before I move on, because 1956 was the last Olympics in which team medals were awarded in the Olympic road race. From 1960 until 1992 there was a separate team time trial in the Olympics. Before that the road race team gold medal was awarded to the team with the three best aggregate times in the race. Schur was the fifth individual rider to cross the line in Melbourne.

Schur won the 1958 and 1959 world amateur road race titles for East Germany, or the German Democratic Republic (GDR) to give the country its proper title, which had by then been recognised by the UCI. And just to underline that recognition the UCI awarded the 1960 world championships to the GDR. The track events were held in Leipzig, and the road races were on the famous Sachsenring motor-racing circuit, near Chemnitz, which was known as Karl-Marx-Stadt at the time. The city's name was changed between 1953 and 1990 to celebrate the father of communism.

It's reckoned that 250,000 people watched the amateur road race on the Sachsenring, which was 20 laps of a 9-kilometre circuit. With one lap to go Schur and his East German team-mate Bernhard Eckstein were ahead of the rest with Willy Van Berghen of Belgium, a renowned sprinter, whom Schur knew very well. Schur decided the tactics he and his team-mate would use, and with a couple of kilometres to go the two East Germans split, Schur choosing one side of the road, and Eckstein the other. Van Berghen now had to pick which one to follow. He picked Schur.

Who wouldn't? Schur was a double world champion going for his hat-trick. Surely he would try to win – but he didn't. Eckstein knew what to do, and accelerated away. Van Berghen quickly realised that if he chased Eckstein, then Schur would just follow and outsprint him. Anyway, he was confident that if he stayed behind Schur he'd beat him in a sprint, and silver isn't gold but it's better than bronze. Unfortunately, the Belgian couldn't even do that and Schur won the sprint, delighting the vast majority of the crowd with an East German one-two.

Schur was always generous with praise for his rivals, and he made friends throughout the cycling world. He held some of the best British riders of his era in particularly high esteem. There was no real pathway into top-level professional road racing in the Fifties, so most of the top British road racers were amateurs whom Schur met regularly in competition. Ian Steel was well known by Eastern Europeans because of his 1952 Peace Race victory, but Schur also knew Stan Britain and Bill Bradley from their Peace Race appearances, and he knew Alan Jackson and Billy Holmes from the 1956 Olympic Games. Jackson took the bronze medal in the Olympic road race in Melbourne and won a silver medal with Holmes and Stan Britain in the team race.

East Germany was awarded the 1960 world cycling championships on the strength of four days of international racing the country had hosted in 1957, to which top UCI officials were invited. They were really impressed by the facilities, and by the quality in depth of the East German riders, who like most athletes in the Eastern bloc had to fight through regional and national races every year to maintain their place in the national team.

The first of the 1957 races, a road race held on the Sachsenring, was won by a Belgian, Emil Daems, who later turned professional and won Milan–San Remo, Paris–Roubaix and the Giro di Lombardia. Alan Jackson was runner-up, and Schur was third. The whole field then moved to Karl-Marx-Stadt for a night-time race, eighty laps of a short circuit around brightly lit city streets.

Schur was determined to win this one. Points were awarded for the first few over the line every tenth lap, the winner being the rider with the most points at the end of the race. Sixty world-class riders lined up, but after two laps there were only fifty-nine of them in the bunch. Schur was missing – but not for long. A few laps later he rejoined the bunch, having gained a lap on them. That was quite something with the class of riders there, but Schur attacked again and lapped everybody for a second time, winning the race by a massive margin.

Through performances like that, through his generous nature and charismatic personality, Schur became well known and well liked throughout the cycling world, receiving invitations to race in many different countries. He was part of an East German team that competed in the Manx International race in 1960 on the Isle of Man, which Bernhard Eckstein won, and there was a plan to get an East German team into the 1961 Milk Race, the stage race that replaced the Tour of Britain. Unfortunately that coincided with the Berlin Wall being built in 1961, which divided the city into East and West Berlin, with East Berlin becoming part of East Germany. The partition meant that for a while East German sports people couldn't get visas to visit any NATO countries. So the 1961 Milk Race was out of the question, although East European teams took part in subsequent years, with Poland, Russia and Czechoslovakia all providing winners of the Milk Race.

Without a trip to the Milk Race in 1961, which he had wanted to ride, Schur announced his retirement, provoking a deluge of tributes in foreign newspapers, with journalists competing to get stories from his rivals about the great German rider. Few knew him as well as the Belgian Willy Van Berghen, who was third behind Eckstein and Schur in the 1960 world road race championships, and third in the 1960 Olympic road race in which Schur was second. The Belgian was also third overall when Schur won the 1959 Peace Race. This is what Van Berghen told the Belgian newspaper *De Standaard* in 1961:

Schur, he was a bike rider; I liken him to and put him in the same class as our own Rik Van Looy. I will never forget when Eckstein became world champion on the Sachsenring. At the time I had a good chance myself as I had been racing quite consistently the whole season, but Schur saw to it that Eckstein got the title, and not me. I have never held this against Schur, for I already knew him from previous combat in the Peace Race to be an honest sporting opponent in the true spirit of amateur sport. It's a pity that not all bike riders in the world race with the same fairness and sporting spirit as Täve. I greet him from Brussels, my home town, and I wish him with all my heart every good fortune in the future.

There were many other tributes, including this one from Oskar Michael from Dresden, a pro road racer in the Twenties who worked in cycling all his life: 'I have known almost all the great bike riders, first as an active rider, later as a trainer and manager, and later still in the cycle business, with which I am still connected. But I have never known such a popular character blessed with such talent and power, who still had time for the youngsters in the street who hailed him as Täve,' Michael told the East German newspaper *Neues Deutschland*. There was also a book about Schur, written by the *Berliner Zeitung* cycling journalist Adi Klimanschewsky, which ran to four reprints and total sales of 100,000 copies.

Although primarily a road racer, Schur was good on the track and filled East German velodromes when they put on races called The Roadman's Hour, which were one-hour scratch races for the country's top road stars. A lot were held at the Werner-Seelenbinder-Halle velodrome in East Berlin, with Schur the main attraction. He would also ride Madisons and pursuit races. In 1960, with East Germany hosting the world cycling championships, they needed to find talent for the 4,000-metre individual pursuit race, because at that time there was only one specialist at the event, Siegfried Köhler. Road racers were asked to give the pursuit a go at the East German national track championships. As the national road team captain, Schur entered to set an example and finished third behind Köhler.

Retirement allowed Schur to focus full-time on his other passion, politics. He was a member of East Germany's Volkskammer parliament from 1959 until 1990. Then on unification he stayed true to his socialist beliefs and was elected to the Bundestag from 1998 to 2002. At the time of writing he is 86, still keeps very fit, and as recently as 2012 he rode two stages of the 1955 Peace Race in memory of Alf Butler, who was the British team manager in many editions of the race. It was organised by Alf's son Allan.

In 1962 Schur had a son, Jan, who also became a great cyclist, winning a gold medal in the 1988 Olympic Games in Seoul in the team time trial with Uwe Ample, Mario Kummer and Maik Landsmann. They were part of the generation that made the transition from elite state-sponsored amateurs to professional road racers.

Jan Schur turned professional in 1990 for the Italian Chateau d'Ax team. He was sixth in the Tour of Flanders that year and took part in the Tour de France, finishing 105th overall. Schur switched to the American Motorola team in 1992 and raced until 1994.

Polish riders were the first from Soviet bloc countries to race as professionals, although as cycling moved to becoming open during the Eighties some Eastern national teams, like Russia, were invited to take part in some Western pro races.

Czeslaw Lang was the first Pole to become a professional cyclist with a Western team when he joined the Italian team Gis Gelati in 1982. Lang raced with Italian pro teams until 1989 and now runs the Tour of Poland, a UCI World Tour race that dates back to 1928, although it was run intermittently until 1947. Lang was followed by his countryman Lech Piasecki, who won the world amateur road race title and the Peace Race in 1985. Lang was racing for the Del Tongo team by then, and they approached the Polish Cycling Federation, which agreed to let Piasecki race for them if the team got its bike suppliers, Colnago, to donate bikes to the Polish national team. A deal was done and in 1986 Piasecki was the first rider from a former Soviet bloc country to win a stage in a Grand Tour, which he achieved by winning a time trial in the Giro d'Italia. The following year he was the first former Eastern bloc rider to wear the yellow jersey in the Tour de France.

After that more and more former Eastern bloc riders turned professional. In 1991 Djamolidine Abdoujaparov from Tashkent, formerly part of the Soviet Union, won the green jersey in the Tour de France. He repeated that feat twice more in 1993 and 1994, as well as winning the points title in the 1992 Vuelta a España and the 1994 Giro d'Italia. Another former Soviet Union rider, Andre Tchmil, was the first Easterner to win one of the monuments of cycling, Paris–Roubaix, in 1994. Then, also in 1994, Evgeni Berzin of Russia became the first from his country to win a Grand Tour, the Giro d'Italia. Berzin was a product of the Soviet system who had previously been an excellent track rider.

The Peace Race survived the fall of communism, although it lost state support so the organisers had to

reach out to businesses for sponsorship. The old Berlin–
Warsaw–Prague route template, which had only varied
slightly, now changed to fit commercial interests. In 2004
the race even reached through the old Iron Curtain and
started in Brussels, finishing in Prague. There was no
Peace Race in 2005, and the last Peace Race as an international elite men's stage race was held in 2006.

However, the Peace Race lives on in spirit as separate
junior and under-23 category races. The junior Peace
Race started in 1965, then petered out, but was resurrected in 1974. It's been held every year since and boasts
Denis Menchov, Fabian Cancellara and Michal Kwiatowski
among its winners. The under-23 Peace Race was born
in 2012, and from 2015 it's been part of the UCI Under-23
Nations Cup.

10

The Great British Anomaly

With James Moore winning the first proper road race, Paris–Rouen, in 1869, you'd expect British riders to feature regularly at the top end of men's road racing, in the story of the Grand Tours and classics, but they don't, or at least not until quite recently. In the early history of cycling British names are consistently there, in many cases dominating European races, but from the turn of the twentieth century they disappear until the late Fifties, when they return, slowly at first but in numbers now. It's a complicated story.

Moore won on both sides of the Channel, on the road and on the track. He set a record of 14 miles 880 yards in one hour at the Molyneux Grounds in Wolverhampton, and he won a race called the MacGregor Cup from 1872 to 1875, and again in 1877. It was held in different parts of France each year, and was regarded as an early world championships.

Track cycling became popular in the UK. The first cycling match between Oxford and Cambridge universities was held at the Lillie Bridge track in 1874. Then, just as it did in Europe, the advent of the safety bicycle made road racing more accessible, and the sport grew in the UK.

In 1885 a British cycling club dedicated to road racing was formed called the North Road Cycling Club. Its stated aim was 'to promote fast and long-distance racing on the North Road and other roads'. The North Road, also known as the Great North Road, was the trunk road between London and Edinburgh – basically what the A1 is today, although sections of the modern A1 follow new routes around towns.

Several North Road members, including George Pilkington Mills, Montague Holbein and H. B. Bates, were invited to take part in the first Bordeaux–Paris, a race still regarded as classic well into the Sixties. They dominated; Mills won, Holbein was second and Bates finished third.

But then in 1894, in a North Road Cycling Club promoted 50-mile road race, a furiously pedalling bunch of riders caused horses drawing a carriage to take fright. They reared up, knocking several racers off their bikes and overturning the carriage. Nobody was seriously hurt, but the woman inside the carriage made an official complaint to the police.

This caused huge consternation inside the governing body of UK cycling, the NCU. The rights of cyclists, and more particularly the rights of cyclists to race on British roads, weren't fully established by law when the accident happened. Some police forces objected to racing, so the

NCU, fearing all cycling might be banned on the open road, both leisure and competition, voluntarily banned racing on all public roads as a goodwill gesture.

The NCU wrote to every registered cycling club asking them not to promote races on public roads, but to use tracks, motor-racing circuits or airfields instead, so that racing was kept well away from the public. However, Frederick Thomas Bidlake, one of the racers who was involved in the overturned carriage incident, thought there was a way to run races on public roads and not cause problems to the public, and thereby avoid the risk of police involvement. Six years previously he had founded the Road Records Association (RRA), and he subsequently set several of their tricycle records. The pre-eminent rule of the RRA, which still exists today, is that all record attempts must be done alone and un-paced. No other riders are involved in record attempts, so they are only races in the sense that the rider is racing against the previous record, but Bidlake thought that the 'alone and un-paced' aspect of RRA record attempts could be applied to races on the road by running them as time trials.

Individual competitors, starting at intervals and riding alone, would attract far less attention than a bunch racing along a road. What's more, if these time trials took place early in the morning on isolated stretches of road, deep in the countryside, they wouldn't attract much attention. The locations of the race routes could even be coded, so only insiders would know where they were. And if all competitors were dressed from head to toe in black, almost total anonymity would be guaranteed. So those were the rules of racing Bidlake proposed, on top of which competitors wouldn't have race numbers, but would start in numbered order and they would have to shout their number to the timekeeper as they crossed the line.

The first race organised under the new rules was a 50-mile time trial run by the North Road Cycling Club on 5 October 1895. Time trials had been organised by the NCU before, but this race was under the new imperative of 'private and confidential', and was overseen by a new governing body, as the RRA's interest was limited to road records. The new body was called the Road Time Trials Council (RTTC), and after a time the NCU accepted it. The two bodies became allies many years later in fighting another rebel cycling body, this time one formed to get massed start races back on British roads, but more of that story later.

Road records administered by the RRA were either place-to-place ones, like Land's End to John O'Groats, or over the set distances or time, which is what RTTC time trials were – 25, 50 and 100 miles, and 12 and 24 hours. However, RRA set-distance and time records could be set on straight-out courses. A rider could start from one place and ride for 25, 50 or 100 miles, or for 12 and even 24 hours, in roughly the same direction. In fact most record attempts did just that, in order to take advantage of wind direction. Riders would pick ideal wind conditions for place-to-place records, so with Land's End–John O'Groats a potential record breaker would wait until a stiff south-westerly wind was forecast. The only time that didn't happen was on 'out and back' records, like London to Brighton and back. Then riders would wait for fairly still conditions, if possible.

The RTTC had its own set-distance and time records, but they had to be set in races, and were called competition records. The move to time trials instead of bunched road races bred some remarkable cyclists. The 12-hour was a very popular time trial challenge, and it's interesting to look at the progress of performance in it. Freddy Grubb set a record of 220.5 miles in 1911. Two years later it was raised to 223.5 miles by H. H. Gayler, who was then killed in action during the First World War. It took a while for racing to get going again after the war, but by 1927 Jack Lauterwasser had increased the 12-hour record to 240 miles, the first 20 miles per hour average. Then in 1935 three riders, Jackie Bone, James McKechnie and Maurice Clark, all rode more than 240 miles in separate races on the same day.

British time trials helped British riders do well when road racing got its own official world championships in 1921. The first world road race championships were held in Copenhagen in 1921. It was for amateur riders only, run as a time trial over 190 kilometres, and Britain's Charles Davey took the bronze medal. The following year, when Liverpool hosted the world championships, British riders took a one-two-three in the road race. Dave Marsh was first, William Burkhill second and Charles Davey took his second consecutive bronze medal. The road race course was based on that used for a 100-mile time trial organised by another very old British cycling club, the Anfield Bicycle Club. The Anfield was formed in 1879, and one of its early presidents, John Houlding, was a brewer and Mayor of Liverpool, who also formed Liverpool Football Club in 1892.

But then the world championships changed to a bunch road race, and Great Britain didn't provide another men's medallist for over forty years. The reason was simple: British road racers were strong, they could ride all day against the clock, but they weren't adept at riding in a bunch; they couldn't cope with the changes of pace, or the bursts of speed that Continental Europeans were used to sustaining. Neither did they have the skills and reflexes that have to be second nature to a good road racer.

Another thing that held British road racers back was that the NCU and RTTC wouldn't allow professionals in races. If somebody wanted to earn a living from cycling, and bike manufacturers at the time were eager to pay them to do so, they could only do it by attacking RRA records. It's something a lot of good riders did, among them Charles Davey, the double world road race bronze medallist. Davey set several records, including Land's End to London, London to Portsmouth and back, and London to Bath and back. By doing so he extended his career and his earnings from cycling until he was 40.

Record attempts weren't kept private and confidential; thousands turned out to watch when one was announced within riding distance – and riding distances were a long way in those days. Cycling clubs boomed, with members taking part in races, going on organised club runs and adventurous tours. Cycling grew as a pastime as well as a sport; couples met through cycling; and people began exploring the wider countryside through cycling.

But if the domestic time trial programme reduced British cyclists' chances in the world road race championships, it boosted them in the 1928 Olympic Games, because the Olympic movement stuck to a time trial to decide their road race medals: a fact that helped the next British road race star to a silver medal. He was substantially behind the winner, although the gap could have been closer – if not closed completely – because it looks like something dodgy happened.

Frank Southall was Britain's representative in the 1928

Olympic road race in Amsterdam. He took the silver medal, but British officials immediately lodged a protest, claiming that the winner, Harry Hansen of Denmark, had cut the course. They didn't see the Dane do it, but their reasoning is hard to argue with. With 50 kilometres of the 165-kilometre course covered, Southall was 90 seconds behind Hansen, but in the next 34 kilometres he lost a scarcely believable seven minutes to Hansen. Why scarcely believable? Because Southall didn't slow down during those 34 kilometres, and the Dane gained no more time on him during the remaining 82 kilometres. Nevertheless, the protest was unsuccessful.

The next British road racing star was Charles Holland from the West Midlands. His parents were keen touring cyclists, and he grew up doing long-distance cycle tours and all-day rides. He started racing at 18, and five years later took the bronze medal in the 1932 Los Angeles Olympic road race, the last held as a time trial. The time trials reappeared in the Olympic programme in 1996, when separate road race and time trial titles became part of the Games.

In 1934 Holland raced in the world amateur road race championships in Leipzig. His diet of racing was typically British, mostly time trials with some closed circuit and track racing, so the experience of bunch road racing in the worlds was quite alien to him. But Holland did very well, especially considering he raced on a single-geared bike. He got into the winning breakaway, but he was up against competitors on multi-geared bikes who were used to racing on roads in big groups. Fourth place was a terrific result for him.

It helped Holland gain selection for the 1936 Berlin Olympic Games, when the road race title was decided by a bunched race on very flat roads, including a long section of dual carriageway through the centre of Berlin. The race ended in a massive sprint, in which Holland finished barely a second behind the winner, Robert Charpentier of France, but was recorded as simply being among the finishers.

In 1930 the British magazine *Cycling*, grandfather of the current *Cycling Weekly*, founded a competition to find the rider who could achieve the best average speed across the three classic time trial distances: 50 miles, 100 miles and 12 hours. Called the British Best All-Rounder (BBAR) competition, it gave British male club riders something to race for in their own areas, while allowing them to be compared with others nationally.

The BBAR predated national titles at the individual time trial distances. Men's national titles at 25 miles, 50 miles, 100 miles and 12 hours were introduced in 1944. Women got a 25-mile title in 1944, and a BBAR over 25, 50 and 100 miles as well as a 50-mile title in 1948. They finally got a 100-mile title in 1950.

Charles Holland was the first to set a 22 miles per hour average when he won the BBAR in 1936. Then, having done everything he could do as an amateur, he turned professional in 1937. His aim was not to attack road records, but to compete in professional six-day track races. In 1937 this exciting form of track racing was returning to its birthplace, London. Not to the Agricultural Hall, Islington, where the first six-day was held in 1878, but to the Empire Pool in Wembley, where a steeply banked track was built for the occasion.

The first six days were individual endurance races, with riders going as far as they could in six days. But they were slow and plodding affairs, and when people grew tired of what was a bit of a ghoulish spectacle, two-man teams were introduced to make the racing faster. One rider raced while the other rested, and they changed when the first rider wanted a break. Banked tracks were built to cope with the faster speeds, and because the constant relay format of two-man teams was invented by the promoters of the New York six-day in Madison Square Gardens, it became known as the Madison.

London 1937 was a Madison-based six-day, so knowing his competitors would be adept at that kind of racing, Holland went to Belgium to train for it. He took part in a few races there to test his new skills, and he got a place in the 1937 London six-day, but he crashed and broke his collarbone on day one. However, while he was training and racing in Belgium, Holland met quite a few pro racers who'd ridden all the big classics and the Tour de France. He would need to be in a European team to ride most of those races, but the Tour de France was open to national and regional teams by then, so he decided to try to get in the Tour. He contacted the Tour's organisers, telling them about a proper road race he'd won on the Isle of Man, which they knew about, and they said they'd accept Holland if he'd join a three-man team with another British rider, Bill Burl, and a Canadian called Pierre Gachon.

The Great Britain-Canada team riders were each given white jerseys with Union Jacks on the sleeves by the Tour de France organisers. They looked good at the start, but faced a huge step up in every aspect of road racing, and they had very little experience to cope with it. Gachon went out on the first stage, Burl on the next, but Holland was a real class act and he battled through to stage 14, Ax-les-Thermes to Bagnères-de-Luchon, where a series of punctures and a broken bike pump left him with no alternative but to abandon the race.

Of the ninety-eight riders who started that Tour, only forty-six finished. There were fifty-six left when Holland went, so he did well, especially with the poor support the organisers gave him. He spoke about the experience in 1989: 'They didn't provide us with a manager, and you cannot look after yourself on a race like that. I think the organisers got all the publicity they wanted out of me first, then they didn't want me to finish. How would it have looked if an individual rider with no support had finished their race?' he said.

Holland spent the rest of his career setting new road records, while the Tour de France stopped for the Second World War, resuming in 1947. By then there was an inspired movement to get road racing back on the open roads of Britain. And the man behind it, the man who lit the fuse to the explosion of British cyclists in the men's and women's professional pelotons, was Percy Stallard.

Stallard started racing the British way, mixing time trials with grass and hard track racing. However, his inspiration came when he took part in a series of bunched races on the Brooklands motor-racing circuit in 1933. They were organised in response to a UCI decision to run the Olympic road race as a bunched race, not a time trial. The NCU actually tried to get the UCI to reconsider, but it wouldn't, so they asked clubs local to Brooklands to organise some bunched races at the venue to give prospective internationals some experience of them.

The series culminated in a 100-kilometre race, which was a trial for the British team for the 1933 world amateur road race championships. Stallard did well enough to get selected, then finished 11th in the worlds, the best of the British team. Later he said, 'I learned more in that one trip than I had in six years as a time triallist.' However, in comparison with the European riders Stallard felt his bike and equipment were outdated and inferior, his skills second class, and the tactics that were second nature to the Europeans were new to him. He also said he'd found the changes of pace in the race difficult to deal with.

Stallard improved the following year when he was seventh in the world road championships race on a very flat circuit in Leipzig. Then in 1936 he raced the first edition of the Manx Trophy, a bunched race on the roads of the Isle of Man. It was a reincarnation of a much older bike race called the Push-bike TT, where after riding a lap of the famous TT motorcycle circuit the riders turned off the promenade in Douglas to finish inside the Palace Ballroom. In 1936 the Manx Trophy was one lap of the TT circuit, in 1937 it was two, and by 1951 it had grown to three laps.

It was the first time most British cyclists had raced in a bunch through towns and villages, and the first time they had raced up and down a mountain. Stallard finished 17th, and although he continued to compete in the NCU races at Brooklands, they weren't real road racing. What's more, after his Isle of Man experience Stallard couldn't see any logical reason why proper road races shouldn't be allowed in the rest of the UK. His chance came during the Second World War.

There was very little motor traffic on the roads of Britain due to petrol rationing. So Stallard wrote to the NCU requesting permission to organise a road race. He pointed out that there would be no need to close the roads, and there would be no real disruption. The NCU refused outright, so Stallard went ahead anyway. He approached the police with his plan for a race from Llangollen to Wolverhampton, and not only did they not object, they promised to help. Stallard announced at Easter 1942 that his race would take place on 7 June that year.

The race route went from Denbighshire into Shropshire, then Staffordshire and finally into Wolverhampton, passing through the towns of Whitchurch and Newport. Stallard obtained permission from the Chief Constables of those areas to stage the race, he got the *Wolverhampton Express and Star* to sponsor it, and he promised that any profits would go to the Forces Comfort Fund. Thirty-four riders took the start, all listed as representing their towns or their branch of the armed forces rather than their cycling clubs. All but one of them used derailleur gears for the undulating course, the exception being Cecil Anslow of Wolverhampton, who raced on a fixed gear of 47 x 15.

Police cars and motorcyclists patrolled the course, and the field steadily broke up under the pressure of attacks from stronger riders. Eventually a group of three escaped the rest, and those riders sprinted to decide the race before a crowd of about a thousand, after receiving a police escort through the streets of Wolverhampton.

Albert Price from the host town beat 'fixie' Anslow, with Jack Holmes of the RAF in third place. Jan Kremers of the Royal Dutch Brigade led in the rest at 53 seconds, and the last of fifteen riders to finish, E. Upton, was just over seven minutes behind. The fifteen finishers were all immediately banned by the NCU and the RTTC from competing in any of their races, which meant all official races in the UK at that time. Stallard's ban was for life, subject to appeal, but he didn't appeal.

Stallard simply ignored the ban, formed a rival body, the British League of Racing Cyclists (BLRC), and encouraged cycling clubs to affiliate to it. And when they did, he got them to organise road races under BLRC rules. At first this caused a big rift in British cycling, but it was necessary. Clubs could affiliate to the BLRC, and many did, or the NCU, but not both. The BLRC was painted as a renegade organisation by cycling's establishment, but that only made it, and road racing, more attractive to young riders, especially those who had read about the Tour de France and the other big European road races.

This is what the editor of *Cycling* magazine, Harry England, wrote in a 1943 editorial:

> Our leniency towards the riders who support the BLRC should have a time limit, from now until the date of the next illegal promotion. After which the mischief-makers should be kept right outside our sport. We can do without men who are thus jeopardising the whole road game, at a time when those away from home look to cyclists who are still able to carry on with their sport, to preserve it with a level-headed and sound policy that will ensure its future.

But instead of withering under attacks like that from British's leading cycling magazine, as well as the NCU's policy of suspending anyone who competed in BLRC events, the BLRC grew. Clubs switched allegiance, and if their club wouldn't switch, then some riders chose to switch to BLRC-affiliated clubs. They had a slogan, 'Up the Leaguers', which BLRC clubs shouted to each other when they met on the road. And members started dressing the way Continental road racers did, with entrepreneurs like Ron Kitching importing European racing jerseys and other clothing to sell in his Harrogate shop.

In 1944 BLRC clubs organised twenty-five road races on British roads, including regional and national championships, as well as place-to-place races like Morecambe to Bradford. The BLRC also oversaw the creation of the first ever stage race held in Britain, the Southern Grand Prix, held in Kent in August 1944. The winners of these races included Stallard, who took the national title; Ernie Clements, who won the first Tour of the Peaks, the Midlands championships and the Tour of the Clees; Geoff Clark, who won Morecambe to Bradford; and Ron Kitching, the winner of the Craven Dales road race in Yorkshire.

Jimmy Kain made the next road racing breakthrough in Britain when in 1945 he organised the Victory Cycling Marathon to celebrate the end of the Second World War. It ran from Brighton to Glasgow in five stages and set out with a budget of £174, which ran out in Bradford. Kain's solution was simple: 'I got out my hat and had a whip-round among the crowd at the stage. They contributed another 26 quid, which got us to Glasgow,' he said in an interview years later.

The race was popular and attracted big crowds, even if the competitors had a really hard time. Some stages were miles longer than billed, and accommodation was difficult to find. In some cases it was impossible, so competitors slept in barns or under hedges. The winner was a Frenchman, Robert Babot, who represented a non-mainstream cycling body in France, the communist-inspired Fédération Sportive et Gymnastique du Travail (FSGT), a workers' sports association that's still going strong today.

The event grew amid the NCU and BLRC conflict, which eventually put sponsors off because of their constant bickering. The *News of the World* gave the race £500 in 1947, then pulled out the following year. The

Daily Express got involved but went the same way, as did Butlins holiday camps. Still the race developed into a Tour of Britain, although some editions called it the Circuit of Britain. Sponsorship stability only came the year before NCU and BLRC amalgamation, when a Derbyshire racer, Dave Orford, got the Milk Marketing Board to take over.

By 1958 there was a category of rider called independents racing in BLRC races, and they raced for money. Orford was one of them, and in 1958 he approached the Milk Marketing Board, the sales body of English and Welsh dairy farmers, and asked its members to pay for the Board's slogan 'Drink More Milk' to be put on every independent racer's jersey. The Board's marketing man was impressed with Orford's pitch, but said he would prefer to sponsor a bike race. So Orford, quick as a flash, suggested the struggling Tour of Britain, and in 1958 the Milk Race was born. The sponsorship lasted for 35 years.

Bickering also held back the development of road racing in the UK, but apart from some understandable intransigence on the part of people who were suspended by the NCU, none of the blame can be laid at the door of the BLRC. On the contrary, they created a wonderful blueprint for British road racing, and they sent teams to compete abroad too, either in races not affiliated to the UCI, or by arrangement with individual race organisers. For example, from 1948 the BLRC sent a team to the biggest bike race in Eastern Europe, the Peace Race, or Berlin–Warsaw–Prague as it was called then.

BLRC clubs modelled their races on what they had seen or read about in Europe. BLRC riders aped the Continental 'look', riding in tight black wool shorts and colourful short-sleeved cycling tops with white ankle socks. They wore little cycling casquette caps and crochet-backed track mitts, and on training rides they wore plus fours with long woollen socks and cycling-specific jumpers, maybe topped off with a black beret. That was how the European pros dressed. They'd seen pictures in French and Italian cycling magazines, some in colour, of famous pros racing in the Alps and Pyrenees, in the Dolomites, and across the plains of France and Flanders, and they were hooked.

Those pictures set the next character in this story on a path to becoming the first British rider to break into top-level men's professional road racing. He is Brian Robinson from Yorkshire, and one of the local cycling heroes who helped Yorkshire's successful bid to host the start of the 2014 Tour de France.

> My older brother Des raced in Europe and he brought some magazines back. It was the early Fifties and I was a keen rider with the Huddersfield Road Club, but my father wouldn't let me race until I was 18, so all I could do was ride my bike and look at pictures, but they must have held some sort of fascination for me.

Robinson was 18 in 1947 and he started racing in time trials. He wanted to do road races but, being ambitious, he also wanted to ride in the Olympics, so he had to steer clear of the BLRC and focus on NCU massed-start races on airfields and such like, and on time trials. Then in the spring of 1952 he got the opportunity to ride in Europe in a race called the Route de France, which was regarded as an amateur Tour de France back then.

> I was doing my national service in the Army, and the Army was invited to send a joint team to the Route de France with the NCU. I did okay, and was lying fifth

overall with three days to go, but then we got to the Pyrenees and I'd never seen anything like it. The only mountain I knew was Holme Moss, which isn't even quite 2000 feet, but the big Pyrenean passes are well over 8,000 feet high. I'll never forget the day we were in the valley riding towards the Col de Peyresourde. You can see the road zig-zagging up that climb from the valley, although I didn't know it then. What I thought I saw was a zig-zag of lights going up the mountain. I asked the rider next to me what they were, and he told me it was the sun reflecting off the windscreens of the cars parked along the route. So I asked him, 'Are we going up there?' And he replied, 'Oh yes.'

At first Robinson was a bit out of his depth on climbs like that – they later became a strength – and he slipped to 40th overall by the end of the race. However, he was good enough to achieve his first ambition, selection for the Olympic Games road race in Helsinki, where he finished 27th, one place behind his brother Des.

Jacques Anquetil, the Frenchman who would be the first to win five Tours de France, was in that Olympic road race and finished 12th. A few weeks later Robinson finished equal eighth alongside Anquetil in the amateur world road race championships. Next year they were both professionals, or at least Anquetil was. Robinson had a sort of semi-pro status, as an independent in the Ellis Briggs team, working winters and racing full-time during the summer.

Ellis Briggs was a Yorkshire bike shop and pretty typical of the early British pro team sponsors, who with one or two exceptions were bike manufacturers, component manufacturers or shops. The team took part in the BLRC road races in the UK, which were open to independent riders. These included the Tour of Britain, where Robinson was fourth in 1953 and runner-up in 1954. Then he went to France, where he reappears in the next chapter.

The Fifties saw road racing take root in the UK, and by the end of the decade the NCU and BLRC came together to form the British Cycling Federation (BCF), which was recognised by the UCI as the official governing body of cycling in Great Britain. It is now called British Cycling (BC) and runs mainstream road racing, along with other disciplines that have been brought under its administrative umbrella.

In 1995 BC started running its own national time trial championships as well, and today there are BC men's and women's elite and under-23 time trial championships. However, the RTTC, now called CTT (Cycling Time Trials), still governs the vast majority of British time trials, a side of UK cycling that is still strong, although nobody who competes in British time trials today is as well known as a gangly studious-looking electrician from Nottingham called Ray Booty who rode during the Fifties.

The athlete Roger Bannister famously broke the four-minute barrier for the mile in 1954, but British cycling had a barrier in the early Fifties too. The 25-mile record had dropped to mid-fifty-minute territory, but nobody had broken four hours for 100 miles. Then in 1956 Ray Booty went close by winning the RTTC's national 100-mile championships in 4 hours, 1 minute and 52 seconds. The next big 100-mile time trial was the classic Bath Road event. In the Fifties it was held at August Bank Holiday on an out-and-back course that started just west of Reading and followed the Bath Road, now the A4. It went through Newbury and turned in the Savernake Forest, a few miles short of Marlborough. Then the riders retraced the outward route back towards the start, but also did a second leg north on what is now the A340, turning short of Abingdon to retrace and finish on Pangbourne Lane.

There was a real buzz in cycling surrounding the possibility of a first sub-four-hour 100. Thousands of club cyclists rode out to see if Booty could break the barrier on the Bath Road, which was a fast course in its day. In typical British club rider style, Booty rode to Reading the previous day, just a bit more than 100 miles from his home in Nottingham.

He had a still morning for the race, and used an 84-inch fixed gear. Gear size in those days was expressed as the diameter of a penny-farthing wheel that would be equivalent to a particular ratio, whereas on the Continent it was expressed as the distance the bike covered during one pedal revolution in that particular ratio. Now cyclists almost universally express gear sizes in the simplest formula: the number of teeth on the chainring by the number of teeth on the sprocket. To give some feel for Booty's gear, 50 x 16 would give a gear of 84.4 inches.

It was the perfect choice for the conditions and Booty never faltered, pedalling with a style that sports journalists of the day described as swan-like – all serenity in his upper body, and furious pedalling below. His reward for textbook time-trial style was a new record of 3 hours, 58 minutes and 28 seconds. The four-hour barrier was a barrier no more.

11

Brentry, Britain Joins Cycling's EU

The two biggest British independent/professional teams of the mid-Fifties were BSA and Hercules. Both were bike manufacturers, and both offered Brian Robinson a contract to race for them in 1955. He chose Hercules, 'because they offered me twice the money', he says. But when he signed his contract Robinson didn't know that Hercules had a plan that would change his life. The company was going to base its team in France for the whole of 1955. It was a ground-breaking idea, and it happened like this.

At the 1954 world championships some of the high-ups from the massive British company Tube Investments (TI), which owned Hercules, spent a convivial evening with

British cycling journalists Jock Wadley and Ron White. The businessmen wanted to know if they could get the Hercules team into the Tour de France, and so have their bikes showcased in the sport's biggest race. The journalists told TI that the Tour was for national and regional teams only, but they would ask the organisers if they would let a British national team ride, and perhaps Hercules riders could form part of it, especially if they raced in Europe before the Tour.

The journalists explained that a British team wouldn't just walk into the Tour de France. British riders would have to prove to the Tour organisers that they could cut it at Tour de France level, and the only way to do that would be to race full-time on the Continent. The guys from TI listened, then said they'd base the Hercules team in France for 1955 and enter every big race in Europe they could. That way they hoped their riders would prove themselves, and would therefore form the bulk of the GB team in the Tour de France. It was the opportunity Brian Robinson had wanted ever since he started cycling. He told me the story:

From mid-January 1955 the whole Hercules team stayed in a bungalow in Les Issambres in the south of France. Lots of French pros went there to train before the season started. Louison Bobet was next door and his brother Jean was opposite. We had a cook who shopped and did all our meals for us, so we were well looked after. All your salary was going into the bank. It was heaven. People say now it must have been hard for us then, but I was doing what I loved and getting paid for it. I didn't see it as hard, it was what I wanted to do.

We did our training in the morning, and we'd get back

to the bungalow by two o'clock, then it was siesta time. But instead of taking a nap I learned a different French sentence every day. The others didn't seem to bother doing that, but I was soon able to converse with the guys in the peloton, and that helped me get accepted.

Learning the language did help, but Robinson's talent helped more. Hercules raced all over Europe, and Robinson was the team's best rider. He finished eighth overall in Paris–Nice, fourth in La Flèche Wallonne, and he led the Tour of the Six Provinces for a couple of stages.

Robinson qualified the British team for the 1955 Tour de France almost single-handedly, but there weren't as many Hercules riders in the team as the company had wanted. Why? Robinson has the answer:

A lot went home. It was understandable really; guys like Dave Bedwell had a good life in the UK, commanding races for four or five years before we went to France. Dave couldn't do that there, although he was still picked for the Tour de France team. Others just missed being at home. Even during pre-season training in the south of France they were saying things like, 'Oh, I wish we could get some Yorkshire puddings.' You can't think like that, you can't think about what you are missing, you have to deal with what's in front of you. My mind-set was different. I just thought: I'm in France so I'll live like a Frenchman, learn the language and eat the food. The ones who went home didn't manage to adapt to life in France, and they didn't step up to the higher level of racing there.

So ten British riders lined up at the start of the 1955 Tour de France as the first all-British team to take part.

They were Dave Bedwell, Tony Hoar, Stan Jones, Fred Krebs, Bob Maitland, Ken Mitchell, Bernard Pusey, Brian Robinson, Ian Steel and Bevis Wood. They fought well, but the Tour de France was a massive step up even for the ones who had raced on the Continent. In the end only two of the team got through to the finish in Paris.

Tony Hoar was last, but last was still 69th overall, and there were 130 starters, all experienced pros. The attrition rate of Tours in the Fifties was terrible. Speaking from his Canadian home a few years ago, Hoar said, 'For most of the race I had riders behind me on the overall standings, but every day one or two of them would pack it in. I'd get near the bottom, move up a bit, then those behind me would stop. Eventually, I suppose, I was last man standing.'

Brian Robinson did better, finishing 29th overall, and with the greatest respect to Hoar that is a world of difference to his dogged but still commendable performance. Robinson wasn't a plucky Brit battling through – he could do this; he could hold his own with the best. 'I think I held my own in the mountains,' he says. 'I can't remember having a really bad day, just not enough good ones.'

Robinson is being typically modest; in fact he made a big impression. No British cyclist had got through the Tour de France before, and suddenly here was one not just getting through but getting through well. Professional road racers were on modest wages in the 1950s, but they made extra money from appearances in the lucrative exhibition races called criteriums, for which they were paid according to how they performed in the Tour de France and other big races. For most professionals of that era criterium contracts made the difference between a living wage and

living well. Robinson received thirty contracts for criteriums straight after the 1955 Tour de France.

But performing well enough to get criterium contracts
was one thing; coping with the extra work they brought
was another, as Robinson recalls:

> I had thirty races in forty days. I didn't have a car to get
> to them, so I went around Europe by train, bike and bus,
> pushing my bike from race to railway station and back
> again, and living out of a rucksack. Once I got better
> known by the riders I made some friends and they started
> giving me lifts in their cars. A few even let me sleep in
> their homes when I had a couple of days spare between
> races. The thing was, I hadn't had anywhere to live prop-
> erly since the start of the 1955 Tour, when we gave up
> the bungalow in Les Issambres. So after the last criterium
> contract was fulfilled in September, I went back to
> Yorkshire.

Robinson returned to Europe in 1956, but without a
permanent team. He was known by then, though; the
European teams knew he was able and dependable, so
he got hired on an ad hoc basis by teams for races where
they had a gap in their roster. Even the top pro teams
were small in the Fifties and Sixties compared to today,
with maybe fifteen riders at the most. Some riders rode
almost every big race, and if a few were sick or injured
the team would hire freelancers like Robinson. Proving
himself in situations like that eventually brought Robinson
a full pro contract with the St Raphael team for 1957.
He was in, the first British cyclist to become part of that
collective body of top-level road racing called the professional peloton.

But before that he had the 1956 Tour de France, in which Robinson rode for the Luxembourg-Mixte team. It had seven riders from Luxembourg, one Italian, one Portuguese and one Brit. The mix of riders was necessary to bring the team up to the ten required by the Tour, because Luxembourg had so few pro riders. Robinson ended up the team's best rider, with 14th overall by the end. That brought him more criteriums and a nice bit of money. Enough to take it a bit easier over the following winter, but easier isn't in Robinson's nature. He had work to do.

'I came home in the winter and dug trenches for the house we live in now. I rode my bike at weekends, then I went back to France in January 1957, when it took me about three weeks to get fit. That's when I beat Louison Bobet to win my first big pro road race, the Grand Prix de Nice.' A few weeks later Robinson became the first British rider to stand on the podium of a monument when he took third place in Milan–San Remo. A great ride, without doubt, but Robinson knew how pro cycling worked by then.

When I was taken on by St Raphael, Raymond Louviot, whom I knew well, had got the directeur sportif job there, and he told me to look after the Spaniard, Miguel Poblet, in Milan–San Remo. Poblet wasn't in our team, but Louviot wanted him, and he knew that Poblet had trained specifically for the race. He was a good classics rider was Poblet, where most Spaniards were better at stage races.

In the race my team-mate Nicolas Barone was away on his own but got caught on the Capo Berta, so I attacked straightaway. I led over the top, then I heard a shout. It was Poblet. I looked back and he was a few lengths behind me, but there was only a couple of riders with him. He shouted at me to slow down, so I did. Maybe if it had been later in the race I would have kept going, but there was a lot of flat after the Capo Berta, and no climb like the Poggio just before the finish like there is now. It wouldn't have worked even if I had attacked. I wouldn't have held on.

Anyway, waiting left me in a break with Poblet, Fred De Bruyne, who had won Milan–San Remo the year before, and a rider called Schepens. We all got stuck in and the break stayed away. I led out the sprint for Poblet, and he and De Bruyne came past me, with Poblet winning the race. They were both better sprinters than me, so they would have beaten me no matter how I did that sprint. Third was a good result, though. I was happy, Louviot was happy, and Poblet must have been happy because he gave me a week's holiday in Spain.

Robinson was an astute racer who knew how and when to help his team-mates, but he also knew how to win if the opportunity arose. 'Cycling is a job for a pro in Europe, and the team winning is more important than individual success. Anyway, the team shares the prizes, and in my day contract money, your monthly wage from the team, wasn't what it is now. The prizes were good, and if you were a good team rider in a good team and could win a bit yourself, you got contracts for criterium races. The top riders had a big say in who got contracts for criteriums, so if you fitted in and were respected, you got contracts,' he says.

The following year Robinson became the first British rider to win a stage in the Tour de France. It only merited half a page in the *Daily Express*, but it was big news in

George Pilkington Mills
(1867–1945), winner of the
inaugural Bordeaux–Paris race.

French racing cyclist Maurice Garin,
winner of the first Tour de France in 1903.

Paul Deman (1889–1961) won the
first Tour de Flanders race in 1913.

Team Omega Pharma – Quick Step 2012 Matteo Trentin, holder of the Ruban Jaune.
© Tim de Waele/Corbis via Getty Images

The arrival of the 1929 Tour de France. From left to right: Maurice De Waele, winner of the Tour, Benoît Faure and Jef Demuysere. © Keystone-France/Gamma-Keystone via Getty Images

Beryl Burton (1937–1996), star of women's cycling in the Fifties, Sixties and Seventies, and among the all-time greats of all women's sport.
© Popperfoto

World Champion Marianne Vos (left) of The Netherlands chats to Elizabeth (Lizzie) Deignan (right) of Great Britain at the start of the Prudential RideLondon Grand Prix Pro Women's Race in St James's Park on 9 August 2014 in London, England. © Bryn Lennon/Getty Images

Former East German cyclist Gustav-Adolf 'Täve' Schur poses with his racing bicycle from 1955, the model 'Friedensfahrt' (Peace Race), during a visit to the production facilities of bicycle manufacturer 'Diamant' bicycles in Hartmannsdorf, Germany, in 2010. © DPA Picture Alliance Archive/Alamy

Peace Race 2004 in Meerane, Germany, where cyclists are seen climbing the so-called 'Steile Wand' ('Steep Wall'). © Christian Fischer/Bongarts/Getty Images

Charles Holland, pioneer racing cyclist and first British rider to enter the Tour de France in 1937.
© M&N/Alamy

British cyclist Brian Robinson on a mountain pass during the ninth stage of the Tour de France, between Briançon and Monaco, 15 July 1955. This was the first tour in which a British team participated. © Bert Hardy/Picture Post/ Hulton Archive/Getty Images

Cyclist Tom Simpson (1937–1967) competing in the 1966 Tour de France.

Barry Hoban receives his trophy after winning the 18th stage of the Tour de France in Bordeaux in 1969. He cycled with the Mercier-Hutchinson team.

Race leader Chris Froome of Great Britain and Team SKY in action on Stage Six of the 2016 Criterium du Dauphine, a 141-km stage from La Rochette to Meribel. © Bryn Lennon/Getty Images

Trophy Baracchi 1967 with Jacques Anquetil and Bernard Guyot. © Jean Tesseyre/Paris Match via Getty Images

Fabian Cancellara of Switzerland competes in the Cycling Road Men's Individual Time Trial on Day 5 of the Rio 2016 Olympic Games at Pontal in Rio de Janeiro, Brazil.

© Bryn Lennon/Getty Images

Mark Cavendish of Great Britain: 5th Tour Dubai 2018, Stage Three Arrival.

© Tim de Waele/Getty Images

A breakaway of 23 riders formed an echelon against the wind but were caught by the peloton early in Stage Three of the 2013 Amgen Tour of California from Palmdale to Santa Clarita.
© Doug Pensinger/Getty Images

Norwegian cyclist Sondre Holst Enger of Team AG2R 2017 receiving a massage from a soigneur. © Tim de Waele/Corbis via Getty Images

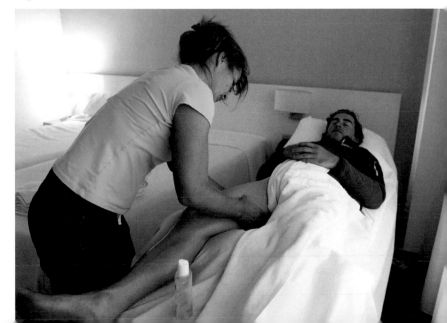

Chris Froome rides during the 78th 'Natourcriterium van Aalst' race on 22 July 2013. The contest is part of the traditional 'criteriums', local races in which mainly cyclists who rode the Tour de France compete. © David Stockman/AFP/Getty Images

A group of riders ready to start a 1930s Australian road race.

Courtesy of the State Library of Western Australia

Sir Hubert
Opperman
(1904–1996),
a pioneer of
Australian
cycling. Courtesy
of the Herald Sun

Sports Illustrated
cover featuring
Greg LeMond
during the 1990
Tour de France.
© Yann Guichaoua/
Vandystadt Agence de
Presse/SI Cover/Sports
Illustrated/Getty Images

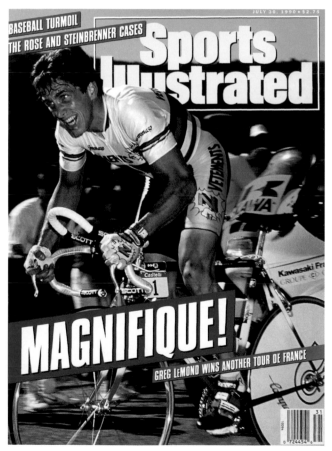

BASEBALL TURMOIL
THE ROSE AND STEINBRENNER CASES

JULY 30, 1990 • $2.75

Sports
Illustrated

MAGNIFIQUE!

GREG LeMOND WINS ANOTHER TOUR DE FRANCE

Luis Alberto 'Lucho' Herrera (born in 1961), the Colombian who first thrust his country into the collective consciousness of cycling.

© CorVos/PezCyclingNews

Italian cyclist Fausto Coppi (1919–1960) during a stage of the 1949 Tour de France. Coppi, one of the most famous cyclists in the world, died of malaria at the age of 40, a few weeks later.

© AFP/Getty Images

André Darrigade, Hans Junkermann and Rik Van Looy during Stage Six of the 1962 Tour de France. © Keystone-France/ Gamma-Rapho via Getty Images

Jacques Anquetil (1934–1987) , supreme stage racer between 1957 and 1964, the first five-time Tour de France winner, the first to emulate Fausto Coppi's Giro/ Tour double, which he did twice, and the first to win all three Grand Tours in his career.

© Horstmüller/ullstein bild via Getty Images

Bernard Hinault leading at Saint Gotthard
Pass, Tour de Suisse in Switzerland.

© Keystone-France/Gamma-Keystone via Getty Images

The great Eddy Merckx, circa 1970
(born in 1945), widely regarded as
the most successful rider in the
history of competitive cycling.

© Jean-Claude Francolon/Gamma-Rapho via Getty Images

Arthur Linton (1868–1896), who won Bordeaux–Paris in 1896 yet died a few months later, and Edward 'Choppy' Warburton (1845–1897), a former top-class runner who trained Linton. Warburton was famous for a black doctor's bag he carried everywhere with him. It held the various potions he used to revive and rejuvenate his athletes. © Jules Beau/Bibliothèque Nationale de France

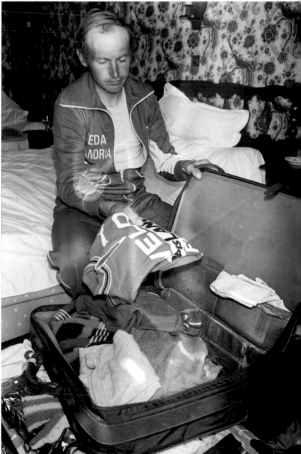

Belgian rider Michel Pollentier packs his suitcase in his hotel room on a rest day, on 17 July 1978 in L'Alpe d'Huez. Pollentier, who won the Tour de France's 16th stage between Saint-Etienne and l'Alpe d'Huez to become the new leader, was caught cheating by medical examiners four hours later during a doping control and expelled from the Tour de France. He was also suspended from cycling for two months.

© AFP/Getty Images

Festina Team's cyclists, among them Swiss Alex Zulle (facing), prepare before the start of the fourth stage of the 85th Tour de France between Plouay and Cholet, as their team faced a doping scandal. © Patrick Kovarik/AFP/Getty Images

Lance Armstrong follows Italy's Ivan Basso during the 15th stage of the 92nd Tour de France between Lézat-sur-Lèze and Saint-Lary-Soulan in July 2005. © Franck Fife/AFP/Getty Images

Europe. 'I didn't expect to win. I was second across the line. Arrigo Padovan beat me in the sprint, but he put me into the barriers. It was quite blatant really, although I didn't expect the decision to be reversed. I didn't even protest, Jean Bobet did that for me. Jean stopped racing quite young and was a journalist with *L'Equipe* on that Tour de France. He got the judges to look at the film, and they agreed with him, so Jean found me and gave me the bouquet saying, "Here, you've won".'

Robinson won another Tour stage in 1959, where this time he did cross the line first, and in fine style after a long lone breakaway that he'd planned the day before.

I was in the top ten overall at the start of stage 14, but I had a bad stomach bug. I was dead really but my team-mate, Shay Elliott from Ireland, we were in another mixed-nations team, stayed with me. I kept telling him to leave me, to ride for himself, because whatever happened I was dropping down the overall standings, but he wouldn't. We ended up outside the time limit. They sent Shay home, but there was a rule in those days that said no one who started a stage in the top ten overall could be eliminated on that stage. So I was still in. I don't know why Shay stopped with me, but he was that kind of person. Too willing to help really.

Anyway, Shay went home and I thought: well, I've got to salvage something. So I looked at the road-book, and the day following the last mountain stage looked good. Escape on the last hill, if you can, then carry on, hoping all the big guys would want to rest for the time trial next day. That was the plan.

At the start of the stage one of my trade team-mates, a Frenchman called Gérard Saint, was lying third in the

King of the Mountains competition. So he approached me, saying that there was one more climb with points that day, and if he could get the points he would move up to second place in the competition. He asked me to lead him out on the climb. I said yes, but only on the condition that he put his brakes on at the top and let me go alone.

And that's what happened. Jean Dotto appeared briefly between us. He was a good guy, but he couldn't descend. I could hear him shouting, 'Wait for me, wait for me', so I put my head down and went for it. The descent was quite gravelly, and I'm thinking: Christ, I've got six-ounce tyres on, my time trial tyres, and I'm going down here like hell. Anyway, I got down, and that was the last they saw of me until the finish.

I put that win down partly to having friends. I mean I never chopped anybody. If anybody wanted something and I could give it to them, then I gave it. The top guys wanted a break to get away on that stage, they wanted a quiet day. It suited them to let me go because I was well down overall, so no danger. In fact they were probably laughing at me for having to ride alone for 130 kilometres in the wind.

Robinson won the stage by 20 minutes. He was well established in the peloton, respected, trusted and dependable. The following year, 1960, saw Tom Simpson ride his first Tour de France. He and Robinson ended up being the only British finishers, with 26th place for Robinson and 29th for Simpson.

Simpson was very talented, but he was also very ambitious. That stood out immediately to Robinson. 'I first became aware of Tom in 1959 when I heard about this

young British lad winning loads of races in Brittany. Tom
came to visit us on the Tour that year, and I introduced
him to Raymond Louviot, who'd heard about him. They
agreed he'd sign for the St Raphael team there and then,
and for more money than I was getting too. But that
was fine by me.'

Robinson was a team man, loyal to the last, and he
knew that his team would be better with Simpson on
board. Loyalty like Robinson's brings rewards in a good
team because, now and again, it brings the chance to
win. Robinson ranks his best-ever victory as the 1961
Dauphiné Libéré stage race, now called the Critérium du
Dauphiné, but he's under no illusions about why he won.
'That was a solid win. Any one of five riders from our
team could have won it, but I got in a break on an early
stage. I was policing it really, riding at the back of the
break so the team was represented, but then Raymond
Louviot came alongside me in the team car and said,
"You can work a bit." That was his vote of confidence,
he was saying I could go for the overall and the team
would back me.'

A lot of things have changed in pro road racing, but
the characteristics of the various countries where racing
takes place haven't changed at all. Robinson enjoyed
racing in France the most, although he found the Tour
de France big and slightly intimidating even then. 'I liked
the Tour,' he says, 'it suited me. Paris–Nice was a good
race too. But I found the crowds and the noise of the
Tour a bit much at times. I liked racing in Italy too, but
I didn't like Belgium, at least not Flanders, even though
I was once fourth in Het Volk (Het Nieuwsblad today).
Racing is hard there, but the people are also hard and
brash, too.'

Robinson's professional career lasted until the end of 1962, when he was still a force to be reckoned with and in demand. He had a place in the Peugeot-BP team for 1963, but he decided it was in his and in his family's best interests to draw the adventure to a close. Robinson returned to Yorkshire to work in the family building business, but he never lost contact with cycling and he's still actively involved in the sport today. And the sporting interest he inherited from his father and shared with his brother Des, who was a good international amateur, continues in the Robinson family. His daughter Louise was a top-class mountain bike and cyclo-cross racer, a world championship silver medallist at cyclo-cross, and his grandchildren, Rebecca and Jake Womersley, are also winning races now.

By the time Robinson retired, Tom Simpson was heading towards the top of professional cycling. If Robinson opened the door, Simpson blew it wide open, walked straight in and sat down at the top table. He was Britain's best until Sir Bradley Wiggins, Mark Cavendish and Chris Froome came along. In fact Wiggins, who admires Simpson a lot, says: 'Tom is still Britain's greatest ever cyclist.'

Even now, when a well-funded British pro team, Team Sky, is one of the best in the world, when British riders are among the world's best in other teams too, especially in Grand Tours, there are big races that Simpson won and no other British rider has. His record proves he is still Britain's best men's single-day racer. Simpson won three of the five biggest single-day races, the monuments. Mark Cavendish is the only other British monument winner, and he's only won one.

Simpson's first pro road race was the 1959 world road

race championships, and he finished fourth. To put that into context only Cavendish (twice) and Simpson himself have done better. In 1964 Simpson was fourth in the worlds again, and in 1965 he became Britain's first ever world professional road race champion. In 1962 Simpson was the first British rider to wear the yellow jersey in the Tour de France, when he also finished sixth overall.

He was a prodigy. He started racing at 14, started winning at 16, then took an Olympic bronze medal in the team pursuit a couple of days past his 19th birthday. Simpson stayed in Britain for two more years, winning national titles and a Commonwealth Games silver medal, then went to Europe to fulfil his destiny. He lived in France, then in Belgium, and remarkably, although he still has the best spread of results of any British road racer, he achieved it at the head of some teams that were not always fully committed to him.

A British winner was a new concept in a sport previously dominated by European racers and European teams, and success in pro road racing depends a lot on teamwork. One man wins, but the team helps him do it. There were no British teams when Simpson raced. He started off well in the St Raphael team, which backed him. But then he found out that Jacques Anquetil was joining the St Raphael team in 1962, so not wishing to limit his horizons and victory chances Simpson moved to another team, Gitane-Leroux. Then in 1963 he went to Peugeot, but he felt they didn't always back him; and that he had to fight to impose his will on the team, which compromised his tactics sometimes, making him attack early, sometimes too early.

Maybe it also made him try too hard. Cyclists are praised for their will to win, but Simpson had more than will; he had a need to win. Right from being a kid he was ultra-competitive at whatever he did, even if he was no good at it. Committed to making early attacks in races so his team were left with no choice but to back him, Simpson often rode to a state of complete exhaustion to make his tactics work. Sometimes it paid, and sometimes it didn't. As well as winning, Simpson's career is littered with races in which he dominated but faltered in the final stages.

And his record has one glaring omission; apart from his good Tour de France in 1962, where his sixth overall could have been third but for a crash and broken finger with a few days to go, his level of success in the Tour didn't match the rest of his career. Simpson didn't ride it in 1963, wanting to focus on the world championships instead. He finished 14th overall in 1964, then crashed out in 1965 and in 1966.

He was 29 in 1967, a good age to have a solid go at winning the Tour de France. So instead of the classics, which suited him better, Simpson focused on stage races, winning Paris–Nice in March, again the first Brit to do so. Then he rode the Vuelta a España, which started in April in those days, winning two stages while getting a solid three-week effort in his legs. After that he trained and rested, won some races but used more as training. By the start of the 1967 Tour de France, Simpson was better prepared for it physically than ever before. He was also going into it better mentally.

In 1961 the Tour de France had switched from national and regional teams to trade-sponsored teams, but in 1967 the Tour co-director, Felix Lévitan, switched back to national teams. That looked bad for Simpson, as half the members of the British team had very little top-level pro racing experience, but at least they were totally committed to him. Plus he'd signed for the Italian team Salvarani for 1968, where his friendship with the great Italian rider Felice Gimondi would have given the team two aces to play, and would have ensured team support.

The future looked good. It looked even better when Simpson got in both important moves in that first week of the 1967 race, and had moved up to sixth overall as the race entered the Alps. Simpson was behind the eventual winner that year, Roger Pingeon, but ahead of the riders who filled the next two places in Paris. An eventual podium was possible, and realistically the podium was his ambition. Simpson acccptcd his tcam wasn't strong enough to protect the yellow jersey, although never wanting to limit himself he also pointed out in a pre-Tour interview: 'Of course I could take the jersey with a day to go and defend it myself in the final time trial.'

It didn't happen. Simpson fell ill the evening before stage 10, succumbing to a stomach bug. He struggled terribly on the next stage, which included the giant Col du Galibier, losing six minutes to the stage winner, Felice Gimondi, and three to Pingeon. By the end of the stage Simpson was in a bad way. He'd been vomiting all day and, according to British team-mate Vin Denson, he couldn't keep any food down that night. Instead he was given a glucose drip by the Italian team doctor, the British team having no medical staff, and he carried on.

Two days later, by the end of stage 12 in Marseilles, he had climbed back to seventh overall. The next stage was Mont Ventoux. Simpson needed to use it to move up; instead he collapsed about 1500 metres from the summit, and died. Heart failure was the official cause, but the report also said that an autopsy found amphetamine drugs in Simpson's system. The news shocked the cycling world as a whole, and hit British cycling very badly.

Lots of British cyclists followed Simpson to Europe in the Sixties, hopeful amateurs looking to make it as pros. Many were based in Ghent, the Belgian city where Simpson lived. Some made it into the professional ranks. Vin Denson won races. So did Michael Wright, although he came up through Belgian racing, having moved there when he was very young. Alan Ramsbottom was a very good pro too. Other Brits managed a year or two in Continental teams, but they were part of the pro peloton, like Robinson and Simpson. But above all there was Barry Hoban, who for a long time after Simpson's death ploughed a lone furrow at the top level in Europe, often the only British rider in big races like the Tour de France.

Hoban is from Yorkshire, three years younger than Simpson, but a lot like him as a cyclist. He was certainly inspired by him, although not in any misty-eyed way, as he recalls.

Tom was winning races on the Continent while I was still racing in the UK, but I was progressing the same way he had as a pursuit racer and all-round track rider who could win time trials and road races. So I thought if he can do well over there, then so can I. In 1962 I went to live in northern France, in the Béthune area, and I raced as an independent in France and Belgium for two years, then I turned professional for Mercier-BP in 1964.

Like Simpson, Hoban won amateur and independent races in France, and he made the big step up to professional racing seamlessly. Too seamlessly as it happened, because he was used too much in his first year.

> I was unlucky when I first turned pro because I had an unsympathetic manager in Antonin Magne, who only had eyes for Raymond Poulidor. He was consumed by Poulidor, and because I was going well he put me in every race to support him. In my first year as a pro I rode all the early-season races, all the classics, the Vuelta a España, the pre-Tour de France stage races, then the Tour de France itself. Then I raced in the criteriums, and continued all the way through to the end of season races and the Giro di Lombardia. It was too much, and I didn't start recovering until near the end of the next road race season.

Hoban won two stages in the 1964 Vuelta a España, and was robbed of a stage win in the Tour de France at Bordeaux when the only man to get past him in the sprint needed a massive hand-sling from a team-mate to do it. He was a key player in Tom Simpson's 1965 world title, working tirelessly to help the winning breakaway get established. In 1966 Hoban won the GP Henninger Turm, a classic in its day. Then he won his first Tour de France stage the day after Tom Simpson died. And then he carried on.

Vin Denson stopped racing at the end of 1968. Allan Ramsbottom had already gone home. A young time trial prodigy, Peter Hill, who had raced as an amateur for Jacques Anquetil's club and was trained by his coach, turned pro for Peugeot-BP in 1967, but his contract wasn't renewed at the end of the year. Still there was Hoban, who took his second Tour de France stage win in 1968 with a long lone breakaway in the mountains, the first British mountain stage success.

Graham Webb won the world amateur road race championships in 1967 in terrific style on what was a red letter day for British cycling, with Beryl Burton winning the women's world road title. Webb turned professional for Mercier-BP for good money, but his pro career got off to a bad start and never recovered. He wasn't cut any slack by the pro hierarchy, and halfway through the following year he stopped racing.

British pros had to be extremely talented, driven and prepared to take big risks, like Simpson, or the managers would use them to support other riders in their teams, as Antonin Magne did with Barry Hoban during his first year. Or they had to fit in, know their place, like Brian Robinson. Hoban was a combination of Simpson and Robinson, in that he knew what to do in support of his team, but he also knew when he could win himself. And when an opportunity arose, he went for it.

The 1968 Tour de France was the last for national teams. Felix Lévitan had to ditch his vendetta against trade teams in 1969. He was under pressure from all sides, because the trade teams funded pro road racing all year but he was denying them its biggest stage. That wasn't right. Plus there was Eddy Merckx. The Tour de France needed Merckx because by 1968 he was the number one bike racer in the world, but he refused to ride the Tour for the Belgian national team. He would only ride for his trade team, Faema. In 1969 the Tour de France went back to the trade team formula, and Merckx won. It has stayed trade teams only ever since.

Hoban found his place in cycling during that 1969

Tour, when he won two successive stages by picking the right breakaway moves and winning the sprint both times. In the following years he won five more Tour de France stages, the last in 1975, winning in breakaways and in bunch sprints, which has led some cycling historians to portray him as a sprinter, but he wasn't. Hoban was a classics racer, as he proved when he won Ghent–Wevelgem in 1974, and with his podium places in Paris–Roubaix (1972) and Liège–Bastogne–Liège (1969).

But despite Hoban's success, during the Seventies there wasn't the flow of British riders moving to Europe, racing there as amateurs and then turning pro that there had been during the Sixties. It looked promising in 1972, when the big British bike manufacturer Raleigh started a project to market their bikes in Europe. They recruited some of the best British pros and talented amateurs and put together a team that rode a few big European races. After two seasons of struggling, however, Raleigh upped the team's budget, recruited a Dutch manager, the former top pro Peter Post, and he started replacing the British riders with Dutch and Belgian ones.

It's said that Post was prejudiced against the Brits, but years later he told me: 'Some were good, some had the ability to make it, [Sid] Barras was a very fast sprinter, but I couldn't get them to understand how a good professional team works. How it's the team that wins, not an individual.' That said, Post was hard to get on with, and not just for British riders. Dave Lloyd, the one British rider who made it through Post's cull in the team until a heart problem put him out of pro road racing in 1976, confirms this: 'Post was against anybody who didn't fit his idea of what a pro should be like, and he was a bully, he picked on people.'

Hoban's last Tour de France in 1978 was the first Paul Sherwen rode. And Sherwen, now half of the TV commentating double act with Phil Liggett, was the first of a new generation of British cyclists in the world's biggest road races. He finished 70th in his first Tour riding for a weak team, but he finished, and he went on to prove his worth in bigger teams winning a few races along the way.

Sherwen got his chance to turn pro by racing as an amateur in France, just like Robinson, Simpson, Hoban and a handful of others had done before him. However, they all did it through different channels. Sherwen opened the door to a regular place for British and/or English-speaking riders in one of France's biggest cycling clubs, the Paris-based Athletic Club de Boulogne Billancourt, almost always referred to by its initials ACBB.

It started when Sherwen moved, and because the club was so happy at his performances he was asked to recommend another Brit to take his place. Sherwen immediately suggested his Manchester-based training partner, Graham Jones. Jones took Sherwen's place in ACBB for 1978 and did even better. He made a solid start to his pro career with the Peugeot team in 1979. Then in 1980, in his debut Tour de France, he was lying 11th overall with one mountain stage and a time trial to go when he fell ill and dropped to 49th. That made the world of difference; if Jones had finished in the top ten in that Tour he could have controlled his career, but instead his team controlled it, putting him in every race they could to support other riders.

Jones admits now that he also had difficulty saying no, which the next British rider to get a place in a big pro team didn't. Robert Millar was a self-contained army of one who knew exactly what he could do, and where he was going. He was a superb climber. He also turned pro for Peugeot, a team with which ACBB had links, but when the Peugeot team manager tried to put him in races that didn't suit him, Millar said no. It didn't make him popular, not at first, but it allowed him to hone his talent, and when Millar made his Tour de France debut in 1983 he won a stage in the Pyrenees.

The following year Millar won the King of the Mountains title outright. This made him the first British rider to win any major Grand Tour competition, and he is still the only one apart from Chris Froome to win the Tour de France King of the Mountains. Millar also finished fourth overall in the 1984 Tour, beating the previous highest, Tom Simpson's sixth place from 1962. Millar's fourth then stood until Bradley Wiggins's fourth place, which was boosted to third after Lance Armstrong's disqualification from the 2009 Tour de France.

Millar was a superb climber and had the best record of any British rider in Grand Tours until very recently. As well as his 1984 Tour de France fourth, Millar finished second in the 1987 Giro d'Italia, winning the mountains title, and he finished second in the 1985 and 1986 Vuelta a España. What's more, in 1985 he could, no, should have won. Victory was stolen from him by the Spanish conspiracy that was dealt with in Chapter 5.

Meanwhile other British riders were going through ACBB. In 1981 Sean Yates, John Herety, Jeff Williams and Kevin Reilly raced for the Paris club, Yates gaining a contract with Peugeot and Herety going to COOP-Mercier. Of the two, Yates was the more successful. He was a very good time triallist, and in 1988 he became the first British rider to win a time trial stage of the Tour de France. Yates evolved into one of the best domestiques in the sport, but he had a personal moment of glory in 1994 when he wore the Tour de France yellow jersey for a day. He was only the third British rider to do that. The second of those three helped sow the seeds of, and later nurture, the success that British cyclists have today. His name is Chris Boardman.

In 1992 Boardman won Britain's first Olympic gold medal in cycling for seventy-two years, and in doing so sparked off a new era of the sport in the UK. The following year his battles at home with Graeme Obree, one of the greatest bike racing innovators ever, went world-wide when first Obree then Boardman set new world hour records. Cycling was stunned. The hour record had been the domain of the greats; the likes of Coppi, Anquetil and Merckx. However, the man who beat Merckx's record, Francesco Moser, although a top road racer, a classics and Grand Tour winner, had prepared very specifically for his hour record attempt, whereas the others more or less tagged it onto the end of their road race season. Moser used specific training methods to help him set his record, using a heart rate monitor and trainers who understood the relationship between heart rate and lactate levels, as well as other performance-limiting factors in the body. These methods removed some of the mystique from training, and certainly removed it from the hour record.

Beating the hour record means maximising a simple equation: power output divided by aerodynamic drag; with weight, atmospheric pressure, friction and other factors playing lesser but still important roles. But the main things are power and drag: increase the first enough and reduce the second enough, and the record is broken.

Obree thought up a whole new bike design to reduce drag, and he had the power, and he broke Moser's hour record first. Boardman used a more orthodox riding position, but he refined it and had a natural body shape and flexibility to reduce drag as much as possible in it. Then Boardman employed pin-point training methods to increase his sustainable power, and later the same year he broke Obree's record.

Their 1993 records put Obree and Boardman on the world stage. Obree's bike design limited the impact he could make on top-level road racing, but he was offered a place in a pro team, Le Groupement, which turned out to be totally the wrong environment for him. Boardman was luckier to be approached by a more enlightened set-up, the French Gan professional team, and he continued on to a very successful road race career.

In 1994 Boardman won the prologue time trial of the Tour de France in record speed, and wore the yellow jersey for two stages before losing it in a team time trial, ironically on the eve of the Tour's second ever visit to Britain. The race was in the UK for two days, and in another ironic twist Sean Yates took his yellow jersey as soon as the race was back in France.

Boardman, working with sports scientist Peter Keen, continued to make progress in top-level pro road racing, winning the world time trial championships in 1994, and two more stages in the Tour de France. But what was probably more important for British cyclists was that Boardman succeeded in demystifying the world's biggest road races, and in so doing gave British racers confidence again. Lottery funding, and the sensible spending of it by British Cycling, did the rest.

A new era of cycling in Britain was born in 2000, when

Team GB cyclists won four medals at the Sydney Olympic Games, including a gold on the track for Jason Queally.

Success bred more success, and with the employment of David Brailsford as performance director at British Cycling, a plan began to take shape for a British cyclist to win the Tour de France. The objective was finally delivered by Bradley Wiggins and Team Sky in 2012, and both Brailsford and Wiggins were knighted as a result.

The British success story continues. Chris Froome won a second Tour de France for Britain in 2013, then won three more, in 2015, 2016 and 2017, taking his own total Tour de France victories to four. In 2017 he won both the Tour de France and the Vuelta a España, the first rider ever to do that since the Vuelta switched to its August berth, and the first since Marco Pantani in 1998 to win two Grand Tours in one year. His Vuelta victory was the first by a Briton in the Spanish Grand Tour.

Froome was born in Kenya but qualifies as British through his parents. He was recruited into the British Cycling system by Sir David Brailsford, and was one of the original Sky riders when the team formed in 2010. But Froome didn't deliver on the potential Brailsford and British Cycling saw in him until the Vuelta of 2011 when, working for eventual third-placed Bradley Wiggins, Froome finished second.

That was a massive breakthrough, and the change has been put down to Froome finally bringing a tropical disease he suffered from, bilharzia, under control, as well as a concerted and very successful effort to lose weight. He went on to finish second behind Wiggins in the 2012 Tour de France, and is without doubt the best Grand Tour rider of his generation, and arguably one of the best ever.

With his five Grand Tour victories Froome currently lies equal seventh with three Italians, Gino Bartali, Alfredo Binda and Felice Gimondi, in the all-time Grand Tour winners list. Above him are Fausto Coppi, Miguel Indurain and Alberto Contador, each with seven wins; Jacques Anquetil is in third place with eight; Bernard Hinault is second with ten; and the all-time leader is Eddy Merckx with eleven Grand Tour victories. Froome is 32 as I write this, and seems to be getting better with each passing year.

But if British cyclists have slowly carved out a place at the top of men's road racing, there was a short time in the 1980s when Ireland was at the top of men's road racing.

The Irish pioneer, a contemporary of Brian Robinson and Tom Simpson, was Seamus 'Shay' Elliott. Like Robinson for the UK, Elliott was the first Irish rider to earn a regular place in a big European team. He was an extremely strong rider who won the cobbled classic Het Volk (Het Nieuwsblad now) in 1959, as well as stages in every Grand Tour; one each in the Tour de France and Giro d'Italia, and two in the Vuelta a España.

He was the first Irish rider to do any of those things, and the first to wear the yellow jersey in the Tour de France, which Elliott did with his stage win in 1963. He kept it for three stages too.

Shay Elliott was also very loyal to the teams he rode for, but it's fair to say that his loyalty was sometimes abused. His career petered out after the mid-1960s, and after his marriage ended and the business he hoped would support him in retirement failed, Elliott returned to Ireland in 1967. He set up a metalwork business with his father, living in a flat above it. Then in May 1971 he was found there, dead from shotgun wounds; it was either an accident or suicide.

The next two Irish greats are road race superstars. Sean Kelly was the King of the Classics, and Stephen Roche the only man ever to equal the great Eddy Merckx when he took cycling's Triple Crown; the Giro d'Italia, the Tour de France and the World Road Race Championships in the same year.

Kelly, the Waterford farmer's boy, and Roche, the Dublin city boy, represented two faces of the same country. And while they raced, Ireland dominated cycling for four years in a row, from 1984 to 1987. The world's number one male road racer was an Irishman.

Kelly was the first to have an impact. He became a professional after racing in France in 1976 when he won a number of good French and international amateur races. At first Kelly appeared happy in the role of a sprinter, helping others when he could. Soon, though, he was winning bigger and better races, and over a wide variety of terrain.

By 1982 Kelly was leading a team built around him. He started winning big consistently and he didn't stop for the next ten years. Classics, stage races, a Grand Tour, the 1988 Vuelta a España, Kelly hammered out success in them all. His best year was 1984, when in the space of 14 days he finished second in the Tour of Flanders, won the overall and three stages of the Tour of the Basque Country, and achieved wins for Paris–Roubaix and Liège–Bastogne–Liège.

In the end, this rock-hard racer won nine monuments, putting him equal third in the all-time winners list with Italians Fausto Coppi and Costante Giradengo. Kelly also won the green jersey in the Tour de France four times, as well as a staggering seven consecutive victories in Paris–Nice. These are just some highlights of what was an amazing cycling career.

Stephen Roche turned professional in 1981, when he had one of the most incredible debut seasons ever. His success wasn't as broad as Kelly's, and he didn't win anywhere near as often or as many times. Roche was more fragile and more prone to setbacks than Kelly, but when the planets lined up for him in 1987, Stephen Roche did what only Eddy Merckx had done and won the Giro d'Italia, Tour de France and world road race championships in the same year. Merckx is the greatest cyclist ever, and emulating his Triple Crown achievement is Roche's cycling legacy. Nobody has done it since. Roche's talent was that deep.

He won other races, among them Paris–Nice in his debut year, the Tour of Romandie in 1983, 1984 and in his 1987 super-season, Criterium International in 1985 and 1991, and the Tour of the Basque Country in 1989. He will be remembered most, though, for 1987 and the Triple Crown.

There have been good Irish road racers since, and Ireland has a team, Aqua Blue Sport racing at UCI Continental Professional level, one tier down from the World Tour. Irish riders are a strong presence in the 2018 World Tour too, with Liège–Bastogne–Liège and Il Lombardia winner Dan Martin, and with Nicholas Roche, Stephen's son, Philip Deignan, as well as two very promising young riders, the sprinter, Sam Bennett and the time triallist and developing all-rounder Ryan Mullen.

12

Time Lords and Ladies

Time trials have been part of road racing since its earliest days. The first place-to-place road race in Italy, from Florence to Pistoia, was a time trial. For reasons discussed in Chapter 10, from 1895 onwards the only races on open roads in Great Britain were time trials, and that remained the official line until the late Fifties. Some early Tour de France stages were run as team time trials. The first individual time trial in the Tour was held in 1934, and went from La-Roche-sur-Yon to Nantes. The first two official world road race championships, in 1921 and 1922, were run as time trials. The 1931 amateur world road race championships, which were held in Copenhagen, was also a time trial. There were even time trials that became regarded as classics, and the biggest of those was the Grand Prix des Nations.

The first Grand Prix des Nations was held in 1932, and it was another race invented by journalists trying to promote a newspaper. Gaston Bénac and Albert Baker d'Isy were the journalists, and *France-Soir* was the newspaper. Bénac and Baker d'Isy covered the 1931 world road race championships in Copenhagen, and they were impressed by the racing. They told *France-Soir*'s readers that in their opinion competing individually against the clock, so that a rider couldn't shelter behind anyone or use tactics to defeat a stronger opponent, was the best way to find true champions. The fact that time trials are cheaper to organise than road races sat well with *France-Soir*'s accountants, so the Grand Prix des Nations was born.

René de Latour, who wrote for top French cycling magazines as well as the British magazine *Sporting Cyclist*, designed the race route. It started in Versailles, crossed the Chevreuse valley twice, taking two bites out of the tough hills there, before heading into Paris to finish on the Vélodrome Buffalo, where many early world hour records were set. The total distance was 140 kilometres, and the first winner was Maurice Archambaud, a future world hour record holder. The race was deemed a success and another edition was sanctioned by *France-Soir* for 1933. Raymond Louviot won it, then Antonin Magne scored the first Grand Prix des Nations hat-trick by winning from 1934 to 1936.

Although time trials had been used to decide the occasional world road race championships, there was no separate official time trial world title in the Thirties, and there wouldn't be one until 1994, so Bénac and Baker d'Isy hoped that their race would become an unofficial world time trial championships, and it quickly did. Entry was by invitation only, and while the pro event did spawn an amateur Grand Prix des Nations, unfortunately there was never one for women. They had to wait until the first official world time trial championships in 1994 to get an equivalent race. Still, although all-male, the Grand Prix des Nations winners were quality. Some were time trial specialists, but others were great all-rounders. In fact, one woman did compete in the Grand Prix des Nations, but more about her later.

One of the keys to winning the original Grand Prix des Nations, which later moved to other courses and was diminished as a result, was mastery of the hills around the Chevreuse valley. Some of the first road race encounters with this valley, lying just southwest of Paris, were made during Bordeaux–Paris. The main road from Bordeaux to the French capital crosses the Chevreuse hills, and the climb from Dourdan was the last big obstacle in that race. It was 50 kilometres from the finish, so for riders with 500 kilometres of non-stop racing in their legs it must have hurt like hell.

The Fifties, Sixties and early Seventies were the golden age of the Grand Prix des Nations. Then the only time trial aerodynamic touches were silk jerseys, which seemed to glow in the sun; and bikes with lighter frame tubes and maybe higher gears, perhaps a single chainring, and wheels with fewer spokes and the lightest silk tubular tyres, which sang and swished to the beat of their rider's pedalling.

After the Seventies it grew increasingly difficult to use the roads into Paris for races, so in 1977 the Grand Prix des Nations moved to the Cannes area in the south of France. Then from 1993 until 1997 it was held near the Lac de Madine in the east. And from 1998 until the final

Grand Prix des Nations in 2004 it was held in the Seine-Maritime area of Normandy. Races need a sense of place to thrive, so moving it around didn't do the Grand Prix des Nations any good. And once the official world time championships were up and running, the Grand Prix des Nations began to lose its allure.

But in its pomp this race was special, and the man who dominated it in those days was Jacques Anquetil. Anquetil was a master of the time trial, always happiest riding on his own at the furious metronomic pace he would set. He was unbeaten in the Grand Prix des Nations, winning nine times out of nine between 1953 and 1966.

The 1953 route, a variation also devised by René de Latour, started in Versailles and went west into the Chevreuse, climbed out at the other side, then went southeast, around Rambouillet, into the forest, and on to St Arnoult-en-Yvelines to begin a northeast run, through the Chevreuse valley again, and into Paris. Over the years Anquetil came to know this route so well, as he also trained on it before each race. However, it was all new to him in 1953; he was 19 years old and had turned professional especially for the Grand Prix des Nations, which in those days was always held in October.

It was his first full professional race, but the way he did his route recce says a lot about how Anquetil approached his profession. He set off for his first look at the Nations course about one month before the race, taking some stamped addressed postcards with him. As Anquetil rode the route, from start to finish, he would stop at a post office, write down on a postcard details of what he'd just ridden and post it home. Then he carried on riding, sending postcards from each section, and once back in Quincampoix near Rouen, he put the postcards together as an *aide-mémoire* to use in the run-up to the race.

The route was tough to memorise because it was tough to ride. That's what made the Grand Prix des Nations so special. It went through towns and villages, over rail lines, across cobbles and along smooth roads. It went up and down hills of all shapes and sizes. There were long draggy straight hills, some were short and sharp, while others twisted and turned upwards, doing the same on the descent. It required a talent for finding the right line and analytical riding combined with brute strength; the key elements of success in a time trial.

When the race was shortened to 100 kilometres, and later 75, the Chevreuse valley section was kept in. It began at Rochefort-en-Yvelines, where an old church dominates the top of the village hill. From there the route headed north, descending at first, then climbing through Bullion on a steep straight road that goes on for ever. The road tops out on a plateau, and the route then went southeast to Limours and La Roncière. That bit started out flat, but a succession of ups and downs soon took over, including up a dusty narrow back lane climb to Roussigny.

From La Roncière the route went northeast, and hit one of the toughest parts of the course, a long, back-breaking drag. Then the next section passed Montlhéry motor-racing circuit, where the Critérium International was born. Several French road race titles were decided on these roads too, and they all ended on the race circuit, which had bankings just like Monza and Brooklands.

The Critérium International has an interesting story. It was once seen as a better way of finding a world road race champion than the 'one race in one place on one day' formula it's always been. Personally I think that's the best way, because a road race is all about getting it together on one day and winning whatever the conditions or whatever the other competitors do. Still, some were adamant that the Critérium International's eventual formula was better.

It started life in 1932, when it was the Critérium National and restricted to French riders. It was a single-day race at first, but from 1963 through to 1966 it was a two-day race, with three stages consisting of two road race stages over contrasting terrain, and one time trial. The race location changed from year to year as well. The Critérium International was a single-day race from 1966, then the two-day, three-stage format was reintroduced in 1978.

For a long time the Grand Prix des Nations was a graveyard for British ambitions, which is surprising because for a long time Britain was a nation of time triallists. But British time trial courses were a lot different to the Grand Prix des Nations. Also, for a time triallist to really achieve his or her potential, until training was better understood, riding road races was necessary to hone the physical and technical abilities necessary to excel on a course like the Grand Prix de Nations. Britain didn't have proper road races until the Fifties, and when it did they were a league below the level of European ones.

Bob Maitland and Ken Joy were two of the best British time triallists of their day, and raced in the Grand Prix des Nations in 1953, when Jacques Anquetil won. They ended up finishing over twenty minutes behind the teenage time trial prodigy. It took until 1962 for a Brit to break into the top ten, when Vin Denson, a full-time European pro by then, finished seventh behind Belgium's

Ferdi Bracke. Peter Head, a valued domestique to the great Belgian classics racer Frans Verbeek, was fifth in 1970. Peter Hill did well in the amateur Grand Prix des Nations. Then Chris Boardman became the first British rider to win the Grand Prix des Nations, but that was in 1996, when it had moved to a circuit near the Lac de Madine in the eastern region of Lorraine.

Another British name associated with the Grand Prix des Nations is Beryl Burton. She was the only woman ever to take part in the race, and she did so during its heyday on the Chevreuse valley course. French bike fans were fascinated by Beryl Burton and her exploits during the Sixties, having read about how she beat men in incredibly long time trials, in articles written by René de Latour. He encouraged British riders to race in Europe and, knowing her strength in a time trial, De Latour asked the Grand Prix des Nations organisers to let Burton ride their race in 1968.

The organisers were intrigued, so they allowed her in the race, but decided that Burton should start 12 minutes before the first professional rider, presumably to save her the embarrassment of being passed by all eleven male pro riders who'd been contracted to ride. In fact, she wasn't caught by any of them. The winner, Felice Gimondi, was 12 minutes quicker than Burton, but he was the only one who was 12 minutes quicker. Gimondi's average speed was 47.518 kph for 73.5 kilometres of undulating, twisting roads, to Burton's 41.583 kph. But Luis Ocana, who went on to win the 1973 Tour de France, was only eight minutes ahead of Burton, and the last pro, Jean-Claude Genty, gained less than five minutes on her.

Grand Prix des Nations fields were always small and select. The professional riders in the 1968 race were among the best of their generation; even last man Genty won two stages of the Critérium du Dauphiné during his career. They were full-time racers, backed by big teams and earning good money. Beryl Burton balanced her training with working on a farm, and looking after her family, on top of which she paid most of her racing costs herself.

Once an official world time trial title was established in 1994, the Grand Prix des Nations grew progressively less important, and it was last run in 2004, when a German time trial specialist Michael Rich won. However, the race still lives in a way, in the Chrono des Nations, a hybrid of two races.

Chrono des Herbiers was a time trial held around Les Herbiers in the Vendée department of France. It was established in 1982, and the first two editions were won by British riders, Gary Dowdell in 1982 and David Akam in 1983. The inaugural women's Chrono des Herbiers took place in 1987. Then in 2006 it took over the space left by the Grand Prix des Nations and changed its name to Chrono des Nations. A men's under-23 race was added to the programme in 2010. Alex Dowsett won it, while David Millar won the men's elite version that year. The Chrono des Nations continues today, although for the last two years there has been no women's or under-23 race.

The first official world time trial championships were held in Sicily in 1994. Chris Boardman won the men's elite title, US racer Karen Kurreck won the women's elite, and Dean Rogers won the men's junior title. The following year saw a women's junior title added to the programme, then the men's under-23 world time trial title was born in 1996. So today there are world time trial championships for male and female juniors, for under-23 men, and for elite men and women. They are all held in the same week as the bunched road race world championships.

Fabian Cancellara of Switzerland and Tony Martin of Germany are the dominant figures in the men's elite winner's list, with four world time trial titles each. Cancellara also won two junior world time trial titles. Jeannie Longo of France heads the women's roll of honour with four titles.

The official world titles, as well as European and national titles for most categories, have replaced the time trial classics. As well as the Grand Prix des Nations there was the Gran Premio di Lugano. It dated back to 1950 and has a glorious list of winners, including Fausto Coppi twice and Jacques Anquetil seven times. Eddy Merckx won it in 1968, but then there was no GP di Lugano time trial in 1972 and 1973. It was run in 1974 and 1975, but that was the last of the race as a time trial. The GP di Lugano returned in 1981, and is still run today, but as a bunched road race.

The Cronostafetta was a very unusual race. From its first edition in 1966 until 1981 it was contested by teams of three, but on three different courses, with a shared start and finish. Each team member raced individually on one of the three separate courses. Their times were then added together, and the team with the fastest total time for the three courses won. It was a bit complicated, never mind hard to watch, so after 1966 the Cronostafetta reverted to a regular team time trial format, with teams of between four and seven competing in different years. The last Cronostafetta was held in 1992.

Since 2012 there's been a world team time trial title

for elite men's and women's trade teams, which usually kicks off the world road race championships week. Before that the team time trial world title was for national teams; the men's title running from 1962 until 1994, and the women's from 1987 until 1994. From 1960 until 1992 there was a men's four-man team time trial in the Olympic Games. The distances of the four-up world and Olympic title races were 100 kilometres for men and 50 kilometres for women. The distance for the new world team time trial title race varies.

The most remarkable team in team time trial history came from Sweden. It was made up of four brothers: Erik, Gösta, Sture and Thomas Pettersson, all from Vargarda in Götaland. They were world champions three years in a row from 1967 until 1969, as well as taking a silver medal for their country in the 1968 Olympic Games team time trial. After the 1969 worlds all four Petterssons turned professional. The oldest, Gösta, was the most successful, winning the 1971 Giro d'Italia, as well as finishing third in the 1970 Tour de France.

There's something special about the symbiosis of a team time trial. Success requires the same attributes as an individual time trial: power, stamina, speed, concentration, good technique and spot-on calculation; but it also requires honesty and self-sacrifice. Egos should be left in the start house. Of course they aren't always. One place where they would emerge from time to time was in the two-man time trial classic, the Baracchi Trophy, which had similar status to the Grand Prix des Nations.

It was created by Mino Baracchi, a rich Bergamo businessman who wanted a race to honour his grandfather, a true cycling *tifoso* or fan. The first Baracchi Trophy was an individual time trial for amateurs held in 1941. From

1944 until 1948 Mino Baracchi opened his race to professionals, but it was still an individual time trial. Then Mino decided to change the format of his race and base it on a much older one. It was a two-man time trial for professionals, but not any professionals – only the best of their generation were invited to compete. They were paid to do so, then paired up by the organisers, so each could end up riding with a team-mate or a rival, a friend or an enemy. The race was called the Giro della Provincia di Milano, and it ran from Milan to Como, then back to Milan, where it finished on the Sempione track.

The Sempione was demolished in 1928, leaving Milan without a banked cycling track until the Velodromo Vigorelli was built in 1935. But the Giro della Provincia di Milano continued until 1937 when it was won by a Frenchman, Maurice Archambaud, who was just days away from setting his world hour record of 45.767 kilometres on the Vigorelli. Archambaud's racing partner that day was Aldo Bini, a top man who won Il Lombardia twice, the Giro del Piemonte three times and five stages in the Giro d'Italia, as well as several other good Italian races.

Mino Baracchi decided to use the Giro della Provincia di Milano as the template for the 1949 Baracchi Trophy, and worked out a testing 100-kilometre route that was a nice mix of hills and flat roads around Bergamo. Then he paid the best racers to ride it, and to attract even more attention he made the Baracchi Trophy the last big pro race of the year.

It worked, and they didn't come much bigger than one of the winners of the first two-man Baracchi Trophy. He was Fiorenzo Magni, the Lion of Mugello, who in 1948 took one of his eventual three victories in the Giro d'Italia, and in 1949 the first of three consecutive Tour of Flanders victories. Magni's partner in the 1949 Baracchi Trophy was Adolfo Grosso, and Magni won with two different partners for the next two years.

After that, Nino Defilippis from Turin won in 1952, and then it was Fausto Coppi's turn. He won in 1953 with that year's amateur world road race champion, Riccardo Filippi, who stayed in Coppi's teams for the rest of his career. Filippi partnered his boss to Baracchi Trophy victories in 1954 and 1955. But when Coppi won again in 1957, it was with Ercole Baldini.

Jacques Anquetil won the Baracchi Trophy three times, but he didn't like it. As the number one rider in the world during the 1960s Anquetil was paid well to take part, but he preferred riding time trials on his own. He was never more uncomfortable, maybe in any race in his life, than he was when winning it in 1962. Egos definitely weren't left in the start house that day.

Anquetil could drive himself as hard as he needed to, so long as he dictated the pace and so long as that pace was constant. He had a computer for a brain that helped him spread his effort as far as he needed to spread it. But he didn't like it when someone else set the pace, especially if that pace was erratic.

In 1962 Anquetil was paired in the Baracchi Trophy with his German team-mate, Rudi Altig, who was a monster in a two-man effort like this. A great track and road racer, Altig injected pace into any breakaway he was in, and he would thunder through to do his turn at the front. Just to add spice, Anquetil and Altig had a bit of history in 1962. They were in the same team, St Raphael, but Anquetil thought Altig was trying to usurp him as its leader. And just to top it all, this time Anquetil had a bad day, a very bad day. They won, but Altig nearly killed the Frenchman. Soon after the start, Anquetil couldn't do his turns at the front. Altig remonstrated with him, encouraged him, but it was no good. Eventually the German just hit the front and stayed there, pacing and sometimes even pushing Anquetil to the finish, where he had to be lifted off his bike.

That was an eventful Baracchi Trophy, and a rare moment of weakness from Anquetil, but mostly the events were a catwalk for talent. Eddy Merckx won three times, Felice Gimondi won twice, but the King of the Baracchi is Francesco Moser with five victories between 1974 and 1985. They make up the bulk of the Moser family total of seven Baracchi Trophy victories; the eldest Moser, Aldo, won twice.

But even towards the end of the Moser streak the Baracchi Trophy started looking like a race from another age. It certainly came from an age when the calendar was less crowded. The last two-man Baracchi was run in 1990. They ran the race as a solo time trial in 1991, but that was it. The end. Tony Rominger of Switzerland was the last winner of the Baracchi Trophy.

Another race that has died out in professional road racing at world level is the hill climb time trial. There are occasional uphill all the way time trials in stage races, and time trialling in general is very much part of stage racing, but races like the GP Mont Faron hill climb, which took place in the south of France, have gone from top-level men's professional cycling.

The Mont Faron race was 5.5 kilometres long with a height gain of around 500 metres. The finish line was at 508 metres, but the race started almost at sea level in the busy port of Toulon. Riders went up one by one, making their way to the top as fast as they could. It was a pure climber's test; very steep and not too long. On longer but steadier climbs Grand Tour winner types tend to dominate. Climbs like Mont Faron favour the best climbers; not good climbers who can time trial, but real climbers. Federico Bahamontes won Mont Faron several times, as did Charly Gaul and Rene Vietto. They are three of the best climbers ever.

Here's what a modern climber, Dan Martin, says about Mont Faron: 'It's a good one for me. Having the hardest part early gets rid of anyone who's not climbing well. Then because it's still quite steep after that, they can't catch you back up. The problem for me in the past was getting to the start of it with the leaders. The stages I've done that have ended on Mont Faron have been like two races, one to get to the bottom of the climb and then the race to the top.'

As Martin points out, Mont Faron is still used for stage finishes, in Paris–Nice for example, but the GP Mont Faron was a straightforward time trial, not pushing and shoving, not tactics, just a contest to see who could climb up it quickest. That made Mont Faron a pure fight against gravity, a sort of world championship for climbers. It's definitely a race that would be worth bringing back. Just like another, slightly unusual, race called A Travers Lausanne.

It must have looked great. A Travers Lausanne was always run the day after the Giro di Lombardia. A number of the best pros would be contracted at the finish of that race, and they would drive northeast from the Lombardia's finish in Como to Lausanne in Switzerland. They would then line up the following day on the north shore of Lake Geneva for A Travers Lausanne.

Lausanne is built on the southern slopes of the Swiss

Plateau, and there is about 300 metres' height difference between the lake shore at Ouchy and the city's northern edge. A Travers Lausanne means Across Lausanne, and the race was just that, a mad uphill slog across Lausanne from the lake shore to the top of town.

The first A Travers Lausanne was held in 1940; the great Swiss racer Ferdi Kübler won the professional category, and then won it for the next five years. Amateurs, juniors and even veterans had separate races. The contestants started together in what must have looked like a cavalry charge with forty riders going elbow to elbow across the road. But soon after the start the gradient would bite and the bunch would explode into little groups, with each rider giving all the uphill thrust he could to get to the top. It was like natural selection for cyclists. Film-clips from this extraordinary race can be found on YouTube.

A Travers Lausanne was abandoned after 1949, and didn't get going again until 1967. Then from 1968 the pro race was run over two stages, a bunch race then a time trial, which is why I've included its history in this time trial chapter. The distance for each leg was 4.5 kilometres, and there was 265 metres of height gain, so the riders climbed an almost six per cent average gradient. The only thing is, the gradient never stayed at its average. The course was a series of steep ramps linked by false flats. It was great for spectators, and the streets were packed each year it was run. The times of the two legs were added together to produce a winner. For spectators it was a double treat. They got a rush of colour and excitement with the stage one stampede up the climb. Then they got a closer look at individual riders in the time trial.

Some great names are on the A Travers Lausanne winners list, some of the very best more than once. Ferdi

Kübler won six times, Fausto Coppi won in 1947, Eddy Merckx also won four editions, and the Dutch rider Joop Zoetemelk had five consecutive victories from 1975 to 1979. The last winner was Cadel Evans in 2001. The race hasn't been run since.

Today uphill time trials in professional road racing are rare outside of stage races, but one place where they thrive is in the United Kingdom. They are called hill climbs, and are traditionally held at the end of each road racing season, although they have been spreading throughout the season recently.

Hills chosen for these very British races tend to be short and very steep. Trying to ride up one of them as fast as possible is a painful, often mentally bruising experience, but it's something some racers are very good at. In the UK there is a history of riders who specialise in this brutal branch of cycling, and their names dominate the roll call of the race that is the culmination of each year's hill climb season: the British national championships.

The first British hill climb title race was held in 1944 on Brasted Hill in Kent. The following year the championships were held in Derbyshire, and the race stayed there for three years, during which the first hill climb specialist emerged. His name is Vic Clark of the Coventry Cycling Club.

In his excellent book about British hill climbing, *A Corinthian Endeavour*, Paul Jones describes meeting the 95-year-old Clark: 'He has a glint in his eye and the compact muscular build of the racing cyclist,' Jones writes. He also puts his finger on what makes hill climbers like Clark so special: 'They have the power to weight ratio of a small garden bird, able to take flight and lift upwards with grace and ease.'

Clark was the first of many compact, sometimes painfully thin little men who were impervious to wind, weather and gradient. They fizz uphill with animal power, emptying every bit of energy along the road, sucking in great gulps of air as they push into the ever darkening place of oxygen debt. At the summit they collapse on their bikes, and are wheeled away to be laid down in the shelter of a wet stone wall or a muddy bank to recover.

Men like Robbie Stringwell, champion in 1950 and 1951, Eric Wilson, Peter Graham and Granville Sydney with thirteen titles between them, spanning 1955 to 1973, and Gareth Armitage dominated early hill climbing. Then, slowly, road and track racers started to become the more dominant force, with Jim Henderson and his five titles between 1998 and 2003 flying the flag for hill climb specialists.

Hill climbs have always have been popular in the UK, especially with club riders who take delight watching their braver club-mates suffer. There's a grim sadism to watching hill climbs, and when races are on the most famous hills – and for most famous climbs read most brutal climbs, the likes of Winnats Pass, Nick O'Pendle and Rosedale Chimney – thousands line the slopes offering their cheers, support and not always well-taken advice.

13

D is for Domestique

Road races vary in distance, terrain, and in the demands they make on competitors, so the types of riders who do well in different races vary too, mentally and physically. Broadly speaking, riders fit into one of the categories discussed in this chapter, although many combine facets of two or more. Let's start at the finish of a race with the sprinters – an English word that everybody uses to describe men and women who can pull out short bursts of great speed, power and energy at the end of races.

A sprinter's life in cycling is much more complicated than it is in athletics. Not even the shortest event in cycling, the track sprint, is as short and uniquely a sprint effort as the 100 metres in athletics. The 100 metres is a purely anaerobic effort, which means the energy to run even a national class 100-metre sprint is almost entirely produced inside the runner's muscles without oxygen delivered to them by the cardiovascular system.

This is less true for track sprinters in cycling, who, although they are timed over 200 metres, which the world's best men and women do inside 10 seconds and 11 seconds respectively, are often racing flat out, or close to flat out, before they get to the last 200-metre timed section. That means track sprints in cycling lie just outside of being totally anaerobic. Track sprinters require some of their energy in a race to be produced by burning sugar in the presence of the oxygen delivered by their cardio-vascular systems.

Now, take that outside to a road race and a road sprinter has to be a very aerobic athlete just to get to the end of a race and do his or her own thing. Like a track sprinter, a road sprinter's speed is natural; it has to be there when they take up the sport, but unlike a track sprinter, road sprinters spend only a small portion of their training time working on their sprint. The rest is about getting into shape to contest the sprints at the end of stages. Experience of how bunch sprints pan out is important too, which is why the best road sprinters study race finishes on DVDs like scholars mugging up for an exam.

But on top of the distance they have to get through, and the final frenetic rush for the line, there are the five to ten, sometimes twenty kilometres of high-speed hectic racing leading up to a road sprint to train for. The effort required to survive these is essentially aerobic, but with little anaerobic spikes. A sprinter's power profile in the final kilometres of a Grand Tour sprint stage looks like an upturned saw, with big power spikes all through the finale as the sprinter makes sudden accelerations, to close gaps or to fight for a better wheel to follow. The cumulative effect of these pre-sprint power spikes shouldn't be under-estimated, because they are often higher than the power required to win the final sprint. They take a lot of training time, to help the sprinter survive them.

Bunch sprints in top-level road races are faster and go on for longer than they used to. Teams with the best sprinters have trains of riders who try to keep their sprinter near the front, and then release him at the optimal moment to go for the line. It's an art and a science. The science is about going as fast as possible, the art is getting the timing right.

Once the last sprint lead-out rider has done his or her bit it's down to the sprinter, and there are two types. Both start their sprint with an explosive acceleration, but the extra speed gained by the acceleration has to be held. Many sprinters do that with pure physical grunt. They are big and powerful, very muscular, and they use their muscles to power them to the line. The two German sprinters, Marcel Kittel and André Greipel, are great examples of this kind of rider. The other way to hold speed gained by an explosive jump is to have great aero-dynamics and slip through the air like a speeding bullet. The fastest bullet today is Mark Cavendish. His nickname, the 'Manx Missile', was well chosen.

Cavendish is arguably the greatest ever road sprinter. There have been other great ones. Mario Cipollini, a sprinter in the Kittel/Greipel mould, ruled in the Nineties and early Noughties. The Belgian Freddy Maertens was incredible in the Seventies and early Eighties. Going back further, André Darrigade was fast in the Fifties and Sixties. And before him there was Charles Pélissier, the first really successful road sprinter who in 1930, like Maertens in 1976, won eight stages in one Tour de France. That's the record for stage wins in one Tour, which Maertens and Pélissier share with Eddy Merckx, a very different package of talent whom we'll get to later.

But even in the aforementioned company, Cavendish's statistics stand out. His total of stage wins stands at forty-eight across all three Grand Tours, in which he's also won all three points titles. He's won many other races, including the 2011 world road race championships and Milan–San Remo in 2009. Mario Cipollini comes closest to Cavendish. He won a total of fifty-seven Grand Tour stages, but forty-two were in his national Tour, where he won the points title twice. Cipollini also won the world road race title in 2000 and Milan–San Remo in 2002, and his record is better than Cavendish in another race that sprinters can win, Ghent–Wevelgem, which the Italian won three times. But Cipollini didn't win all three Grand Tour points titles, and his twelve Tour de France stage wins don't stack up so well against Cavendish's thirty.

So let's look at Mark Cavendish through the eyes of somebody who coached and counselled him when he was younger, Rod Ellingworth. Ellingworth was in the vanguard of British Cycling's success story as a coach, and now works for Team Sky. He founded the British Cycling under-23 academy, which developed riders like Cavendish and Geraint Thomas, and continues to do sterling work as part of what has become a production line of British world and Olympic medallists.

The first time I met Mark there were things that stood out. He was fast, yes, but I'd seen plenty of fast young kids. He had a great work ethic, which is the thing that makes the difference between having potential and delivering success. But the biggest thing that hit me about him, and it has bearing on his sprinting, is how aware of his surroundings Mark is. Even as a teenager he took in everything around him, and he remembered it so well he could recount it perfectly. It's not just a photographic memory, either. Mark's awareness is something deeper.

His judgement of speed and distance borders on the uncanny. In his early years as a pro, when we talked about a sprint he'd just done, Mark would say things like 'I moved one metre this way, or half a metre that.' Or he'd say that something happened 75 metres from the line. And when you played the sprint back and measured what had happened, it was one metre, or 75 metres, or exactly what Mark said it was.

And the other thing, something I think is crucial: Mark says that for him sprints happen in slow motion. It's like he can slow down what's happening around him and run it inside his brain at half speed. It gives him the time to make good decisions. It helps him map a way through, measure distances, and do what he needs to do. Everybody might be sprinting at 70-plus kilometres per hour, but what happens in split seconds of real time gets stretched out inside Mark's head.

It's a remarkable gift, but it's something almost everybody has experienced. Think about when you've fallen off your bike, or crashed, or simply had a fall anywhere, or a road accident. When it happened, did it feel like it happened in slow motion? If so, then you've experienced heightened awareness. For most people it's brought on by the stress of going through something traumatic. Mark Cavendish can switch it on whenever he wants. Top racing drivers, cricket players, and many who excel at racket sports can do the same. Sportspeople sometimes refer to heightened awareness as being in the zone.

So, we know how Mark Cavendish gets in the right place at the right time and sees gaps opening before they do, but how does he convert good positioning into victory? Ellingworth again:

> He's naturally fast and probably has a fair bit of fast-twitch muscle, although we've never done tests to find out. He sprints a lot in training too, giving it full gas every time he does. That's something British Cycling coaches do with track sprinters, they train them to give 100 per cent every time they sprint. But what's also very important is how small Mark gets when he sprints. He isn't tall off the bike, but he has the knack of getting so low and narrow when he sprints he just causes a lot less drag. Mark's frontal area when he's sprinting is tiny compared to big sprinters, so where Cav produces 1400 to 1500 watts to go 75 kilometres per hour, they need 1700 watts or more, and still don't go quite as fast.

There are other tools in Cavendish's box: 'Great recovery, a big capacity for hard work, and he can sprint when he's on his knees, but all sprinters can do that,' says Ellingworth. However, he reckons the most important thing, after his power to frontal area ratio and spatial awareness, is Cavendish's ability to accelerate very quickly. 'His acceleration is phenomenal; nobody can jump from 60 to 75 kilometres per hour quicker than Cav,' says Ellingworth.

So that's Mark Cavendish's sprint; some of it is a natural gift, and some of it requires work. But it's the tip of the iceberg when set against the problem all road sprinters face. They have to get to the end of long and often arduous races in order to use their sprint, and they have to get through mountain stages in Grand Tours to continue using their sprint on the flat stages after them. 'That's where I've done my work, getting Mark to the end of stages and through three-week races. It's where Mark has worked hardest too,' says Ellingworth.

> We've worked for hours on his climbing. Not by doing classic uphill intervals but by recreating what happens on a climb in a race, and practising the different scenarios that play out in races at race speed or faster. Mark isn't going to win a race on a hill, he's only got to be still there, or close by, at the top. That's what we've worked on. In groups or with me motor pacing him, we practised hitting a climb hard, or picking up the speed on it. We practised answering attacks, practised accelerating over the top. We practised everything we can think of that will happen in a race at as near race conditions as we could set up.

Road race sprinting has changed a lot over the years. The lead-out trains that are normal today on sprint stages, or at the end of races that suit sprinters, didn't exist until the late Eighties. Before that, most sprinters had to fend for themselves, and the final kilometres before a sprint finish were very stop and start, with riders attacking and closing gaps all the way.

Some riders, often good track pursuiters, were experts at launching late lone attacks on sprint stages with between three kilometres and one kilometre to go. Britain's Barry Hoban won his share of Tour de France bunch sprints, and he remembers the late lone break artists very well:

> Willy Teirlinck of Belgium was one. He won three stages in the 1972 Tour by shooting out of the group with no more than three kilometres to go. It wouldn't happen now. The lead-out trains are going 60-odd kilometres per hour now and nobody can get away like a Teirlinck or a Fedor Den Hertog could. We didn't have lead-out trains, everybody was going for it alone, jockeying for position, and the final few kilometres would be stop-start, stop-start, so the average speed was more like 50 kph. If they timed it right, the moment the speed dropped, riders like Teirlinck and Den Hertog could jump away with a burst of 55 kph and hold everybody off.

Rik Van Looy is a bit of an outlier in the development of lead-out trains. His teams used to lead him out in bunch finishes in the Sixties, although Van Looy always tried to win without using his sprint, which he often did. Lead-outs became more of a feature in the Eighties, with the Dutch Superconfex team using its riders to set a high pace at the front of bunch finishes, each rider going flat out for about 500 metres then dropping back, all for the benefit of the team's sprinter, Jean-Paul Van Poppel.

Then through the Nineties more teams realised that if they had a good sprinter, using riders to lead him out was the best way to win. Mario Cipollini had a fearsome lead-out train. And as women's road racing developed, so did the idea of a lead-out in bunched sprints. But even now, women's teams in top races are smaller than men's, which reduces the size of their lead-outs.

Lead-outs eat up man or woman power, so a sprinter

has to be very good before a team will commit riders to his or her service. Not all sprinters get one, which means they have to go old school and use other teams' lead-out trains to get them in the best position. Some sprinters even seem to prefer that way of working. The Australian sprinter Robbie McEwen was very fast and very good at freelancing in bunched sprints. McEwen won twelve Tour de France stages and the green jersey three times between 2002 and 2007.

Okay, I've taken a long time talking about sprinters, but that's because their life is complicated. What they do is balance two opposite aspects of sports performance: endurance and speed. Add in the tactics that play out in a sprint, the spatial awareness required, the pressure to get results, and sprinters live in a tricky world. But so do our next group, the pure climbers, or *grimpeurs*, to give them their French name.

Like sprinters, pure climbers must ride a fine line to nurture and preserve their gift while coping with the slings and arrows fired at them by terrain and conditions in the rest of a race. But when they get to terrain that suits them, and have the condition to use it, pure climbers can be devastating. They are also poetry to watch.

At its most basic level cycling is physics. A cyclist's power output to the pedals can be measured in watts, and with good aerodynamics in the mix, power to the pedals determines a cyclist's speed on the flat. However, when a cyclist goes uphill gravity comes into play, and with gravity a rider's weight gains importance. Going uphill, the watts a rider puts out, divided by their body and bike weight combined, determines speed.

So, pure climbers are skinny. Some notable ones in years gone by even looked frail. But pure climbers are also capable of terrific changes of pace uphill, a gift they have on top of their great power to weight ratios, and one far less quantifiable. Even now, when cycling is dominated by talk of numbers, pure climbers talk of sensations instead, and about things like the feel of their pedals. They seem to operate in a world beyond the science of training manuals and numerical definition, and do things on intuition. They are a living reminder of an old way of cycling, the spiritual descendants of mountain kings like Federico Bahamontes, Charly Gaul and Lucien Van Impe, who could turn a Grand Tour upside down with one big attack in the mountains.

The problem for pure climbers now is that power to weight is a number, and numbers can be worked on by anyone. The general standard of climbing in professional cycling has improved a lot. So good all-round riders with Grand Tour ambitions get as light as they can, while working on the power output they can maintain for 30 to 40 minutes. Then with the help of strong team-mates they set a constant brutal pace on the climbs, which can draw a climber's sting before he or she gets the chance to use it.

There are still plenty of pure climbers in pro cycling today, although they don't win as much as their forebears did, but now and again they still succeed and are always exciting. One of the best pure climbers today is Ireland's Dan Martin. After several years of development he can live with the hard pace the all-rounders are capable of setting, and is starting to use his natural climber's change of pace uphill to devastating effect in Grand Tours. I'm writing this shortly after the 2017 Tour de France, which Martin animated in the mountains, and on some flatter stages. He finished sixth overall, but it could have been much higher if Martin hadn't been taken out by Ritchie Porte's crash on the descent of Mont des Chats on stage nine. He cracked two vertebrae, which hampered him for the rest of the race.

It's taken Martin a lot of work to get into positions where he can use his climber's talent. Just like Mark Cavendish with his sprints, Martin had to get better at all the stuff that precedes a climb, riding on the flat and getting faster and strong enough to turn big gears comfortably. His labours began to pay in 2009, when Martin went to live in Girona in northeast Spain. I visited him there that year, and this is what he said about his training, and about climbing. 'I have to get to the climbs before I can do anything. That's been my biggest jump this year, the difference I can feel. I'm stronger on the flat and can handle the speed and big gears. I'm maybe climbing a bit better, but the big difference is I'm getting to the hills in better shape,' he said.

Then he talked about his training for the hills, which was done almost exclusively on his bike. No core work, no weight training.

I think it's even more important for me not to do anything that might upset my body balance. I don't have much muscle, not even on my legs. I weigh 61 kilograms and I'm about five feet ten inches tall. If I isolate a muscle group, like my core, I reckon I could make them stronger than they need to be, and that could cause problems elsewhere, maybe pulling something out of line. I know I use my core muscles a lot when I ride, because I feel them get sore when I've done a lot of climbing, but I leave it at that. I think that what I do on my bike is the right amount of training for my core.

Martin often referred to harmony and balance, which are two words that pure climbers use a lot. Lucien Van Impe, six times King of the Mountains at the Tour de France, says they are elusive too. Van Impe says he would spend weeks alone in the mountains before each Tour de France trying to find harmony and balance.

> I had to rediscover the rhythm of climbing before each stage race. Rhythm isn't something you can point at or give a number to, it's something you feel. You develop it by riding the climbs and focusing on the way you pedal, harmonising your pedal revs with your breathing. You focus for days, then one day you have it. It's there in your legs, and you can climb like you have jets in your feet.

Being in tune with his body, monitoring it both on and off the bike, is something Martin prides himself on.

> When I climb it's all on feel. When I was an amateur my directeur sportif had a theory, he said that cycling was just a matter of managing pain. He reckoned that you should be able to hold for 20 minutes the pace you can hold for five, all you have to do is focus. In a way I believe that. Obviously not for the 4,000-metre pursuit guys or prologue specialists. They have something else going on physically, different muscle fibres maybe, and couldn't possibly hold their 4k pace for 20 minutes, no matter how much they suffered. But I believe you can go deeper than you think, you just have to focus and have self-belief. For example, I can hold my 20-minute pace for a long time, 40 minutes maybe, on a climb by digging deep, focusing and managing the pain. I never go on power or heart rate.

Pure climbers are able to soak up pain. Shared wisdom in top-level road racing is that everybody in the front group on a mountain climb is five minutes from letting go. It's a belief that helps riders cope by focusing on what they are doing there and then, not the top of the climb or the rest of the race. Sports scientists call it focusing on process not outcome. Riders break long climbs into five-minute chunks, or whatever they decide, and soak up the pain for that five minutes, then they go on to the next, and the next, and the next, until they get to the top.

But pure climbers can also do something else. They can attack from a high pace, from all the suffering and focusing, and forge gaps on the others. It's one of their defining characteristics. As well as being light, having great power to weight ratios and an ability to soak up pain, pure climbers are quite fast. Not sprinter fast, but they have a snappy acceleration uphill. Martin agrees. 'Yeah, I can sprint. I've probably got a few fast-twitch fibres, not like sprinters have but the types of fibres that can be slow-twitch and fast. I've always been able to ride hard on a climb then put in an extra burst then recover quickly from it.

Martin also talked a lot about rhythm, about feeling the pedals and spinning his legs:

My upper body moves in time to my legs, it just feels natural. And I pedal fast, I use the 25 sprocket a lot. It's my default gear. In training, when I come to a climb I just drop into the 25 to get my rhythm right, then click up through the gears. But I still pedal, I still stay on top of the gear and keep my upper body to lower body rhythm matched. My legs feel blocked if I push a bigger gear, they only work when they spin fast. I don't know whether it's the spinning or something to do with my muscles, but I never really need massage after a race. Some people say that having a high cadence disperses lactate better, so maybe that's it.

Martin sets up his bike to suit his pedalling style when climbing. 'I've set my saddle quite far forward because I think that helps you pedal quite quickly. It also has the added advantage of making the switch to a time trial bike easier. The saddle position on my time trial and road bikes is exactly the same relative to the cranks. I'm really comfortable on my time trial bike and don't have to spend ages getting used to the position.'

Lucien Van Impe calls the supple pedalling style when climbing – a style that Van Impe had in spades – 'coup de pédale'.

It's something rare. Something only pure climbers have. Richard Virenque [eight-time Tour de France King of the Mountains] never had it, but he wasn't a pure climber. It's also something that's difficult to train and easy to lose. I spent the weeks before the Tour de France finding it each year, but it's so fragile I could lose it in the first week of flat stages before we even got to any mountains if I used the big gears too much.

Van Impe really rates Martin. He's a pure climber from the old school, whose relaxed, bobbing style makes riding uphill look easy. In and out of the saddle, it doesn't seem to matter, Martin flits between the two with ease. 'If I'm going to be in and out of the saddle a lot, I ride with my hands on the brake hoods because the transition is easier,' he says.

And although Martin says he rides on feel a lot, he has applied some science to his choice of climbing position. 'I try to stay sat down for as long as possible. If you watch your heart rate, it always goes up when you are out of the saddle, even if you stay at the same power output. That means you must be making more effort out of the saddle, which costs energy. It can't be much but it makes a difference,' he says.

Martin is very aware that focusing on the little things, like riding position and choice of gear, is what make the difference in modern cycling. 'The way racing is now there are maybe fifteen to twenty riders who can finish within thirty seconds of each other at the top of a long climb. The margins are that small, so anything you can do to keep or gain something is crucial,' he reckons.

Martin changed his diet quite drastically in 2009, just to improve his general health and recovery. He also went against the trend and used fixed cleats instead of ones that allow his feet to move on the pedals. 'I don't like to feel my feet move, and they splay out at the heels if they do. I hate that. I like to feel my foot is being held tight and in line. It's a bit of bother when I fit new plates to get them lined up, but it's worth it. It's another one of those micro things that make a difference.'

A lot of Dan Martin is nature, a gift from his parents, Neil, who was a good pro racer, and Maria, who is Stephen Roche's sister. Roche was one of the best, and when your maternal uncle has won the Tour de France, the Giro d'Italia and the world championships in the same year, you should be able to ride a bike fast. The great Italian coach, Aldo Sassi, liked to quote the famous training advice attributed to Fausto Coppi: 'Ride your bike, ride your bike, and ride your bike.' But Sassi added his own proviso: 'Coppi was right, you must ride your bike a lot, but he should have added that if you want to be a champion you should also choose your parents wisely.'

There's now no doubt that athletic ability is inherited. For example, scientists have determined that genes controlling endurance are inherited from mothers, so to build on Sassi's quote, if you want to be a good endurance athlete then choose your mother wisely. Genetics are now so important in sports like cycling that many top-level coaches talk about gene expression, and the training they prescribe is designed to switch on genes that control different physiological responses and processes.

Moving on from the pure climbers, the next cyclist type we'll discuss wins the biggest races. They are the all-rounders, men and women capable of setting a brutal pace over a wide range of terrain, and who keep doing so. They are some of the greatest ever road racers, and they are called *rouleurs*.

Some will say that my classification of a rouleur is too wide, but I see the powers of a rouleur as a spectrum of ability. For example, the way I see it, Jacques Anquetil and Miguel Indurain were pure rouleurs. They were capable of setting a hard constant pace that made them very difficult to drop, and made them superb time trial-lists. Anquetil and Indurain are two of the four five-time Tour de France winners. The other two, Eddy Merckx and Bernard Hinault, were primarily rouleurs, but they were explosive as well, so they won a wider range of races. Rouleurs have big engines. They have the physiology to provide lots of oxygen to their muscles, and the physique to use it to power their pedals.

In many ways they are the simplest road racers to understand. They make everybody else hurt by riding hard. They are always good time triallists, which means they gain time in Grand Tours in that discipline. Some have the right combination of power output and weight to compete in the mountains, which makes these rouleurs devastating. All of the five-time Tour de France winners have won mountain stages; Indurain early in his career, Anquetil when he had to, while Merckx and Hinault seemed almost to win them when they wanted to.

Another rider I'd place with Anquetil, Merckx, Hinault and Indurain as being among the greatest male road racers is Fausto Coppi, and he was a rouleur too. Coppi also won time trials and mountain stages, often by many minutes, simply by accelerating smoothly away from the rest and then going further away.

But it's not only the greats who are rouleurs. Less gifted rouleurs, who still have the ability to set a high pace and stick with it over varied terrain, are needed by teams to control a peloton. Their high pace-setting makes it very difficult for others to escape. Or they can be used to chase breakaways, or set a high pace between and sometimes on climbs in stage races. They will pace riders who've had problems back to the peloton, and drop back to the team cars to load up with bottles which they then distribute to their team-mates. They are the foot soldiers of cycling, and they are called *domestiques*.

Domestique is a French word meaning servant, and its use in cycling dates back to the 1911 Tour de France, when it wasn't meant as a compliment. It was an insult that the Tour de France founder, Henri Desgrange, threw at a French racer called Maurice Brocco. According to the French cycling writer, Pierre Chany, Brocco had a reputation for hiring himself out to pace others in races. The story goes that Brocco paced the 1909 Tour winner

François Faber, who wasn't going well, all the way to the finish of stage nine of the 1911 Tour de France, which went from Perpignan to Luchon.

That was against the Tour rules in 1911, but although Desgrange suspected pacing, there was no way to prove it. Brocco claimed that he'd been riding along at his own pace, and he could do nothing about who followed him. Desgrange thought that Faber had paid Brocco. So, not having enough evidence to disqualify Brocco, Desgrange poured scorn on him in *L'Auto*, writing: 'He is unworthy, he is no more than a domestique.'

That made Brocco angry, as domestique in those days meant only servant, and he was a good bike racer. At the start of the next stage, the big Pyrenean one from Luchon to Bayonne, Brocco went up to Desgrange and told him, 'Today I will make you eat that word, domestique indeed. We will settle accounts.' Desgrange didn't like cyclists answering back, so he followed Brocco on the stage. When they hit the third climb of the day, the Col du Tourmalet, Brocco was in the second group on the road, and is reported to have started shouting at Desgrange. 'Am I allowed to ride with these men?' Desgrange didn't reply, so Brocco shouted, 'No, well then,' and he attacked. By the next climb, the Col d'Aubique, Brocco had caught the leaders, with Desgrange still following him. 'What about these men then? Do I have the right to stay with them?' he asked. 'No? OK,' he said, and he dropped those riders too, racing away to win the stage alone by 34 minutes.

Brocco was a good rider, and although he didn't like being called a domestique the term stuck, and plenty of strong riders since have been proud to be domestiques. Good domestiques are revered in cycling now. It's no use having the best rider in the world if the team hasn't got strong domestiques. So the best teams snap up the best domestiques whenever they can, meaning that a skilful domestique can command a decent salary for helping others. It makes being a good domestique worth it, even for some who could be challenging for victory.

Eddy Merckx was notorious for buying up good riders, possible challengers even, through his personal manager, who made some very generous offers to join his teams. It was a big part of the Merckx success story. Yes, he was the greatest road racer ever, but he had one of the greatest teams as well. Riders like Herman Van Springel, Rogers Swerts and Joseph Bruyère won big races, but all spent a good portion of their careers in the service of Merckx. And service is what it was; Merckx wanted to win everything.

Many domestiques stay in a team for two or three years then move on. Sometimes they get a better offer to do the same job, sometimes they want to have a go at winning for themselves. Others start out as domestiques in a team, and rise through the ranks to be its leader. Miguel Indurain of Spain is a good example of that. But some stay faithful to a leader through their entire career.

One of those was the Italian pro Andrea Carrea. His career lasted ten years from 1949 to 1958, and he spent almost all of it in the service of Fausto Coppi. *Gregario* is the Italian term for domestique in cycling. The journalist Jean-Luc Galletier wrote: 'Carrea was a gregario par excellence, the incarnation of personal disinterest showing to perfection the notion of personal sacrifice. He refused the slightest bit of personal glory.'

Carrea was so loyal that he couldn't stand the thought of Coppi not trusting in his 100 per cent support, as demonstrated by stage nine of the 1952 Tour de France. Coppi was back to full strength in 1952 after time out through broken bones. He won the 1952 Giro d'Italia and was hot favourite to repeat his 1949 Giro and Tour de France double, but in the Tour he seemed distracted.

Andrea Carrea was worried; the Alps were coming and although Coppi was third overall he wasn't concentrating, and he was particularly bad on stage nine. One of Carrea's duties was to ride near the front to keep tabs on what was happening there, and there were a lot of attacks on stage nine – attacks that Carrea thought the Italian team should have somebody with, but Coppi wanted everyone riding close to him, because he reckoned he was having a bad day. Carrea kept drifting back through the peloton to report to Coppi, who eventually said, 'Look, you go with the next move if you are that worried.' So Carrea did.

But the breakaway was good, it gained time on the rest and Carrea took over the yellow jersey. It would have been the highlight of any other rider's career, his first yellow jersey, but it was one of the low points of Carrea's. He did nothing to help the breakaway, but as the yellow jersey was presented to him, Carrea was worrying about Coppi's reaction. He waited for Coppi to finish the stage, and when he crossed the line Carrea got to him first, apologising for what had happened. Coppi just laughed, but the incident seemed to shake him from his torpor. Next day Coppi won the first ever stage finish on Alpe d'Huez, and after that went on the rampage, laying waste to his rivals through the Alps to Sestrière. Coppi won the stage by over seven minutes, and the 1952 Tour by almost half an hour.

The final type of road racer is the *puncheur*. Puncheurs

are best at single-day races and good for stage wins in Grand Tours, especially when stages are neither flat enough for sprinters nor mountainous enough for the pure climbers and overall contenders. Most single-day classics winners nowadays are puncheurs, although there was a time when the more explosive of the best rouleurs, like Merckx and Hinault, won classics too.

To define the qualities of a puncheur it's useful to compare their physiology with that of a high-class rouleur. This is how coach and physiologist Aldo Sassi explained the difference between rouleurs and puncheurs to me in 2009.

> When performing a test to exhaustion a Grand Tour contender [a rouleur] has a high and quite flat curve of power plotted against time to exhaustion. They typically have a high VO2 max, which is a measure of how much oxygen their body can process, but can access a high proportion of their VO2 max over a long period of time. They are aerobic athletes, and differ naturally from the best single-day riders [puncheurs], who have a much steeper curve of power against time to exhaustion. Top single-day riders also have a high VO2 max, but can access an even higher proportion of it than Grand Tour contenders, which they do anaerobically, although for a much shorter period of time.

Almost all puncheurs have a good sprint. Indeed, some, like the Belgian Johan Museeuw, started their pro careers as sprinters, and their sprint was something they could rely on later if it was needed. Typically, a puncheur will try to break the field down, so the smallest workable number of riders remain to contest the victory. They do this by sound tactical decisions and by making stinging attacks, often more than one, at key moments in a race. It's during those attacks that they access a high proportion of their already high VO2 max, so for a brief time they simply ride too hard for anyone but the best to follow.

So that's a look at the different types of road racer, but it's important to stress that they aren't always unique packages. Okay, there are pure climbers, pure sprinters, pure rouleurs and puncheurs, who only have the strengths typical of their group. Mark Cavendish, for example, has won little else but sprints. Tony Martin of Germany is a great time triallist but so far has lacked the explosion to become a classics winner. Mostly, though, rider types form a spectrum rather than unique packages. This is certainly true for puncheurs.

Puncheurs are the all-rounders of road racing. Somebody like Philippe Gilbert of Belgium, winner of some of the biggest single-day races like Liège–Bastogne–Liège and the Tour of Flanders, is the epitome of a puncheur, but he can ride a good time trial too. At the other end of the puncheur spectrum, the Swiss rider Fabian Cancellara was world and Olympic time trial champion but still explosive enough to win the Tour of Flanders and Paris–Roubaix. Chris Froome is a rouleur who has some characerics of a climber. He could probably do well in some of the hillier one-day classics, like Liège–Bastogne–Liège, but he's never targeted them. Bradley Wiggins is a rouleur with a bit more punch. Towards the end of his career he had a good go at Paris–Roubaix and did quite well. I believe that if he'd have focused on the cobbled classics earlier he could have won one.

14

E is for Echelon

Road racing is full of strange names and terms, more than just grimpeurs, puncheurs and rouleurs. Knowing what the names and terms mean, and using them in the right place, is one of the attractions of the sport, a code bike fans use to converse with each other, and a badge declaring 'we are in the know'. So here's a quick A–Z of the commonly used terms in road racing, with one or two asides into more general road race history.

Starting with the letter A, to ride *à bloc* means going as hard as a rider can for a short period of time. It is not a sprint effort, it's a longer one, like what a lead-out rider does in the final kilometres leading up to a big bunch sprint. Riding à bloc is hard, about as hard as a rider can go for one to three minutes.

The other big A to remember is the *autobus*, a group

formed by sprinters and other heavy riders, or anybody simply having a bad day at the back of a race on mountain stages. The group cooperates to ensure they don't finish outside the time limit, or the *hors delai*, another term that you will come across, for each stage. The autobus, which is also referred to by its Italian name, *grupetto*, is usually under the command of an experienced rider who knows the route, will work out the possible time limit, and try to get everybody riding at the pace needed to just beat it. Bernie Eisel of Austria is currently one of the best bus drivers in the sport.

But if you think the autobus sounds fun, perhaps because it is sometimes referred to as the laughing group, think again. Riders put off forming the autobus for as long as possible, hanging on grimly to the back of the main bunch, or peloton, and often doing some desperate descending to get back to it if they are distanced on the early climbs. They need to hold the peloton's speed for as long as possible to help them beat the time limit, because the cut-off margin isn't big, usually 10 per cent of the stage winner's time. Keeping within 10 per cent of a Grand Tour mountain stage winner is no easy feat for anybody.

When the autobus finally forms, the riders in it must keep pushing, and pushing hard. In the Tour de France, for example, the autobus, and even those who can't quite get in but still beat the time limit, always ends up doing the stage faster than the winner of the Etape du Tour, which covers the same stage. (If you don't know about it, the Etape du Tour is a cyclosportive event that follows the exact route of a mountain stage of each year's Tour de France. Its fastest finishers are often pro riders, which just shows how fast the autobus shifts.) Mark Cavendish, who is often in the bus, has said that the riders in it suffer just as much as the climbers at the front, but they don't get as much encouragement.

Okay, I've already mentioned the word *peloton*, so I'll take that out of turn. You probably know what it is, but do you know where the word came from? Like so many in cycling it's from France, from a French word for 'little ball'; the English words platoon and pellet come from the same source. The peloton is the largest group in a road race, but it means much more. As well as being the mobile base of operations in a race, the peloton is an abstract concept, it's the collective will, spirit and attitude of professional cycling. The peloton has an opinion, and nothing in pro bike racing changes unless there is consensus about it within the peloton.

The international language of road racing is now English, but that change was made only recently. It was French from the day road racing started, which is why so many French words are still used in cycling. So, returning to alphabetical order we have the letter B and *baroudeur*, a breakaway specialist, a rider who is always in the break-away moves or going up the road on their own.

Next is the humble *bidon*, or drinks bottle. Cyclists must drink during long road races, and some of the fluids they need must be carried with them. The first road racers used leather satchels, which they strapped to their handlebars, and carried drinks in them contained in glass bottles or tin flasks or canteens. Cycling-specific bidons appeared just after the First World War. Bidon is French, but derives from the Old Norse *bida*, meaning container or vessel. Bidon is also used in everyday French to mean 'belly' or 'a load of bull'. The first bidons were made from aluminium and had cork stoppers. They were roughly the same shape and size as modern bidons, and were carried, two side by side, in aluminium handle-bar-mounted cages.

Early bottle cages had spring-loaded levers to open and close them. So with a flick of the lever a rider could remove the bottle, have a drink, then place it back in the cage, where it was secured again by flicking the lever the other way.

But two bottles on the handlebars isn't very aerodynamic, and they alter a bike's handling, which got one of road racing's great innovators thinking. René Vietto, known as one of the best riders to never win the Tour de France, also gave us the downtube bottle cage, among other things. When Vietto finished second in the 1939 Tour de France his bike had one bidon centrally mounted on his handlebars, and one centrally mounted low down on the downtube. That arrangement of bidons lowered his bike's centre of gravity, which improved its handling. It must have improved his bike's aerodynamics too.

By the second half of the Fifties all pros had their bikes set up like Vietto's. Riders were also beginning to use squeezable plastic bidons. Then, during the Sixties, they ditched the handlebar cage in favour of carrying one bottle on the downtube. A second, seat-tube mounted, cage was added later when the importance of hydration was better understood.

Moving on to C, *chasse patate* is French for 'potato hunt' and is used to describe the situation where a rider is chasing one group but not gaining on it, while not being caught by the group behind. The rider is stuck in limbo, not gaining or losing, making what almost always turns out to be a futile effort. Although the term is used frequently in road racing today, chasse patate originated inside the velodromes in the early days of six-day racing.

Six-day racing revolves around the Madison, which the old six-day riders used to call chases. The thing was, when pressure was on in these chases, which were much longer than they are today, some less experienced riders ended up many laps behind the specialist six-day riders. The less experienced riders were often popular local road racers, signed up by the race promoters to get their fans into the velodrome and to swell the promoter's take at the gate. But it didn't look good, and wouldn't have made the fans happy, if these road racers ended way behind the best track riders. The solution was the potato chase. In the old six-days there were often several Madison races, or chases, throughout each day, so in some chases the top teams agreed not to attack. Instead they let the two-man teams that were a long way behind regain some lost laps. And just to make sure those teams were recognised by the others, they jammed a potato between the rails of their saddles, signifying to the best teams not to chase when they attacked. Hence the name potato chase, or chasse patate.

After that brief track interlude, let's head back onto the road now with the letter C. Road racers have always worn some sort of headgear. When James Moore won the first ever bike race in 1868, his plus-fours and linen jacket racing ensemble was nattily topped off by a stiff-brimmed hat, rather like a scaled-down bowler. Victorian Penny Farthing racers wore pill-box hats held in place by chin straps, and when the Tour de France started in 1903 most of its competitors wore cloth caps styled like Yorkshire's beloved flat cap.

Cloth caps worked well, their peak offering protection from sun and rain. And while the 1906 Tour winner René Pottier protected his head with a white floppy hat, he wasn't copied. Cloth caps prevailed until the outbreak of the First World War. After it the peloton was split; die-hards stuck with their cloth caps, while young bloods preferred peaked school caps.

The increasing sophistication of professional teams during the Twenties changed things. As the decade progressed, distinctive team jerseys with sponsors' names on them became universal in pro road racing. This was when the cycling cap or *casquette* was born, made from cotton with a stiff peak, and in colours to match a rider's team kit.

Casquettes are really practical. Their long peaks protect a cyclist's eyes against rain, sun and wind; and turned around, the peak protects a rider's vulnerable neck from sunburn. A water-soaked cap, or better still one filled with ice cubes lifted during an old-style Tour de France café raid (more of those in a bit), helped keep riders cool. Another old-style ruse was to slip a cabbage leaf under a cap, to provide extra cooling as well as extra sun protection.

In the Fifties sponsors' names started appearing on caps, and in 1955 the yellow cap was introduced in the Tour de France. The yellow cap was optional, but could be worn by the members of the leading team on combined time. Yellow caps were scratched in 1992, and in today's Tour the leading team has the option of wearing yellow helmets.

Finally there is the supporter's cap, and its heyday was the Sixties and Seventies. Fans of top riders, and even some fairly obscure ones in bike-mad Flanders, could buy cycling caps with their hero's name on them. They were commissioned by supporters' clubs, or could be bought at races from freelance sellers, who were cycling's equivalent of the looky looky man. If you supported a rider and didn't wear a supporter's cap, you didn't really care, man.

I mentioned café raids in passing above. Today riders are allowed to drop back from the peloton to get drinks from their team cars, and in the biggest races there are motorbike-mounted drinks services. None of that was allowed until the Seventies, so before then riders quenched their thirst by stopping at fountains to fill their bottles, or by raiding cafés for cold drinks, even alcoholic ones. They were such a regular feature of road racing in hot weather that café raids had their own name: *la chasse à la canette*. Literally 'hunting for cans', drinks cans.

The other important road racing letter C is *commissaire*, the sport's equivalent of umpire or referee. Commissaires are vehicle based, and they follow races to enforce the rules and catch anybody breaking them. If caught, riders can be fined, docked places or time, or even thrown off the race. In big road races there's a team of commissaires, with a head commissaire in charge of them.

The first of the Ds is *directeur sportif*. It's another French cycling term and it means sports director. In top-level road racing now the directeur sportif directs what a team does on the road. Sports directors may also decide overall strategy for the team, although this is often done in conjunction with an overall team manager. Still, the sports director's number one job is to ensure that the team's plan is executed on the road. They often have to change the plan, or the way it is executed, mid-race, so they need to know the sport inside out. Most sports directors are ex-professional cyclists.

In days gone by sports directors did everything, even in big teams, with maybe an assistant director to share race duties, and always a secretary taking care of admin. The number one directeur sportif was responsible for making sure the team had the equipment it needed, that hotels were booked, and that everybody knew where they had to be and when they had to be there. Now the top teams have overall managers, a number of sports directors, plus people in charge of equipment procurement, testing and logistics, as well as anything else you will think of, and even some you won't.

The other D is *dossard*, the French word for a race number, which is how riders are identified. There are two sorts of race numbers, ones that go on the riders' clothing and numbers that go on their bikes. Competitors in early road races wore numbers on armbands. Bike numbers date back to the earliest road races, when they were used to ensure that riders finished a race on the same bike they started on.

By 1910 Tour de France riders had their numbers printed on cloth squares and pinned to the left-hand side of their jerseys, low down at the back. The number had to be visible, so riders who carried food in bags (there were no rear pockets in early cycling jerseys) needed to pin a number on their bag as well.

Jersey numbers have changed little since the early days. Plastic replaced cloth, but numbers are still pinned to jerseys in all but the biggest road races. Adhesive numbers are used in some big races now. Also, an increasing number of skinsuits have number windows in their design, in the form of transparent pockets that the number is placed in. The pocket keeps the number flat to the rider's body, so the number doesn't disrupt air flow over the rider.

Frame numbers evolved from thin cardboard to metal then plastic plates, always mounted below the top tube where it joins the head tube. Early frame numbers were secured with thin wire. Then, in the Sixties, Tour de France frame numbers were made from very malleable metal, hooked over the top tube, then squeezed to secure the number in place and held fast by a small nut and bolt. From 1970 Tour de France frame numbers were bolted to the frame's top tube through a clamp, and later on in the Tour, and in other big European races, numbers were bolted to mounts brazed under the bike's top tube. Nowadays frame numbers are attached to the seat bolt or a bracket at the rear of the bike.

Some numbers have special status. The winner of a previous year's race is often given the number 1. Team leaders are generally given the first number in each block of ten. A red number indicates the Tour de France rider who was judged the most combative on the previous stage. Then there's the myth of number 51 in the Tour de France. It grew out of the Seventies, because Eddy Merckx was number 51 when he won in 1969, and Luis Ocana was number 51 when he won in 1973, as were Bernard Thévenet in 1975 and Bernard Hinault in 1978. That was the last time; rider number 51 hasn't won the Tour since, yet the myth still persists. The most regular Tour-winning number is number 1.

Moving on to the letter E we have *echelon*, a word describing the formation road racers use to combat cross-winds. If the wind blows head-on or from behind, the riders in a breakaway, or in the peloton when it's going fast, form a pace-line. In a pace-line one person leads while the others follow in their slipstream. When the front rider wants to stop setting the pace, he or she moves to one side in the road and drops back to join the end of the line, or at least somewhere further down it. The next rider then takes over pace-setting at the front of the group or the peloton.

An echelon is used when the wind blows from the

side, or in crosswinds as they are commonly called. An echelon works the same way as a pace-line except the leading rider rides on the side where the wind is blowing from, while the others line up inside and behind, a bit like geese do in flight.

But if that description of an echelon makes it sound sedate then it's misleading, because when the pressure is on, life in an echelon is about as far from sedate as it gets. Although the peloton forms a loose echelon shape in crosswinds, tight echelons are used to break up races, and while riding in them is hard, outside it's brutal. Knowing a crosswind section is coming, a team might go to the front of the race, and when the crosswinds hit, the lead rider takes a position on the road on the side the wind is blowing from, but only far enough from the other side to allow his or her team mates to join the echelon and share its shelter.

Riders behind the echelon get no shelter, so if the leading riders go hard, splits occur. The only option for the other riders then is to force their way into the front echelon, which can be done with craft and/or brute force, or form another echelon behind. Both options are fraught with problems. Try the first, and the teams which are really good in crosswinds often leave one rider at the back of the echelon to prevent anyone else joining it. With the other option, the riders who get in the front echelon during the initial scramble are usually the strongest, so natural selection means the front echelon tends to draw clear of the rest.

The word 'echelon' is French. It was originally used in English, according to the *Oxford English Dictionary*, to describe 'an arrangement of troops in parallel groups each with its end clear of those in front or behind'. It can be applied to ships too. It's used by English speakers in cycling now but, confusingly, an echelon is sometimes called a *bordure* in French, although that usually means the echelon is filling the road from edge to edge. Meanwhile, an echelon is a *waaier* in Flemish and Dutch, and cyclists from both nations are masters of the echelon.

Rounding off the letter E we have *espoir*, the French word for hope, which is sometimes used to describe the under-23 age group of bike racers, the 19- to 22-year-olds. From 1971 until 1984 there was also a stage race called Etoile des Espoirs, which was launched by Jean Leulliot to encourage young riders. However, to gain publicity quickly for his race, and to ensure it would be covered by the media, Leulliot invited the biggest name in French cycling at the time, Raymond Poulidor, to take part in the first edition, which he duly won. Poulidor was 35. All other winners over the years have been much younger riders.

Jean Leulliot also played a part in the wider story of road racing. He was a political left-winger with fiery loyalties whose career suffered because of them, but they motivated him as well. Leulliot enters the story during the Second World War, when the occupying German forces wanted French life to continue as close to normal as possible.

The Germans approached the organiser of the Tour de France, Jacques Goddet, who had replaced Henri Desgrange in 1936 when Desgrange fell ill during the Tour de France, and asked him to revive the Tour and run it in 1942. Goddet had previously cooperated with the occupying forces. He supported the Pétain government, which wanted peaceful coexistence with the Germans, but this was too much and Goddet declined.

However, Jean Leulliot did offer to run a shortened

version of the Tour called the Circuit de France. It wasn't something Leulliot did lightly or as an act of collaboration, because French left-wingers were dead against German Fascism, but he thought it unreasonable that people who made their living from cycling should be deprived of doing so just to support Goddet's lofty stand.

After the war Goddet, who was Leulliot's political opposite, founded the daily sports newspaper *L'Equipe*, which is still going strong today, and took over the reins of the Tour de France once more. However, Goddet and Leulliot's enmity grew as the Tour de France, and *L'Equipe*, and with them Goddet, became more successful with each passing year.

Leulliot formed his own sports organisation, Monde Six, and in 1951 he became race director of Paris–Nice, which was revived that year. Paris–Nice, now the first really big stage race in Europe each year, was born in 1933. It was the idea of another newspaper man, Albert Lejeune, who wanted a race to promote two of his papers at different ends of the country. One was *Le Petit Journal* in Paris, and the other was called *Le Petit Nice*, so a race between those two places was ideal. Paris–Nice ran every year from 1933 until 1940, when it was cancelled because of the Second World War.

There was another edition of Paris–Nice in 1946, and then none until the race was revived in 1951 by the mayor of Nice, Jean Medecin, who renamed it Paris–Côte d'Azur. It was run by the weekly magazine *Route et Piste*, which Jean Leulliot wrote for. The race's name changed back to Paris–Nice in 1954, and then in 1957 Leulliot bought the rights to it. In 1959 a few more stages were added and Paris–Nice became Paris–Nice–Rome for one year.

Monde Six and Leulliot also organised the Route de

France, a Tour de France for amateurs. But then *L'Equipe*, under its editor Jacques Marchand (Goddet was full-time director of the Tour de France by then), started the Tour de l'Avenir in 1961. The Tour de l'Avenir was intended to represent the Tour de France of the future. It was originally for amateur riders and it ran for two weeks within the framework of the Tour de France, using a shortened version of some of its stages. It slowly eclipsed Leulliot's Route de France, which was last run in 1992. The Tour de l'Avenir was opened to professionals in 1981, and is still going strong today as a stage race for elite under-23 riders, espoirs, but is run quite separately from the Tour de France.

The Route de France name was revived as La Route de France Féminine, a stage race for women that ran from 2006 to 2010, then made a comeback in 2012 after the demise of the Tour de France Féminine in 2009 and another big women's stage race in France, the Tour de l'Aude Cycliste Féminine. Leulliot would be pleased about his Route de France becoming a women's race because he had a plan for a women's Tour de France way back in 1951. And as well as Etoile des Espoirs, he organised the Grand Prix de France time trial and the Trophée des Grimpeurs. All good races, but all overshadowed by those organised by *L'Equipe*.

Leulliot died in 1982 and his daughter Josette took over Monde Six, selling the rights to Paris–Nice to the 1983 and 1984 Tour de France winner, Laurent Fignon, in 2000. But when Fignon lost money on his new venture he was forced to sell it to the present Tour de France owners ASO, who took over Goddet and *L'Equipe*'s cycling interests when ASO's founder, Emilien Amaury, bought *L'Equipe* in 1968.

Right, after that short diversion into history, back to

etymology and the letter F. First there is the *Flamme Rouge*, also called the Red Kite. It's a red flag, often triangular and usually suspended over the road one kilometre from the finish line of a race. It's there to give the riders solid visual evidence of where the final kilometre starts. In many races there are countdown boards at the side of the road, sometimes one per 100 metres. Traditionally in British road races there was a yellow flag hung by the side of the road 200 metres from the finish line.

The next F is *feed zone*, the designated place on a race route or on a circuit where team staff are allowed to hand supplementary food and bottles to their riders. In France the sign for a feed zone is *Ravitaillement*, a word which means resupply and is also used in the military.

While talking about feed zones let's jump to M for *musette*, because musettes are the little cloth bags that extra food and drink is put into, and are then handed to riders in feed zones. Each bag has a single strap, which the riders put around their neck so they can transfer the contents, usually a bidon of drink, some gels and a few energy bars, to the pockets of their racing jerseys. They then discard the musettes, which become nice mementos for fans.

The final F is *la fringale*, better known as bonk, or bonking, also known in France as *l'homme avec le marteau*, the man with the hammer. Bonk is experienced – suffered is a better word – when a road racer runs out of immediately available fuel to burn. The fuel is glucose, stored as glycogen in the body. Unfortunately the human body can only store enough glycogen to work reasonably hard – not flat out, it's much less for flat out – for about two hours. That's why on-the-bike feeding is vital in long road races.

La fringale, the bonk, or getting hit on the head by the hammer, was a regular occurrence in road racing until recently, especially early in the season when riders' bodies weren't used to racing, or they weren't as fit as they could be. It's a horrible experience, but some road racers welcomed it. An old lore of racing held that a rider went much better and was stronger after suffering from the bonk. It was true too, and now we know why.

Fewer cases of bonk occur to top-level road racers now because they train to become fat adapted. Fat adaptation means they burn a greater percentage of fat as fuel at higher and higher power outputs. To do that they use dietary manipulations, like restricting the total amounts of carbohydrate they eat, timing what they do eat correctly, using fewer carbohydrates as fuel during training, and training in a fasted or part-fasted state.

I could go on, for there is lot more to this area of nutrition and training, but the overall aim is to get the body to use fat in preference to glucose (carbohydrate) at higher and higher power outputs. The reason the old racers went better after they'd bonked was that by doing so they got a crash course in teaching the body to use fats as fuel, because running out of available glucose meant their body was forced to switch to fat.

The reason why fat is a better fuel for endurance cycling is that even the skinniest cyclist has about forty hours' worth of fat reserves, but only those two hours of glucose. So the harder they can ride using fat for fuel, the more they preserve their glucose stores for use in the most intense parts of a race.

Moving on to H, the main term to know and understand is *hors catégorie*, used for the longest, highest and/or hardest climbs in the Tour de France. The Tour organisers number the significant climbs in each year's race route from fourth to first, according to increasing severity. Points are awarded at the top of each categorised climb, and they count towards the King of the Mountains title. Taking the 2014 Tour de France as an example, the points ranged from one point for first to the top of a fourth category climb, to ten points for first to the top of a first category climb. The points spread increases with severity too, from just one point for the first to the top of a fourth category climb, to the first six riders at the top of a first category climb getting points.

Hors catégorie means beyond categorisation, i.e. the hardest climbs in the Tour. In our example, the 2014 Tour, the first rider to the summit of a hors catégorie climb was awarded 25 points, second place got 20 points, third got 16, and so on down to two points for the tenth rider to the top. Also, in the 2014 Tour de France any second, first or hors catégorie climb that was also the stage finish, attracted double points. So the stage winner on top of a hors catégorie climb would have also won 50 points towards the King of the Mountains title.

Hors catégories also had another meaning in road racing, referring to riders of a special status. Up until the end of the Sixties there were three categories of senior male road racer: amateur, independent and professional. Independents were a halfway house between amateurs and professionals. They could race against professionals in some of their races, and against amateurs in some of theirs. In Europe there were cash prizes for both, so some independents were reluctant to turn professional because they could win more money as independents. They also got to pick and choose the races they did, so could stay around where they lived, and made decent money while not having to travel all over Europe.

However, in 1969 the UCI declared that the independent category was to be scrapped, and independent riders had to either turn professional or return to amateur status. They were given a couple of years to sort themselves out, and the UCI created a short-lived category called 'senior amateur hors catégorie' for them to race under while they did so. A few chose to go pro, but most went back to being amateurs.

The two main road racing Ls to remember are *laché* and *lanterne rouge*. Laché describes a racer who has been dropped from a group. It's from the French verb *lacher*, which means to release or abandon, and is very descriptive because it sounds painful, which being dropped is.

Lanterne rouge is the title of the last rider in the overall classification of a stage race. It was born in the Tour de France, means red lamp and refers to the red lamps or lanterns that were hung on the last carriage or truck of French trains. Traditionally, on the final road race stage of the Tour the lanterne rouge posed for photographers carrying a red lantern while ambling along at the back of the peloton. He was often joined for the photos by the yellow jersey too.

Moving on to M, we've talked about *musette*, which is a word also used to describe a canvas bag with a shoulder strap carried by soldiers, and a small French bagpipe. The other big road racing M is *magic spanner*. Magic spanner refers to cases where a rider, who is perhaps chasing back to the peloton after a mechanical incident, asks for his or her team car's attention because, they will say, something needs adjusting on their bikes. A brake pad might be rubbing after a wheel change, something like that. Once alongside the rider, the mechanic leans out of the car, and fiddles a bit with the rider's bike while the rider holds on to the car. Sometimes the mechanic fiddles for quite a long time.

Holding on to a car for a tow is against the rules of racing, but commissaires tolerate a bit of magic spanner, so long as there's no abuse of it. If there is, and the commissaire sees it, the rider gets a warning and it has to stop. The riders and team can be fined too. Still, once warned, the mechanic often gives the rider a big shove forward as a parting gift.

Magic spanner is closely related to sticky bottle. A sticky bottle is where a rider drops back to the team car for a new bidon, but when it's passed over and the rider grabs it, the person passing the bidon keeps hold too. The net result is another tow.

From time to time commissaires get tough with magic spanners and sticky bottles. Just before the 2015 Paris–Nice the UCI commissaires on the race reminded teams of a UCI rule that says: 'It is forbidden for mechanics to hang out of vehicles to work on a bike or a rider.' The commissaires warned the teams they would enforce the rule in Paris–Nice. If the warning was heard, in some cases it wasn't received. Two team managers were fined 1,000 francs each on stages one and four. The rule is there for the safety of riders and team personnel. A good few riders have crashed while hanging on to cars. Strictly speaking, if there is something wrong with a rider's bike in a race, they should call for their team car, and when it gets close they stop and the mechanic fixes it by the side of the road.

So, leaving the rights and wrongs of magic spanners and sticky bottles, let's move on to the letter O and *on the rivet*, a term used to describe a rider making a very big effort on the flat. When cyclists ride very hard on the flat they tend to sit a bit further forwards on their saddle; it's a consequence of trying to get low and aerodynamic, pulling extra hard with their arms on the handlebars, and trying to get all their leg power down into the pedals. The term 'on the rivet' comes from the old days, when racing bike saddles were made of leather. The leather was fixed to the metal saddle frame by copper rivets, and all saddles had one rivet right on their nose, which is what the very front of a racing saddle is called. So when flat out on a road, and sitting right at the front of the saddle, the rider was on the rivet.

There are a number of Ps. We've dealt with *peloton* and *puncheur*, but not *palmarès*. It's another French word, literally meaning a list of achievements, and a road racer's palmarès is his or her career record of race wins, placings and other notable performances.

Panache is another French word, meaning dash, verve, style or *élan* – which is yet another. In cycling it means winning in style. It can also mean doing anything with style, for the show, for the entertainment. It doesn't mean clowning about, though. It means doing something outstanding, but looking cool while doing so.

Parcours is the race route, its course. The parcours for big races is always published in the road-book, the instruction manual for that race. The parcours will be shown in map form, in profile, and as a list of points passed through and the times when the race is expected there, sometimes based on different average speeds. Feed zones, hills and other race details are also listed on the parcours, as well as the positions of *primes*.

Primes are intermediate prizes, either points or cash, which can be won along the parcours. The primes may be awarded at hill summits, or on the finish line of circuit races. Sometimes in circuit races primes are given each lap, or every two or three, or at whatever intervals the race promoter or organiser can afford to give them. In criterium and kermesse road races, both explained in the next chapter, primes are also donated by spectators. Most European criteriums and Belgian kermesse races have people collecting prime cash from spectators.

S stands for *soigneur*, from the French verb *soigner*, which means to care. And that's what soigneurs do; they care for riders in a team by making sure they have food and drink for the race, by handing up extra supplies during it, then meeting them off the bike at the end of races, making sure they are okay and giving them recovery drinks. Back at the team hotels, soigneurs use massage and other therapies to help the riders recover. And as well as looking after the riders physically, they are often the glue that holds a team together, patiently listening to complaints and grouches in their role as team confessors.

There's no doubt now that in the past some soigneurs overstepped the rules and helped some riders take banned substances. You'll see later on in this book that in the very early days of road racing, when soigneurs were also referred to as trainers, many of them dealt in the dark arts of doping. Nowadays soigneurs are carefully vetted by teams, which has helped make men's professional road racing a much healthier place to work in.

The other S-word you'll hear used a lot in professional road racing, particularly during the second half of each racing season, is *stagiaire*. A stagiaire is an amateur rider who is selected by a professional team for a trial in some races. It's a chance for the team to get to know the rider in more depth, and a chance for the rider to experience pro racing and life in the team before either of them commits to a full-pro contract.

The two road racing T terms to remember are both Italian: *tempo* and *tifosi*. Riding tempo is the pace the peloton goes when it doesn't want a breakaway to gain any more time. Riders from one of more teams will do long turns, turn being short for turn on the front, at a pace just below their time trial pace, which is also known as anaerobic threshold. Tempo is also used to describe a training session that every professional road racer does a lot. It's riding at a hard pace, but a hard pace that's manageable and feels good, for an extended period.

Tifosi are fans, Italian fans to be precise. They are noisy, opinionated and in the past have exhibited extreme nationalistic tendencies. In 1960, when he won the Giro d'Italia after coming second the year before, Jacques Anquetil became so frustrated by fans pushing his Italian rival Gastone Nencini uphill for long stretches of time that he remarked bitterly: 'If the tifosi could get away with it they'd put Nencini in a car and drive him to the top of each climb.'

Many non-Italian riders have experienced the same level of, shall we call it passion, down the years. This is Vin Denson, the first English-speaking winner of a stage in the Giro d'Italia, talking about his experience of that race in 1966:

> We had the lead, the pink jersey, in the Ford France team through Julio Jimenez that year, so we were on the front every day working for him. The day we went into Napoli was amazing. I was leading, riding between the tall houses all with Romeo and Juliet type balconies on them, and the Italians were stood on the balconies pelting me with the contents of their rubbish bins. They did it just because I was in a French team, and because we were winning. At the finish I was covered with rotten fruit and veg and old spaghetti sauce.

Tête de la course means the front, literally head, of the race. On the other hand, *la course en tête* describes a way of racing, or an attacking rider who is always at the front. And the final T you need to know is exactly the opposite; it's the *ticket collector*, a term used to describe a canny rider who always sits at the back of the peloton but is comfortable doing so.

Being the ticket collector doesn't mean a rider is lazy or unambitious; it's quite the opposite. It takes skill to be at the end of the peloton, stay there and remain relaxed while riding there. It takes supreme confidence and a high degree of awareness, because when under pressure the peloton can split near the back. Being the ticket collector is often the mark of a rider who knows their own ability, and uses it decisively when the opportunities arise.

The number one ticket collector in men's pro road racing at the moment is Britain's Steve Cummings. He will spend whole Grand Tours riding right at the back, except when his team needs him and when he knows the terrain is right for him to win a stage. Then he is right there, right in the mix, grafting to make the perfect move to give him the best chance of winning. And when Cummings gets in such a move, more often than not he wins.

So, that's my A–Z of road racing terms. I think I've covered the main ones, and the more puzzling ones. There are others, of course, and when French was the language of road racing there were many more. However, there are still enough French terms to add a bit of Continental glamour, and enough special knowledge for fans to be sages of road racing.

15

Round the Houses

This chapter is about two kinds of circuit races; one is called a *criterium*, and the other is a *kermesse*. Criteriums are found all over the world, and there are quite wide variations on their central theme. Kermesse races, true kermesses (you get other countries saying a race is a kermesse when it's actually a criterium – don't worry, there'll be a handout at the end), were born in Flanders and they are only found in Flanders.

We'll start with criteriums because of their universal nature. Almost any country that has road races has criteriums in some form or another. In some countries they are very important, in others less so. The USA and UK have always had a healthy number of criteriums, and specialists who are very good at riding them. However, criteriums in those two countries differ from those you'll find in mainland Europe. Basically, though, all criteriums, with one notable exception explained in the next paragraph, are multi-lap circuit races. It's just the size of the lap and the overall distance that differs.

Criteriums were born in France, where the word *critérium* originally just meant competition, which explains the anomaly I alluded to above: a stage race called the Critérium du Dauphiné. About a week long, it's a race in and around the French Alps, and the organisers have always used criterium in its title in the word's literal sense. When it was created in 1947 by the regional newspaper *Le Dauphiné Libéré*, it was called the Critérium du Dauphiné Libéré. It didn't run in 1967 or 1968, but returned in 1969, by which time it had merged with another old race in the same part of France, the Circuit des Six Provinces. Then, like many big French races, it was slowly taken over by ASO, the organisers of the Tour de France. In 2010, when *Le Dauphiné Libéré* handed over the reins of the race fully to ASO, its name was changed to Critérium du Dauphiné.

Okay, with that anomaly explained, on with the history of criteriums as most of the world knows them. As the name suggests, they were born in France as local, easy to organise bike races. Having found a circuit, often a triangular one in France, the organisers then decided on the number of laps, the date of the race, which often coincided with saints' days and holidays, co-opted some people to help close off the circuit on the day, publicised what they were doing – and local riders would turn up and race. It was the way most French cyclists got into the sport. Same in the Netherlands, where there is a great tradition of criterium racing.

Criteriums grew to be very popular in France, especially

in certain areas: Brittany, for example. And as early as the Fifties and Sixties, British club racers were making the short trip over the Channel and a little bit down country for some Breton criterium racing during their holidays. What they experienced when they got there was a far cry from the racing they were used to in the UK, which was time trials, circuit races on windy airfields, or a few fledgling road races far out in the countryside watched by club-mates, family and friends.

Mike Breckon was one such club racer. In May 1960 he took his annual holiday in Loudéac, travelling with a friend from York, Tony McCarthy. They took a French-English phrasebook, a copy of *Cyclisme*, the French racer's handbook, with a list of races inside it, and their bikes. Breckon wrote about the experiences in the British cycling magazine, *Sporting Cyclist*. The following is an extract from that piece.

Our first race was in Loudéac, on a short for a Breton criterium three-quarter mile circuit which had to be covered 60 times, each lap passing right in front of our hotel. There was a crowd of 3,000 by the time the race started at two-thirty on Sunday afternoon. I was amazed by the pace. The field was about 90 strong, and there was always someone trying to get a breakaway going.

The only way to finish such a race is to stay near the head of affairs to keep an eye on things. But don't try going with all the breaks, because it will kill you. Both Tony and I managed to feature in a number of attacks, Tony doing particularly well as he has a strong sprint developed from years of track racing. He picked up one or two primes and became tremendously popular with the locals, who shouted 'Toni' and 'Michel' at the tops of their voices.

I was amazed to discover after the first race that the average speed was 27 mph. When you are making an attack off the front, the speed must be quite something, though this is not really noticeable at the time. The riding was generally of a good standard, with only one crash during the event. That was on the last lap when riders were jockeying for position. We learned a lot of things quickly, like how to use our gears like the French riders do. They all use close-ratio gears, maybe one tooth difference on each sprocket, and are constantly changing to get the very best out of their gears. We also found out the Breton riders used much lighter frames than ours, which must have helped their sprinting.

I hope that extract helps convey some of the atmosphere and nature of standard French criteriums. Even races for ordinary club racers are a real occasion in their locality, with circuits closed off, not just for rider safety but so the organisers can charge admission fees. That last fact was responsible for creating the biggest criteriums there are, where promoters engage local help to close off a circuit and charge admission, then pay the best professional road racers they can to ride their race.

Professional criteriums became big business in Europe, because in the days before the blanket TV coverage of big road races, locals wanted to see the stars they'd only read about in newspapers. And they were quite happy to pay to stand in their own village or on their own town streets to do so.

The post-Tour de France criteriums were the first big pro criteriums, and they still exist in a reduced form today. They grew from and over time replaced post-Tour track meetings, where the stars of each year's Tour de

France, the overall and stage winners, plus others who had achieved something notable, were invited to race in velodromes in front of paying spectators.

Post-Tour de France track meetings are nearly as old as the Tour itself. The Tour organising newspaper *L'Auto* carried details of a post-Tour track meeting at the Parc des Princes velodrome in its 15 August 1913 issue. The first three overall in that year's Tour de France were contracted to ride: Philippe Thys, Gustave Garrigou and Marcel Buysse, along with stage winners like François Faber.

There were lots of velodromes in France back then, but their owners always charged promoters a fee to use them, and there was a limit on the number of spectators you could get in. So small velodromes without much space for a crowd weren't viable for post-Tour track meetings. But people in a place with a small velodrome still wanted to see the riders, and criterium circuits had plenty of space for people to watch them. Soon the best professional road racers were racing all over France in criterium races. The promoters paid them, often through agents, men who represented a string of riders and would negotiate their criterium contacts for them, taking a cut themselves of course. And the promoters charged the public to watch.

That's how post-Tour criteriums got started, and they proved so popular that soon there were early-season criteriums, post-classics ones, post-Giro criteriums in Italy, post-world championships ones, often billed as revenge races, and end of season criteriums: all so that fans could see the stars of road racing where they lived.

Professional criteriums became big business, growing throughout the Fifties, Sixties and into the Seventies.

The post-Tour criteriums in particular were another world. This is the British rider Barry Hoban talking about his first experience of the post-Tour criteriums, when he was a new professional in 1964, and had just finished his first Tour de France. He explains their importance, how they worked and how they varied between countries. He also talks about the atmosphere of the criteriums, and the camaraderie of the pro riders who took part and moved around Europe like a travelling circus on wheels.

When the Tour de France was over we carried on racing. Basically, we just entered another phase of it. In those days the contracts we had with teams were our bread and jam. They fed you, they kept you, but they didn't provide any of life's luxuries. If you were going to make extra money you made it in the criteriums after the Tour. You were given your contract to ride, then there was a chance of winning cash prizes and primes in the races. They were quite lucrative for all of us, and very lucrative if you were one of the stars.

They weren't easy, though. Nowadays the criteriums in Belgium and Holland seem to be choreographed, because you get guys like Chris Froome and Vincenzo Nibali winning; you know, real climbers. Well, the likes of Federico Bahamontes, José Manuel Fuente or Julio Jimenez, the best climbers of my era, never won a Dutch or Belgian criterium in the Sixties or Seventies.

Belgian and Dutch criteriums were always about 100 kilometres in length, mostly in the evenings in Holland, where circuits were about one kilometre in length, so 100 laps with between five and seven corners every lap. Boy it hurt, accelerating out of all those corners, and if you couldn't win you didn't win, there was nothing given, no freebies. Yeah, sometimes we'd cooperate, riders would band together and share prize money between us. If one rider attacked, a few others might have agreed to block for him for a share of what he won. But the circuits were sealed off, and everybody watching paid to get in, so they didn't want to see anything that was rigged.

The Belgian criteriums were slightly different. They still had a paying public, but sometimes they were on bigger and more adventurous circuits. The post-Tour criterium in Ronse had a quite long drag on the circuit, so did the one in Geraardsbergen. And the criterium at Poperinge in West Flanders had a good cobbled section, which was interesting when it rained.

Over the years I rode a few criteriums in Belgium and Holland, but mostly I rode in France, and there the criteriums were more like road races. Once again, the village or a small town was closed off and everyone had to pay to get on the circuits, which were longer than elsewhere, three to five kilometres. More often than not, a French criterium circuit had three sections: an uphill, a downhill, and a flat section. So a triangle, and the race distances would be 130 to 140 kilometres. You really knew about it when you'd been up the same hill thirty to forty times. And in Brittany in particular, where top criteriums like those in Callac or Châteaulin had 30,000 plus paying spectators, the public wanted value for their money.

They had what we called mafias in the pro criteriums. Groups of riders, who although they raced for different teams the rest of the year, banded together to help each other in the criteriums. So the guys who'd just done the Tour would normally ride together. The top guys, the Tour contenders, were in one group, while others changed from race to race. But there were always some other riders contracted for criteriums to make the fields bigger, riders like local independents and amateurs, and some of those were really good and had their own mafias. So you had the Breton mafia in Brittany, and the Bordeaux mafia, and others.

The organisers always wanted a Tour rider to win their race, which the Tour riders tried to arrange, but it was never easy. As well as experienced riders in the mafias you got young ambitious riders thrown in too. I was like that in 1963 when I got a ride in a post-Tour criterium in northern France. I kept attacking and attacking, and in the end I got told off by one of the most experienced pros, Jean Stablinski. I hadn't realised that most of the Tour de France pros had driven through the night to be at the race, and they were tired.

I also remember a young Bernard Hinault in the Seventies riding with the Breton mafia, well before he was known as the great rider he was. He screamed at us, he stuck his elbows out, attacking and fighting like only a Breton can. It took the combined efforts of me, Walter Godefroot and Jacques Esclassan to put him in his place. Later on he realised it was part of his apprenticeship.

Anyway, being a young pro doing the Post-Tour criterium round for the first time in 1964 I travelled with my mate, a French guy called Jean-Pierre Genet, who was a Breton. Well, actually his parents were Breton, and much like the Irish who came to live in Liverpool for work, the Bretons went to live in Paris, and Jean-Pierre was born in Paris. But he was Breton in every other sense. Bretons know everybody. Everywhere you go they'll have a relation there. So I latched on to Jean-Pierre and I stayed where he stayed, and we struck up a bond. It was great, we were two young men getting around

France doing something we loved. I vividly remember him saying to me one day: 'It's amazing isn't it, they pay us for doing something we like doing.'

That year we had beautiful weather too, we just wore shorts and T-shirts all the time, and as well as racing we met all these people whom Jean-Pierre knew. One day we were in the Loire valley going to a race and Jean-Pierre says: 'Look I've got some friends, a cousin of mine, they've got a vineyard near here, let's go and taste some good Muscadet wine. So we went off the main road into this maze of little lanes until we found a tiny farm track, and at the end of the track there was a small farm with a little French guy there at the gate, really rural French, with his beret on and stubble on his chin.

He greeted us, and we went down to the wine cellar. All the wine cellars around there, in the Loire, are basically man-made caves hewn out of the rock. The idea of a wine cellar is that you have, within a degree or so, constant temperature all year round. So even in the middle of summer, when it's boiling hot upstairs, you go down and it's nice and fresh. Anyway, we started tasting this Muscadet, and I didn't know much about wine so I was drinking it like lemonade. Great stuff, great stuff, I'm saying to each one they gave me to try. I ended up buying two or three boxes of it, and in old money I paid one French franc per bottle, that's like seven and a half pence. But remember, this was on our way to a criterium, we still had to race later that day.

So eventually we got there, and criteriums had a special atmosphere. It was one of the few times people got to see the cycling stars they read about close up. And I mean really close, like you could shake hands, get an autograph, and have a quick chat. And the biggest stars were something special back then. They had star quality. We called them Les Gros Bras, the Big Arms. They all looked the part too. They had star quality.

Anquetil would turn up with his wife Janine and their entourage. They filled two cars wherever they went, and their life looked so glamorous, but behind the scenes Janine might have driven all through the night while Jacques slept. That's how they got from one criterium to another, because Anquetil did all the big ones, not just in France but in surrounding countries. That's how he made most of his money.

They drove through the night, then they'd get to the town where the next criterium was at about eight or nine o'clock in the morning. They'd check into a hotel, and that's when Janine slept. She was something else. I was only 24 years old and Janine looked so elegant. She was quite a bit older than Jacques, but she looked super glamorous. Although all the top riders' wives looked like that then, or they seemed to. They all had these big cars too, big Mercedes or what have you, while we'd be crammed into whatever car we had, an old Opel Record or whatever.

But as you went round the criteriums you got to know them all a bit better, although Anquetil remained a bit of a demi-god to me. I never had a real long conversation with him. Some who came later, like Eddy Merckx, I was a bit in awe of him too because he was so good, the best ever, but I could chat with him. Luis Ocana was easy to talk to as well, and from the Anquetil era so was Rudi Altig.

Nowadays the teams almost segregate themselves, but in the Sixties and Seventies you mixed, and in the criteriums you mixed a lot. If you weren't rushing off to do another race you'd sit down with ten to fifteen others and have a meal together, a league of nations all from different teams.

But there was one criterium in Brittany that was always a bit special. Callac was near the home of André Foucher, a great Tour de France rider but also a proper Breton farmer. So we finished the criterium in Callac and Jean-Pierre said to me: 'We're all going round to Foucher's afterwards because we've not got a race tomorrow.' First I'd heard of it, but okay, let's go. About ten of us turned up at Foucher's farm, and they had this big kitchen dining-room where everything in the family happened. There was a huge table and there were stable doors at the bottom of the room. If you opened the top half of the doors you could see through to the cows, and above the cows' heads was the hay-loft.

André's wife was busy cooking when we got there, so André took us all down the street to the local café for an aperitif, then we went back to the house for this meal. We all sat round the table and André's wife brought a great big cauldron and plonked it down in the middle, and it was full of cooked crabs. You just reached in, picked a crab out, put it on your plate, cracked it open and delved in. It was true peasant food, but the way it was cooked, the fresh crabs were delicious, and there was wine in abundance.

It was great, a great atmosphere, plenty to eat and drink, but after a while I started wondering where we were going to sleep that night, so I asked Jean-Pierre. 'Up in the loft,' he said. 'There's plenty of hay, we'll be fine up there.' So we slept up there in the hay-loft, with all the cows sleeping below us.

So, that was life in the post-Tour criteriums of the Sixties, and it stayed very much like that through the Seventies and into the Eighties. Riders were contracted on a race by race basis, and often paid in cash, significant amounts of cash when a share of the prize money and primes collected from the crowd were added in. The Danish former world hour record holder Ole Ritter remembers that carrying lots of cash around Europe was a problem – a nice one, but still a problem:

> After the 1975 Tour de France I had contracts for 23 criteriums in 21 days. Francesco Moser was my team-mate, and he'd had a good Tour de France, he won the best young rider's white jersey. We had the same contracts, so we travelled to all the races in my car, and we earned so much cash that Moser asked my wife Marianne, who was with us, to buy a big aluminium suitcase with a lock on it. We had no time to go to banks, and the banks weren't as connected as they are in Europe now. Plus different countries had their own currencies still in those days. So we put all our money in the suitcase, and while Francesco and I raced Marianne sat on it.

The criteriums continued to be important for most pro road racers until 1990, when the tectonic plates of pro bike racing tradition were changed by an American, Greg LeMond. And if life for the average pro didn't get easier, at least they were paid more, in many cases a lot more.

The best riders always got fairly good salaries from their teams, but they got rich from prize money and from criterium and track contracts, as well as product endorsements. Many less well paid riders depended on the criteriums to boost their wages. As Barry Hoban mentioned, the criteriums were the difference between just paying your bills and having enough money to buy a new car or put down a deposit on a nicer house. That's why professional criteriums were so important to everyone.

As time passed, salaries rose, just as basic pay did in other jobs, but there was a definite upward jump after Greg LeMond hit the scene in the Eighties, especially in 1986 when he joined the La Vie Clare team that was created by the multi-millionaire French businessman Bernard Tapie. LeMond won the Tour de France that year, the first American to do so, but his second victory made an even bigger difference to team salaries, and to the way teams were run.

After an amazing comeback from severe injuries sustained in a hunting accident in 1987, LeMond won the 1989 Tour de France by the narrowest ever margin of eight seconds. A few weeks later he won the world professional road race championship. Doing that double boosted LeMond's criterium earnings from 10,000 to 30,000 dollars a race. Criterium earnings were still the barometer of a pro road racer's worth, but during the following winter two teams started talking numbers of a very different magnitude to Greg LeMond.

He had a year of his contract with the Belgian ADR squad left to run. It was one of the very few that wanted him by 1989, after his long fall from the top due to his injuries and associated health problems that slowed down and often halted his comeback. However, although LeMond received some money from the team, they were consistently late in paying him, which breached the terms of their contract. LeMond was free to move.

In September 1989 it was announced that the American had been offered a three-year deal worth 5.5 million dollars by Peugeot's replacement, the Z team. The American 7-Eleven team wanted him too, and LeMond was inclined to sign for the Americans, but they couldn't possibly come up with anything like Z's offer.

Five and a half million dollars was a whole order of magnitude bigger than the salaries teams had previously paid their best riders. And LeMond didn't stop at his own salary; he negotiated victory bonuses with Z for his team-mates, and he had the whole deal underpinned by a bank guarantee. LeMond changed professional cycling in many ways, but this was probably his biggest contribution.

When LeMond signed a one million dollar deal with the La Vie Claire team in 1986 he dragged up every other pro road racer's worth in his wake. It happened again after the Z deal, but introducing a bank guarantee to make everyone in the team more secure was another big step forward. All top-level professional cycling teams are financed that way now.

The general increase in riders' salaries was good for them, but it was bad news for the professional criteriums. Riders no longer needed criteriums to top up their pay, and missing out on a taxing round of criteriums allowed them to focus on training and preparing for big races. Doing well in big races, which also means doing their job well as domestiques, increased their market value. And that reduced their reliance on criteriums even more.

As the importance of professional criteriums, especially the post-Tour de France ones, dwindled in continental Europe, so did their number. Nowadays the post-Tour criterium round focuses on northern Europe and takes place over the two weeks immediately following each year's Tour de France, not the four to six weeks it used to be.

There are post-Tour criteriums elsewhere, but the big budget races are in Belgium and Holland now. And because they are successful, well sponsored and well attended by the paying public, they pay the riders very well. When the Australian sprinter Robbie McEwen won the second of his three green jerseys in 2004, it was rumoured that he got a good six-figure sum for ten post-Tour criteriums. McEwen used to say that he didn't consider his Tour de France over until well into the second week of August. So it's still worthwhile for the top riders to extend their Tour and stay in Europe for another week, or maybe two, depending on what other objectives they have that year.

After the 2008 Tour de France, when he set a British record of winning four stages, Mark Cavendish was in great demand with the criterium organisers. He had the Beijing Olympics coming up, but he agreed to five races in five days following the Tour de France. After that he returned home for a short rest, then some specialised track training. I spent those five days following Cavendish, so I could write an article about the post-Tour criteriums for *Cycle Sport* magazine. These are the highlights of my little road trip.

It's Monday, 28 July, the day after the Tour de France, and I'm in Aalst, an East Flanders town halfway between Ghent and Brussels. This race is always held the day after the Tour de France. Aalst is a short hop from Paris, and it's not unusual for the Tour winner to ride this one. Indeed, the 2008 Tour winner Carlos Sastre not only raced in Aalst but won, which gives a little context to Barry Hoban's earlier remark in this chapter about there being more fixing in the post-Tour criteriums than there used to be. They are still good fun to watch.

Aalst is one of the oldest races on the criterium circuit and dates back to 1934. It's hugely popular, and a crowd of seventy thousand packed the town centre streets in 2008 to watch a good race over a very twisty but flat circuit. It's a real show too. First off, the star riders are presented to the crowd by being driven around the circuit in open-topped sports cars. In post-Tour criteriums, or nartourcriteriums as they are called in Flanders and the Netherlands, the riders often race in the jersey they won in the Tour de France, so in Aalst Sastre wore yellow and Oscar Freire wore his green jersey. And although Sastre outsprinted Mark Cavendish and Freire to win, which was fixed, the race was still exciting and fast. 'The crowd doesn't want to see a load of guys riding round talking, so you have to race,' Cavendish said afterwards. Most of the recent Tour de France stars showed themselves in a short solo or small group breakaway, while the Belgian national champion, Jürgen Roelandts, did quite a few laps on his own before the big sprint at the end.

The crowds certainly enjoyed it. The pro criterium at Aalst is a real spectacle, as it's run off at high speed under floodlights, which add atmosphere. But the other highlight at Aalst is the race for ex-pros on the same circuit before the main event. In 2008 it was won by Sean Kelly from the 1992 Liège–Bastogne–Liège winner, Dirk De Wolf, and Jan Janssen, who at the age of 67 looked as silky smooth as he did when he became the first Dutch winner of the Tour de France way back in 1968.

Next day I hopped across the border into the Netherlands, and to the village of Stiphout for its nartourcriterium, the Bavaria Profronde Stiphout (Bavaria is a beer brand). It was great. The Dutch really know how to party. If you ever get the chance to visit Alpe d'Huez when the Tour de France climbs it, get as close as you can to Dutch Corner. You can't miss it; it's noisy, surrounded by a distinctive beery aroma, and very orange. Dutch fans made the corner their own after several Dutch riders won stages on Alpe d'Huez in the years after the climb found a regular slot in the Tour in the Seventies. The fans get there days ahead of the race, many in camper vans, and have a three-day party. That, basically, is what Dutch criteriums are: parties.

The atmosphere at Stiphout in 2008 was electric. Thumping music, live and recorded, plenty to eat and drink, and a bike racing sideshow. There was a full programme of races, starting in the afternoon with juniors, then the women raced, then the under-23 men; and in the evening Tour de France riders took to the streets with a sprinkling of local heroes to fight out the pro race.

Andy Schleck won the 2008 Bavaria Profronde Stiphout from Carlos Sastre, after Schleck and Sastre had broken away from the rest. So that was two Tour contenders leaving the rest, and sorting the race out between them. It pleased the crowd no end, as did a rip-roaring bunch sprint behind, in which Mark Cavendish defeated Robbie McEwen. And they both looked like they enjoyed it.

Wednesday, 30 July, and it's back in Belgium, but only just. The next race was in Peer, about 50 kilometres south of Stiphout. It's the birthplace of the artist Pieter Brueghel, home to the Brueghel Foundation and to a very modern rumour. In 2009 Wikileaks claimed that American nuclear weapons were stored at the Kleine Brogel Air Base, just outside of town.

Anyway, Cavendish was the undisputed star at Peer. Gert Steegmans was second on the bill, but even in his

308 THE CALL OF THE ROAD

home country his one stage victory in the Tour, albeit on the Champs-Elysées, couldn't stack up against Cavendish's four. After the usual solo and small group attacks, which in these criteriums are often local riders showing their face to please their fans, a breakaway group formed that contained Cavendish, Steegmans, Philippe Gilbert, local Limburg champion Sébastien Rosseler and mountain bike pro Roel Paulissen. They stayed together until the finish, where Cavendish's sprint took him two seconds clear of Steegmans, with the rest close behind the big Belgian.

Afterwards Cavendish said that he was enjoying the races, and that he felt they were good training for the upcoming Olympic Madison. 'I'm doing 60-kilometre rides each day, as well as the race. There's a lot of sprinting out of corners in the criteriums, which is good training to keep my speed.'

On Thursday, 31 July we were in Herentals, Belgium, home of Fifties and Sixties cycling legend Rik Van Looy. Herentals is also near to Mol, where the then current, now just retired Belgian classics legend Tom Boonen is from. The programme consisted of a women's race, followed by the men, who did fifty laps of a 1.84-kilometre very fast circuit. It only had four 90-degree corners and three sweeping bends each lap. Very different to Aalst, where there were eleven sharp corners.

Britain's Jo Rowsell won the women's race, while local interest was focused on Katrien Van Looy, Rik's grand-daughter. Katrien was 18 and in her second year of racing. She won three races in 2007 and was in the thick of the action at Herentals before finishing 16th out of 41 riders in the elite women's race. She won a few more times in subsequent years but left the sport in 2012.

After each of the big names in the men's race was introduced to the enthusiastic crowd, with Cavendish and
Boonen getting the noisiest reception, the riders got under
way just after 7.30 p.m. The sun was setting behind tall
town buildings, with growing darkness making the fast-
moving bunch lit by banks of powerful floodlights really
stand out. For two and a half hours they raged around the
circuit, riders going off the front and getting reeled back
in, as the bunch expanded and contracted from a knot of
colour to a long snaking line, and back again.

It looked tough, and with the field made up of riders
who were really good at this kind of race, they really
ripped into each other. The bunch was pretty spread out
when Cavendish, Boonen and Philippe Gilbert prised
themselves clear towards the end. On the last lap
Cavendish lit his after-burners to launch another super-
fast sprint, more than enough to beat Tom Boonen to the
line.

Heerlen is in the hilly part of Holland, and on Friday,
1 August it hosted the last nartourcriterium Cavendish
did in 2008. The Profronde Heerlen had Cavendish,
Steegmans, Frank Schleck, Martijn Maaskant and Lars
Boom as its big names. Heerlen is very close to Luxembourg
so Schleck drew a crowd on his own. All the stars were
active in the race, with Schleck spending enough time
off the front to tie up the 5,000 euros sprints prize to
put with his contract fee.

Lars Boom made a serious lone effort close to the
finish, but was brought back by Servais Knaven, who
was trying to set up the sprint for his Quick Step team-
mate Gert Steegmans. The plan worked, but only up until
Cavendish shot past the Belgian to win his third criterium
in three days. And that was the end of my five-day trip

to the post-Tour criteriums, which although not as important as they used to be, are still a vibrant part of cycling in Europe.

It's a different story in the USA, Australia and the UK, where there are pro criteriums throughout each road race season. In the UK criteriums are a lot shorter than they are in mainland Europe. Time is often used to define the length of a race, so a professional criterium might be one hour plus one lap. Criterium circuits in the UK are usually around one to 1.5 kilometres in length.

During the Eighties televised city-centre criteriums became popular in the UK. The first big series of televised races was sponsored by Kellogg's, and it was created by Allan Rushton, a man who did a lot to raise the profile of road racing in Britain. It was Rushton who got Kellogg's to sponsor a stage race, the Kellogg's Tour, in which some of the biggest teams took part. He also promoted a single-day race in the UK called the Wincanton Classic as part of the UCI World Cup, the equivalent of the World Tour today. Unfortunately, and Rushton says this himself, he racked the races up from one-hour criteriums to long-distance races and stage races too quickly for the UK cycling market, which wasn't as big then and didn't have the support from business and local authorities it has today.

British professionals were very good at city-centre criteriums, and when Rushton brought over big European stars like Francesco Moser to the Kellogg's city-centre series, they didn't get their own way at all. The tradition of these fast, exciting races continues in the UK today through the Tour Series televised city-centre criteriums for elite men and women, which are a highlight in each cycling year.

That's a quick look at the worldwide phenomenon of criteriums. Now for Flanders and its very special kind of circuit races, the kermesses. Their roots are in religious celebrations held all over the Low Countries, but in Flanders those celebrations became a reason for carnivals, then for funfairs, and finally for bike races.

Kermesse, which you'll sometimes see spelled *kermis*, is a word made from two other words: *kerk*, meaning church, and *mis*, which is the Dutch word for the religious celebration of mass. So the original kermesses were masses to celebrate the anniversaries of building a church. The tradition started in the twelfth century, and almost every village and town in the Netherlands, Belgium and in the far north of France had an annual religious festival or kermesse.

However, Flemish people must have always liked a party, because by the fourteenth century many religious kermesse celebrations in Flanders were also marked by the holding of a carnival. Marten Van Cleve was a late fourteenth-century artist from Antwerp, and one of his most famous paintings is a 1541 Flemish carnival scene entitled *A Village Kermesse*. In more modern times kermesse carnivals became funfairs, and once road racing took hold in bike-mad Flanders, circuit races based on the town square, with a short loop into the local countryside each lap, were run alongside the funfair on kermesse day.

This is Barry Hoban again, talking about the professional kermesses he rode in the Sixties and Seventies:

I've got a theory about why kermesse circuits are the length they are, around about ten kilometres. Traditionally, when there was kermesse the local firms closed for the day, so most people got the day off. There was a fairground, there were stalls and loads of other attractions, and all the pubs were open and they were packed. I reckon that the length of a kermesse lap was made just long enough to allow someone to get a glass of beer and drink it just in time to watch the riders come round. Then they realised their glass was empty, so they went back inside the pub, ordered another beer, and they'd nearly drunk that one by the time the riders came round again. So they watched the riders pass, and then it's time for another beer, and so on. If it's fifteen laps they have fifteen beers. That's my take on it anyhow.

Hoban raced at a time when the professional kermesse calendar was big enough to support, if not a richly funded, then adequately funded, world of its own within professional cycling. Between May and September there was a pro kermesse somewhere in Flanders on almost every day of the week. There were kermesse teams that rarely raced outside Flanders, and riders winning twenty to thirty kermesses per year who were stars at home but hardly known to the rest of the cycling world.

Hoban lived in Ghent, the capital of Flanders, for most of his career, which he spent with top international teams riding the Grand Tours, classics and other races on the wider pro race circuit. He used pro kermesses as training, because they were hard and fast, a really good workout for a top international rider, but when Hoban rode them they were nearly impossible for an outsider to win. Hoban won eight stages of the Tour de France, but he only ever won one professional kermesse. He explains why:

It was difficult for me or anyone outside the pro kermesse world to win because, just like they had in the criteriums, they had regional mafias in kermesses. They were only Flemish and made up of guys who'd come up from the junior ranks together, and even though they rode for different teams they rode together. They also had bookmakers at kermesses, and the mafias worked with the bookmakers.

It was hilarious at times. I knew it was going to be very difficult to win a kermesse race, but I used to know the guys who were aiming to win a particular race. You knew the local guy was going to really try, and he'd always have guys in his mafia helping him. So a break would go up the road with the local guy in it, and his mates behind wouldn't work, which caused a gap. Then it was up to the local guy in the break to sort out payments to the other guys in it. The trick was to get in the break with the local guy, and I wasn't going to work to take anyone to the finish line if they weren't going to pay me.

That was what kermesse racing was about. It was near impossible to beat the mafias, because as well as working together the best kermesse racers were really good at what they did. Over 150 kilometres, on a typical kermesse circuit, the kermesse guys were very fast. So I claim it as a real big feather in my cap that I actually won a pro kermesse. I only ever won one, and I was really flying when I did it.

It was at Oostkamp, and I was away with five or six riders on the last lap, but nobody was talking about money. Maybe they thought they could beat me anyway and didn't need to pay, but they didn't beat me. I attacked and kept on attacking, eventually leaving them all for dead to finish on my own. I reckon that was probably the only kermesse race at that time where the winner didn't pay one penny to the guys behind.

Kermesse racing threw up its own legends in Flanders who were known as the Kings of Kermesse. The first was Fred Hamerlinck, from Assenede in East Flanders, who was so prolific that in 1929 he won five kermesses in one week. He was third in the Tour of Flanders that year too, and he was so good, so highly regarded, that eventually the Belgian cycling authorities talked him into riding the Tour de France in 1931, the second year it was restricted to national teams and individual entrants.

Hamerlinck won the first stage, and he won again a few days later in Bordeaux, but he didn't enjoy the race one bit. He didn't like racing in France, and he didn't like the heat of the south, so he abandoned the race on stage 12, Montpellier to Marseilles, along with seven others, and went home. He carried on winning kermesse races for a few years, and became so popular that he packed out the Ghent Sportspaleis when he raced on the track there. Along the way Hamerlinck won enough money to buy a café near Ghent, and he spent the rest of his life listening to his customers tell him how good he was.

Moving on through the years, it was more difficult for one rider to dominate when the mafias that Hoban talks about were at their strongest during the Fifties, Sixties and Seventies. But through that time Flemish cycling became progressively more outward-looking, as more and more Flemish riders were making their mark on the wider cycling world. The mafias became less of a force, and it was possible for talented riders who wanted to stay in the kermesse world to win lots of races.

In 1982 Jonny De Nul won twenty-three kermesse races. In 1995, by which time most kermesses were open and the number of pro-only races had dropped drastically,

Ludo Giesberts won a record fifty-eight kermesses, adding to a career total of over five hundred. His kermesse year record lasted until 1996, when Benny Van Itterbeek won sixty races.

Kermesse races are slightly shorter now than in Hoban's day, and average 120 kilometres. The laps still include the village or town's main street, with a little loop into the countryside. Laps are between five and ten kilometres long, and the roads are closed by a rolling method, where traffic can use junctions when the race isn't passing. Also, there is less cash for riders to win, with total pay-outs of 670 euros across the first thirty-five finishers, or in richer kermesses 800 euros going down to the fiftieth finisher. But there are cash primes too. So, kermesse races are not what they were, but are still very much alive. They are also a great place for young riders to learn skills and build strength and speed.

16

Aussie Roules

With its population of Europeans who emigrated for a
better life, the establishment and growth of bike racing
in Australia pretty much shadowed Europe. Track cycling
was very popular, especially at agricultural festivals and
city sports days, but there were road races too, mostly
run as handicaps to attract a good entry from racers of
all abilities. And Aussie cyclists were adventurous.

It wasn't long before the best of them were racing in
other countries, especially when they'd heard about the
chance of earning fame and fortune. During the first
decade of the twentieth century six-day track racing got
established in Australia, and after winning the 1912
Sydney and Melbourne six-days with Paddy Hehir, Alf
Goullet went to race in North America, where the six-
days were really big. Goullet eventually won fifteen

six-days there, including New York seven times, and he made a great deal of money. There were other Aussies on the American six-day circuit, including Alf Grenda and Reggie McNamara, and they all did very well.

By the Twenties and early Thirties, news of big races like the Tour de France had filtered through to Australia, and some ambitious racers wanted to have a go, in particular a New Zealander called Harry Watson and three Australians, Perry Osborne, Ernest Bainbridge and Hubert Opperman, forever known as Oppy in Australia.

Opperman's introduction to cycling was delivering telegrams by bike. He finished third in his first race, and by 23 he was the best road racer in Australia, with three national titles won by 1928. That's when the *Melbourne Morning Herald*, the *Sporting Globe* and the *Sun* in New Zealand started a fund to raise money and send Opperman, Watson, Osborne and Bainbridge to Europe so they could try to get into the Tour de France.

They had to prove themselves first, and Opperman did it in style by taking third place in Paris–Brussels behind Nicolas Frantz. They were invited to the 1928 Tour de France as the Ravat-Wonder-Dunlop team, but with four riders instead of the nine or ten some of the bigger teams had, the Australians were at a disadvantage on flat stages, which were run as a sort of team time trial with the teams separated on the road and each member timed from start to finish. Riders could go ahead of their team, and many did, but by sharing the pace the strong teams ensured their members posted the fastest times. Opperman's team wasn't strong, and he had to leave his team behind early on the team stages so he wouldn't lose time by staying with them. He eventually finished 18th overall, winning the admiration of many. At the end of the road race season readers of *L'Auto* voted Opperman Europe's most popular sportsman of the year.

He also won the Bol d'Or 24-hour track race in 1928, even after his bike was sabotaged by a rival and he had to stop for repairs. He got back on terms by riding seventeen hours straight before a call of nature forced him to stop to answer it. But Opperman's biggest cycling achievement came in 1931, when he won Paris–Brest–Paris.

He set his sights on winning the race after the 1928 Tour de France, and when he returned to Australia he started preparing for it. It was still another three years to the next edition of Paris–Brest–Paris, but Opperman realised that to win it he had to be in the saddle for two days and two nights solid. He had to train his body to cope with that but, even more important, he had to train his mind. So he decided to attack the Sydney to Melbourne road record in 1929.

Opperman set a new record of 39 hours and 42 minutes for the 560 miles, and recalling it thirty-four years later in an interview with *Sporting Cyclist* magazine, he said:

That event alone gave me the second night in the saddle without rest. And believe me, there's no other feeling in cycling like it. It's on that second night that you really learn what fluctuation of energy is. Sometimes you feel that you have really drained all your resources, but then as the hours pass, the energy returns. And it's on the second night that you find yourself becoming colder, when, in fact, it's not really colder.

That second night will always live in my memory as a horrible nightmare. In my semi-consciousness, I fancied that I was in a competition race, that the others had left me. And chase and pursue as I might, I would never

catch them. The lights of cars threw curious shadows on
the road and my blurred eyes made animals and humans
suddenly spring up in front of me, causing some seconds
of horrible suspense until they would dispel just at the
moment a collision seemed inevitable.

Opperman got so low at one point that he pleaded with
his manager, 'Let me have a rest. A lie-down. Just for
ten minutes. Just for a little time, please.' But his manager
just told him to keep going. He sympathised, but later
told Opperman that if he'd stopped he might never have
got going again, and if he kept going then his strength
would return.

'And how right he was,' Opperman said. 'To stop when
in the throes of a flat period is fatal. So on I had to go,
a balloon head floating in the clouds, legs as long as
chimney stacks and pushing pedals in a weary circle. But
hammering into my brain there was one comfort and
inspiration: this is for Paris–Brest, for Paris–Brest, for
Paris–Brest.'

Opperman returned to Europe in 1931 and finished
12th overall in the Tour de France. But instead of cashing
in on his result and taking contracts for criteriums and
track meetings, the Australian continued his training for
Paris–Brest–Paris. One of his sessions was actually riding
the full route, so when he lined up for the start of the
race he was the most confident rider in the field, despite
having no team support.

The race started at the Pont Noir, near St Cloud on
the outskirts of Paris. The crowd was massive, and thousands lined the streets out of Paris, despite the falling
rain. The riders weren't daunted by that, and when
Maurice Garin fired the starter's pistol they set off so fast

that you'd have thought the race was 100 kilometres long, not 1,120 kilometres.

The early miles were a selection, so that when they left the string of towns west of Paris, twenty-eight top riders were clear, and they settled down for the long haul to Brest. This is how Opperman described going through the first night.

The sombre clouds brought darkness at an early hour, and soon the following cars were playing their powerful lights on the shiny surface of the macadam road. The road twisted and dipped, and despite the efforts of the drivers the field would constantly plunge into inky blackness, causing frantic braking and shouting until the blessed illumination lit up the highway to reveal a confusion of riders who could not see. And when we bunched up again, a hurried head-count would ensue just in case someone had taken a long, bold chance and flown away into the night.

Very few spoke, each content to pedal along with his own thoughts, pleasant or unpleasant. Like animals who shelter from the elements we instinctively rode closer to the hedges to gain shelter from the howling wind, which at times almost brought us to a full stop. We passed through villages, bumping over cobblestones, and villagers, lanterns in hand, would rush to their doors and shout 'Bon courage.' Then, we were out into the black night again.

The Bordeaux–Paris winner Bernard Van Rysselberghe gave us a temporary scare on the first night. Springing away like a stag, he had a three-minute lead in a few kilometres. The news of the break caused a rapid pace to be set up by the Alcyon team, and after half an hour the fugitive was seen in the distance, leisurely eating and waiting for the field.

Their blood warmed by the exertion, several others made an effort to become the hare, but soon the excess steam was blown off, and everyone settled down again to the regular crank turning, broken only by calcium-lit controls where a signature had to be left and a food bag procured.

It was at the first control that I heard that Marcel Mazeyrat had abandoned. 'Punctured three times and could not make up against the wind,' someone said. Poor Mazeyrat, I mused. How hard it must have been back there on his own, fighting against the gale. Then I gasped, for I could not believe my ears, Benoît Faure announced that Jef Demuysere had quit. Never. Demuysere was a favourite. I was more afraid of him than any other rider. But I checked again and again, and Jef was not to be seen.

After dawn, the approach to Brest heralded a revival in the flagging spirits of the bunch. Fifty kilometres from the port Nicolas Frantz, the hope of Luxembourg, made his first appearance and rocketed up to high speed. We all buzzed into activity, and soon he had company. From this point to Brest, despite the retarding wind, which came with cyclonic force from the sea, the riders were nervous, jumping like cats.

We arrived at the Brest control so fast that onlookers must have thought it was a one-way race. There was a two-minute neutralisation during which arms flapped like Dutch windmills. What a relief to be going in the opposite direction. The sea was now behind us, and thankfully so was the gale. Frantz made the first breakaway. His face flushed a healthy red, eyes gleaming with satisfaction, he soon had us strung out in a kilometre-long line. But he was only testing. Then the wind dropped, the rain clouds broke up and for the first time in thirty-four hours we could doff our waterproofs.

With the exception of a noticeable shortness of temper, I observed that at least a dozen appeared to be still enjoying the race. Evidently, it would be left to the second night to cull the weak from the strong. Marcel Bidot, alone of the favourites, gave the impression of being fatigued at this point, but he would be dangerous before the end.

Midnight again and bitterly cold. With the others I donned leg warmers, cape and cap, and I looked about me. Eyelids were getting heavy, just as mine were. Frantz, so fresh a few hours ago, was staring fixedly ahead, his bicycle rolling from the right to the left. 'Nick, Nick, wake up,' I yelled. He could only mumble, 'Sleepy, Oppy. I want to sleep.' Then he crashed into the grass and fell heavily.

Maurice De Waele followed suit, crashing a few kilometres further on. I nearly succumbed to sleep several times, but fought it by whistling and shouting and waking others, striving to find something to occupy my mind. Four hours later it was dawn again, and the sleep fell away from my resisting body. The dreaded second night had passed. Paris was 200 kilometres away.

For the first time in the history of the race fifteen men were together so close to the finish, and each one realised that his best chance of victory was to slip away unattended. Just before the control at Rennes, Frans Bonduel started speaking to me but I could not understand him, so he gestured to a man in his support car who knew English. He told me that Bonduel was going to pull out of the race. He had had enough. But before he did he wanted me to know that the Alcyon and J. B. Louvet teams intended to amalgamate against me.

Goodness, what hope would I have now? After 1,000 kilometres I was not quite in the mood to appreciate that. There was but one way to combat it, to attack before those teams had a chance to do anything. I ground to the front, pushed my heart down between my teeth and swung into a steady pace, causing the others to forget attacking for a while.

But immediately I slackened, Frantz, now recovered from his bad night, would be off. When he was caught, De Waele, also recovered, tore up from the rear and commenced another red-hot scrap which lasted until the last control, 100 kilometres from Paris. There we tore off our leg warmers and extra clothing, and prepared ourselves to fight to the bitter end. Only one rider by this time appeared to have any life and vigour and that was the big Marcel Bidot, who had thrown off the weight of tiredness and was riding easily and freely.

Always a support rider for De Waele and Frantz, Marcel was one who seldom endeavoured to break away. But when I saw the Alcyon manager speak to him I moved up to be on his wheel. It was too late. He'd gone and 100 metres lay between the bunch and Bidot. It was maddening, but what could I do? With three teams on my wheel, it would be lunacy to pursue, yet if I did not Bidot must surely win. Then I saw the only clear course I could take. It was to chase, and chase until I dropped. At least I would go down with the knowledge that I had done my best. I took off after him, and when I caught up with Bidot he was at the roadside changing a tyre.

This was my chance. I attacked again. No good, Frantz was there. So I waited, then went again, and this time I was off on my own. What a feeling. Soon I had three minutes on them but they were in hot pursuit; seven riders working together to catch me. Twenty-four kilometres to go and they were one minute behind me. Twenty kilometres to go and my manager, Bruce Small, drove up beside me and shouted in my ear: 'Ride like the devil, Oppy, or you've lost. There are four riders only now, 28 seconds behind you.' My breath sobbed in my throat. Was I to have the race taken away?

The kilometres raced by, then I heard the noise of klaxons behind, which could mean but one thing: the approach of the riders. It was over. I was captured, five kilometres from the finish. How can I describe the bitterness of that moment? I raged at the thought, and attacked as soon as they caught me, but the four clung to me like horrible leeches. But there was still hope, there was still the sprint on the track at the end, and I made up my mind to make my effort just before the last banking.

Into the big cement bowl we sped, with Emile Decroix leading, Léon Louyet riding close behind. But Decroix was tired and could do nothing; instead, Giuseppe Pancera made his bid. I followed Pancera, and soon we were at the point where I would make my effort. Jumping to the front in one effort, we rounded the bend and into the straight. I could hear the others' wheels all about me. Surely I must be beaten. But no, the line shot past and it was my wheel which reached it first. I had won.

There was little time to bask in the glory of having achieved what he'd set out to do three years earlier. It was time to cash in and make some money from criterium contracts. The next day Opperman rode a 100-kilometre one in Antwerp, then another next day in Brussels, then it was back to Paris, then up to Amsterdam. Everybody in Europe wanted to see Hubert Opperman.

So that was how the pioneer of Australian road racers made a name for himself in Europe, but what was early road racing like in Australia? Let's look at a big one, the Centenary 1000 in 1934. It was called Centenary because it celebrated the hundredth birthday of the foundation of the southernmost state of the Australian mainland, Victoria, and a thousand was the number of miles the cyclists did in six stages. It was actually 1,100 miles long, but a thousand looks and sounds better. It was a big race with good prize money, but typical of Australian road races of its time in the way it was run, and in the type of terrain it covered.

Centenary 1000 was a one-off title, but the race was a predecessor of today's Sun Tour, an international ride in its own right. However, the roads and stage distances were not like any found in races today. The average for each stage was about 160 miles, which is long enough, but the roads were 90 per cent corrugated dusty tracks.

One hundred and eleven riders started; all the best Australian road racers, including Hubert Opperman, and a father and son pair Clinton and Jack Beasley, 18 and 45 respectively and the youngest and the oldest riders in the race. News also spread to Europe, where a few riders had competed on Australian tracks. Nino Borsari, Paul Chocque and Fernand Mithouard entered the Centenary 1000, and they were real quality. Borsari was part of the Italian gold medal-winning team pursuit squad at the 1932 Olympic Games, and the two Frenchmen were Tour de France riders, and they both went on to win Bordeaux–Paris, Mithouard in 1933 and Choque in 1936.

The race, like so many in Australia, was a group handicap in which riders started in different groups according to their ability and past performances. The expected slowest riders started first, and the quickest were in the last group to start. First past the post at the end would win. Handicap racing encouraged more riders to try their luck, as even the slow ones had a chance of winning because of the start they were given, but there was also a race within the Centenary 1000. The best riders, the ones who started in the elite last group, contested a separate classification called 'The Championship' which had its own prize list. This was done to encourage top riders to enter.

The press got behind the Centenary 1000, and it completely captured the imaginations of a big sporting public in Victoria. It also produced a new Australian sports hero in the man who won the handicap race, Ted Stubenrauch from Bairnsdale, on the east coast of Victoria.

Stubenrauch left home at the age of nine and worked at all sorts of jobs in the Australian bush. Later in life, after his cycling career and distinguished service in the Australian Air Force, he recalled sleeping outdoors under the Southern Cross, and wondering where his next meal was coming from. He became interested in bike racing, but couldn't afford the expensive equipment that proper racers used. Undeterred, he got an old bike together and started racing, with some success.

After a while he heard about the Centenary 1000 and its near £2,000 prize purse, and started training for the race. Ted told his mates about it, about the possibility of winning life-changing money, and in best bush tradition they had a raffle at the pub, raising five pounds fifty pence, enough for Stubenrauch to travel to Melbourne to buy some bits for his bike and make it good enough to compete. He kept the rest of the money for food to fuel the 1,100 miles of effort he was taking on.

So Ted Stubenrauch the bushman cyclist lined up with some of the best road racers in the world for the big 1,100-mile race around Victoria, but because they'd never heard of him the organisers put him in what was called the limit group (an Australian term for the first group to set off in a handicap road race). There were four groups, and Stubenrauch's got the biggest start in the handicap race, and he made the most of it.

The first stage used the Melbourne–Warrnambool route, which became a classic Australian race that's still going strong today. It's 165 miles long, but in 1934 those 165 miles were on hard-packed stone, dirt and dust roads. 'I had three bob [15 pence] when I turned up at the start, and that was every penny I owned in the world. Later, I had to borrow ten bob [50 pence] from Clyde Palmer, the famous sports reporter, and that got me round the rest of the route,' Stubenrauch recalled in an interview many years later.

There were eight of us left in the leading bunch 16 miles from the finish of the first stage, at which point the other seven started arguing about sharing the prize money between them. Nobody spoke to me, because most of them had never seen me before, but old Jack Beasley knew me, and he said, 'What about Stubey?' at which they all yelled, 'To hell with Stubey.' Well, that made me more determined than ever. I knew I had the form, as I'd been winning most of the town sprints on the stage, and for months before the race I had been doing daily training rides of 120 miles before breakfast. Anyway, the finish was on the Warrnambool horse-racing track. I stayed at the rear all the way round the track, and as soon as I saw them get up off the saddle to start sprinting

I went past them all on the outside, and with very little effort I won the stage.

Stubenrauch crashed badly on stage four to Wangaratta. He struggled through to the finish but his shoulder was damaged, and fearful of reporting to the race doctor in case he was told to quit, Stubenrauch visited a private doctor in Wangaratta. The doctor strapped Stubenrauch's arm, from shoulder to elbow, to his side, and then advised him to quit the race, but his advice wasn't official. To appease the doctor, Ted said he would think about it. He carried on.

The next stage went over three high passes in the Victorian Alps. Stubenrauch missed his start time, but set off anyway, in the dark because of how far they had to ride. 'The hardest part was trying to see, the others had the help of headlights on the following cars. Anyway, I ploughed through the deep gravel of the track that led to the mountains, and hoped for the best. After a few miles I saw the convoy's tail lights ahead. I was saved,' he recalled.

He wasn't saved from the terrible weather, though. A blizzard met the riders on the slopes of the Ovens Valley, then at Porepunkah they started the 18.5 miles uphill to the summit of Mount Buffalo. The blizzard became so fierce that about half of the riders pulled out on this section. It took an even greater toll of the following convoy. All the motor vehicles had to give up, either bogged down in mud in the valley or stuck in snow on the steep climb. But Stubenrauch ploughed on. One by one he caught and passed the field. As it was still dark he couldn't tell how many riders were ahead of him, but halfway to the summit he found out.

'You've only got one other ahead of you,' Jack Beasley called out as Stubenrauch passed the veteran. 'That brought some warmth into my chilled legs,' Ted remembered. Daylight broke as he walked through the deep snow and slush of the last few yards to the mountain summit chalet, where the riders were scheduled to have a meal before continuing on to the other climbs. They ended up staying there; up ahead the road over the next climb, Mount Hotham, was completely blocked.

So the riders slept in the chalet, wearing whatever they could borrow from the owners and other guests: skiing kit, pyjamas, even women's clothes, cardigans and blouses, and some of the catering staff's uniforms. One rider borrowed a complete evening suit. Then, just when everybody was settling down for the night, the phone rang. It was the race organisers. They said they would have to drive around the mountains, and would meet the race after the riders had got themselves off Mount Hotham. They also told them that the next stage was extended to 216 miles, including two more high passes, because they had to be back in Melbourne on schedule. And with that they left them to sort the race out as best they could.

It was dark again when the survivors set off from Mount Buffalo, and they slithered and fell on the dangerous descent in the dark to the township of Bright. The creek crossings were flooded, and one of them nearly did for Jack Beasley. He'd dropped the field on the descent, then plunged through a creek crossing that was much deeper than he thought. So deep that he sank out of sight, and once underwater he couldn't detach his feet from the pedals because they were strapped on so tightly. Luckily another rider who was just catching him saw the splash, and dived in to save Beasley.

From Bright there was the long climb to Harrietville, then over the Little Blow Hard Pass, the highest point on the route at nearly 1,800 metres. Horse-drawn snow-ploughs had cleared the track of some of the snow, but there was still a deep covering. Ted Stubenrauch and forty other riders struggled through it, and fourteen and a half hours after he started that morning, Stubenrauch rode alone into Sale to increase his lead on the handicap general classifications.

The final day to Melbourne wasn't as eventful as the previous two. Stubenrauch was still given a rough ride by some of the professionals in the race, but he kept the lead. Winning the Centenary 1000 brought him the fortune he had been chasing. For his efforts he collected over £1,000, worth many times more than that today.

It was Ted Stubenrauch's first and last big victory. He continued racing for another four years, but only added another £700 to his savings. Then in 1938 he stopped cycling to join the Royal Australian Air Force as a regular, before becoming an air gunner. During the Second World War he was trapped in Java by the Japanese, but got back to Australia by stealing a Japanese warship and sailing it there. Stubenrauch stayed in the Air Force after the war, becoming a squadron leader before he retired.

The Centenary 1000 made Stubenrauch, and the Aussie public loved the race, turning out in their thousands to cheer the riders on, but the star professionals in the field didn't like it one bit. Chocque, Mithouard and Opperman failed to finish. Chocque ended up in hospital in Ballarat after a bad fall, which Mithouard told reporters was caused by 'a leading Australian rider', but quickly adding, 'And it wasn't Opperman.'

The road conditions eventually did for Mithouard. The

rock-strewn passes in the Victoria Alps ripped up five of his tyres before a buckled wheel collapsed, got tangled in his frame, and the resulting fall injured him and damaged his bike irreparably. 'Not even in the Tour de France do they put riders through such a test,' he said after a hospital check-up.

Hubert Opperman got over the mountains then crashed on a flat stage, hurting his knee and cutting his arm badly. Several stitches were inserted in his wounds, and Opperman carried on against doctor's orders, but two stages later the pain became too much and he had to quit 20 miles from the finish. He didn't want to, but he couldn't physically continue, and had to be lifted off his bike and carried to a car. It was the first time Opperman had ever quit a big race.

As you might have guessed from the graphic way he describes his 1931 Paris–Brest–Paris victory (which is why I included such a long transcript), Opperman had a fine command of language, and used it well in later life. The Second World War ended his cycling career, and after it was over he joined Australia's Liberal Party. In 1949 Opperman was elected as the MP for the Geelong district. He was called to government in 1960, and between 1963 and 1966 he was Australia's minister of immigration. Opperman was given an OBE in 1953, and knighted in 1968 after service as Malta's High Commissioner. Sir Hubert Opperman died in 1996, by which time Australian road racers were no longer pioneers but established as part of world cycling.

However, there was still quite gap between Opperman's last participation in the Tour de France and the next Australian to ride it. He was John Beasley, son of the 'old' Jack Beasley referred to in Ted Stubenrauch's account of his experiences of the Centenary 1000, and brother of Clinton, who also rode that race. Beasley was invited to ride the 1952 Tour de France as part of the Luxembourg International team, but he suffered mechanical problems on stage two and finished outside of the time limit. Beasley was a member of the Luxembourg team again in 1955, when he was joined by another Australian, Russell Mockridge, who was better known as a track sprinter, having won gold medals in the 1,000-metre time trial and the tandem sprint at the 1952 Olympic Games. Surprisingly, it was Beasley who withdrew early, and Mockridge who made it through the Tour, finishing 60th overall.

The next Aussie in the Tour was Bill Lawrie, a track and road racer who was primarily in Europe to ride six-day races. He started the 1967 Tour as part of the Great Britain team but went out on stage seven. Australian track racers had been part of the European six-day scene for a long time, and a few – Alf Strom, Reg Arnold and Graeme Gilmore are examples – lived full-time in Europe, riding road races in summer and track in the winter. The next wave of Aussie road racers to make their names in Europe started doing so at the end of the Seventies. In their vanguard were Phil Anderson and Allan Peiper.

Peiper ran away from home in 1977 at the age of 16, no longer wanting to be part of a family shattered by his alcoholic father. He headed for Belgium, where he raced as a junior, living in rented squalor to start with, but then he was taken under the wing of the Planckaert family, a Flemish cycling dynasty.

Peiper fell ill and returned to Australia, but now he'd sampled racing in Europe, and life there, and knew it was where he wanted to be. In the meantime Phil Anderson, super-strong and a natural-born athlete, won the 1978 Commonwealth Games road race title in Canada. The following year Anderson joined the ACBB cycling club in Paris, which was sponsored by Cycles Peugeot. He had a terrific time, and joined the Peugeot professional team along with Britain's Robert Millar in 1980. They led the way for more English speakers to race for ACBB and some of them become professionals for Peugeot. Stephen Roche did so in 1981, Sean Yates in 1982, and then in 1983 the move was made by Allan Peiper, who had rebuilt his body in Australia.

Anderson became the first Australian ever to wear the Tour de France yellow jersey, in 1981. He wore it again in 1982, this time winning two stages, another first for Australia, keeping the jersey for nine days, and ending the race with the white jersey of the best young rider. He also finished fifth overall in 1982, a feat he repeated in 1985. They were the highest overall finishes by any Australian until Cadel Evans's fourth place in 2006. But more of Evans later.

The following year Anderson scored another Australian first when he won a classic, the Amstel Gold Race in the hilly southeast corner of Holland. 'I was so proud to play a part when Phil Anderson won the Amstel Gold Race in 1983,' Allan Peiper wrote in his autobiography *A Peiper's Tale*. 'It was really emotional seeing Phil on the podium. We trained together in Belgium, riding 53 x 15 all the time in five-hour sessions, uphill and down with Phil ripping my legs off. He was awesome, as strong as an ox.'

Anderson returned to Australia in 1994, after a long and distinguished road race career, the best by any Australian road racer for years. Now other Australians have won big races: Stuart O'Grady was the first Aussie monument winner with the 2007 Paris–Roubaix; Simon

Gerrans has won two monuments, Milan–San Remo in 2102 and Liège–Bastogne–Liège in 2014; and Matt Hayman won Paris–Roubaix in 2016. And there have been, and there still are, some very good Australian women competing in top-level road races: the likes of Sarah Carrigan, Anna Wilson, Kathy Watt and Oenone Wood.

But none of the men really eclipsed Anderson for all-round performance until Cadel Evans switched from mountain bike road racing in 2001, when he was 24. Evans finished eighth overall in his first Tour de France in 2005, and then was fourth in 2006 and second in 2007 and 2008. He won the 2009 world road race title, then after a lacklustre Tour de France in 2010 he won the race in 2011. It was Australia's first Tour de France win, and first Grand Tour win.

Evans is still his country's only Grand Tour winner, but Richie Porte from Tasmania looks capable of winning one, especially since leaving Team Sky to head up BMC Racing Team's stage race squad. Porte was extremely good in the 2017 Tour de France, a possible threat to Britain's Chris Froome, before crashing out on stage nine. He'll be back soon, and there are plenty of good young Aussies to keep their flag flying high.

Australia also has a UCI World Tour race, the Tour Down Under. Based in the Adelaide area of South Australia, it began in 1999, with Stuart O'Grady the first winner. It gained World Tour status in 2008, and its January date means it opens the men's World Tour each year. A women's criterium series has run alongside the race since 2007.

17

American Flyers

American Flyers is a film released in 1985, when the USA was emerging as a major force in world road racing. It tells the story of two brothers, Marcus and David Sommers, who take part in a race called The Hell of the West. The back story is that the brothers' family have a history of cerebral aneurisms, their father having died as a result of one.

Their mother suspects her youngest, David, may be prone to having an aneurism, so Marcus, played by Kevin Costner, convinces him to go for tests. Later David over-hears Marcus in a private conversation telling somebody he doesn't want to worry David about something. So David assumes that Marcus has been tested and it has been discovered he could suffer an aneurism.

Anyway, they take part in the race like you do, Marcus

does suffer an aneurism and David wants to quit, having already lost time through a crash. Marcus convinces him to carry on, and on the final stage David attacks early, which his rivals put down to youthful exuberance, but he carries on to win. Again, like you do. Or rather like they do in Hollywood.

Some race footage was included in the film, taken during the 1984 Coors Classic on the Morgul-Bismark circuit in Boulder, Colorado, as well as on the Tour of the Moon stage that runs through a park called the Colorado National Memorial.

The film is a bit schmaltzy, but just the fact that Hollywood was using road racing as a backdrop for a plot showed that awareness of the sport had grown in a country where it had been a very minor minority sport. The film is also worth seeing because of this: the starter who drops the flag on stage one is none other than Eddy Merckx. Blink and you'll miss him, but it is Eddy Merckx.

Road racing started in the United States the same way it did in Australia, through the efforts of expat Europeans who wanted to enjoy the sport they'd done in the old country. And what a terrific canvas they had to paint on. The wild American countryside has been a stunning setting for some terrific races.

Road cycling was a popular leisure activity at the end of the nineteenth century, and at the start of the twentieth, but America quickly fell in love with the motorcar, and except for errand boys and kids riding in the suburbs, cars replaced bikes on US roads. But even when cycling was popular, the only racing that really caught on was track racing, and in particular six-day racing.

Then, after the Second World War, road racing gained a foothold, particularly in California where a lot of expat

Italians lived. By the Sixties about 300 riders had organised themselves into eighteen clubs in and around San Francisco, with a similar number in the southern half of the state. Road races were mostly criteriums then, and few Americans competed in Europe except in Italy, and sometimes Belgium, where descendants of immigrants still had family connections.

Then, almost out of the blue, in 1969 Audrey McElmury won the women's world road race championship title in Brno, in what was then Czechoslovakia. Born in Massachusetts, McElmury grew up in La Jolla, California, where she took up cycling after a skateboard accident. As a self-supported athlete she had finished fifth in the world road race championships in Rome in 1968. That proved she had a realistic shot at winning in Brno, but the American cycling federation refused to fund a women's team on the grounds that they had only a few women members. So McElmury paid for a team of three to go to Brno, at a cost of 10,000 dollars. She won brilliantly, and was an inspiration to others.

In 1976 George Mount finished sixth in the Montreal Olympic Games road race. Mount later turned professional, following in the footsteps of Jonathan Boycr, who in 1973 went to live in Paris to race for the amateur club ACBB. Boyer turned pro in 1977, and in 1981 he became the first American to ride the Tour de France. He completed the race a further four times, with a best placing of 12th overall in 1983. Boyer was fifth in the 1980 world road race championships, and he won a stage in the Tour of Switzerland in 1984. But by then Greg LeMond had taken the presence of America in European cycling to another level, and given a massive boost to road racing in his own country.

LeMond was born in Lakewood, California, on 26 June 1961. He didn't live in California for long, because when he was nine he and his family moved to the Washoe Valley in Nevada. That's where he entered his teen years, on the eastern slopes of the Sierra Nevada Mountains, an outdoor sports paradise.

LeMond's first sport was skiing, and his hero was Wayne Wong, a pioneer freestyle skier and inductee of the Canadian Ski Hall of Fame and the US Ski and Snowboard Hall of Fame. Wong led a training camp LeMond attended in 1975, where he told the young American that he should ride a bike as much as possible during the ski off-season, because it was what Wong and a lot of top skiers did to keep fit during the summer.

So as soon as the roads were free of snow, LeMond rode his bike at every opportunity. He rode to and from Earl Wooster High School in Reno, a round trip of 36 miles, as often as he could. And if time allowed he would return home by a long detour over Mount Rose, then alongside Lake Tahoe to Carson City where he was left with another tough climb to get back to the Washoe Valley.

Soon it wasn't just cycling to get fit for skiing; LeMond had found something in cycling. 'I was sold on it as a way to exercise, and soon found it had many benefits for me beyond the physical. I think I suffered from Attention Deficit Syndrome, although it didn't have a name back then, and my triumph over the symptoms was founded atop two thin tyres over many dusty miles. Even an hour of exercise cleared my head and sharpened my focus. I was transformed,' he says now.

Then LeMond saw his first road race and it was an epiphany. It was glorious, fast, noisy, raw and colourful. He started training harder, and started hanging out at

Rick's Bike Shop in Reno, where the staff encouraged LeMond to have a go at a local training race. He did, showing up on a heavy bike and wearing sneakers, while the rest were on genuine lightweight race bikes and dressed in proper cycling kit. LeMond finished second, and Rick the shop owner talked Greg's father, Bob, into buying his son a proper race bike, a red Cinelli.

Greg LeMond started racing in official events in 1976, and won the first eleven races he entered. He was so good he was given permission to race with the next age group up, the 16- and 17-year-olds, despite still being 15. He was a natural, a born champion, and he was encouraged by his father, who on seeing the enjoyment his son discovered in cycling, bought a bike himself.

Bob LeMond was in his mid-thirties, and his idea at first was to ride with his son and maybe lose a bit of weight. But then he started training, and then he started racing. At 38, and with only three years' riding behind him, Bob LeMond finished fifth in the Red Zinger Classic. And the Red Zinger was a big deal. It was a stage race born in 1975, promoted and sponsored by a Boulder-based herbal tea company called Celestial Seasonings, who named the race after one of their tea brands. It grew and grew over the years, eventually becoming a big international stage race called the Coors Classic.

In 1977 Greg LeMond won the American junior road race championships. He crashed three times in that race in Seattle, but each time he got up and caught the rest, eventually leaving them to win alone. He was unstoppable. In fact the only thing that could stop Greg LeMond then were the rules. He won two out of three American selection races for the junior world cycling championships, but he couldn't be picked because he was a year too young.

LeMond's first world championships were in Washington in 1978, where he took a bronze medal in the team time trial. Then he made his first trip to Europe. The father of one of his cycling friends, Kent Gordis, had a house in Switzerland. Using that as a base, and with Gordis's mum driving, they did a whirlwind tour of Europe. LeMond won races in Switzerland, France, Belgium and Italy. And in Belgium, where they really know their cycling, some were saying they'd seen the next big thing in the sport.

That European trip was when the desire to be a pro really took hold. In Switzerland LeMond met the French Olympic downhill skiing gold medallist Jean-Claude Killy, who is an avid cyclist. Killy had a chalet on the Col de Joux-Plane and invited LeMond and a few others to ride out to his place, where they could watch the Tour de France tackle the Joux-Plane climb. When LeMond saw the Tour he was certain it was where he should be. 'I didn't believe it was a dream, either. I was winning most of my races, and I'd beaten the European juniors, riders who were serious and who knew they would become pros. For me it was a reality. I could do it,' he says.

Just to be clear about his ambition, LeMond wrote down exactly what he wanted to achieve:

It was on a yellow legal pad, I wrote a list with four things on it. The four things I wanted to win as a cyclist, and I also wrote down when I wanted to achieve them by. They were winning the junior world road race title in 1979, bringing home the Olympic gold medal in 1980, win the professional world road race title by the age of 23, and the Tour de France by the time I was 25.

In 1979 Greg LeMond ticked the first target on his list when he became first American male to win a world road race title. He also won a silver medal in the track pursuit and a bronze in the team time trial. It put him on the world cycling map, and invitations to race in Europe were rolling in.

He couldn't tick the next target because the USA boycotted the 1980 Moscow Olympic Games, but he augmented his reputation in Europe during a racing trip there in April that year. LeMond won a stage and finished third in the Circuit des Ardennes in Belgium; then in France he won the Circuit de la Sarthe. Both were big results, especially the second one. Cycling was still split into amateurs and professionals, but the Circuit de la Sarthe was an open race, meaning top amateurs could face professionals who'd ridden the Tour de France. The other teams in that race were national amateur squads, including the fearsome Eastern bloc teams. Greg LeMond beat them all.

Cyrille Guimard was a recently retired pro racer who managed the Renault-Elf pro team in the early Eighties. He'd been a good rider who could have won more but for chronic knee problems that eventually forced his early retirement from the sport. He was a master tactician and great motivator. Bernard Hinault had already won the Tour de France twice under Guimard's guidance, and Guimard was very impressed when he heard about Greg LeMond, and by what he saw:

> LeMond's next race was the Ruban-Granitier Breton, so I went to see him. He got in the winning break with five Russians and a Belgian, and they had a good lead, so he only had to stay with them in the breakaway to win overall. Unfortunately he punctured and his team car was

nowhere to be seen. I think he got a wheel from another team. He started to chase but when his team car caught him he stopped riding. He threw his bike at the car and asked them where the hell had they been. He told them he'd lost the race because of them. He was talented, but more than that I liked his attitude. He cared, he really wanted to win; it mattered. I liked that, so I made up my mind I would have him in my team.

Guimard offered LeMond a pro contract with Renault-Elf right there at the Ruban-Granitier Breton, and they signed an agreement in principle. Then during the following winter, as Guimard recalls, he and Bernard Hinault travelled to Nevada to meet LeMond and his family, and to talk money.

Greg had another offer from Peugeot, and it was for more money, although I knew he would rather ride for me and ride with Hinault. But I didn't want to just leave things to phone calls. I always invested in my riders and I wanted to meet Greg's family. I knew I could afford to offer him a little more, which was good because I remember Greg telling me he could earn more money collecting golf balls at his local golf club than I originally offered him.

So Greg LeMond joined the professional ranks in 1981, and in 1982 he won the prestigious Tour de l'Avenir. Then the following year he won his first world road race title. He was 22, and another objective on his list was ticked. There was one more left.

LeMond made his Tour de France debut in 1984, finishing third overall and taking the best young rider award. In 1985 he supported team-mate Hinault to his fifth and final Tour de France win, and the following year, as we will see later, LeMond became the first American to win the Tour de France. He's the only American now, after Lance Armstrong was stripped of his wins, but more of Armstrong too a little later in the book. Nineteen eighty-six was the first of three victories for LeMond, but the relationship between him and Hinault went sour that year, as became very apparent during the 1986 Coors Classic.

The seed of the Coors Classic was planted in 1979 when the public relations officer for the Red Zinger Classic, Michael Aisner, bought the rights to the race from one of Celestial Seasoning's owners, Mo Siegal. Then with Siegal's agreement Aisner took the idea of creating a much bigger race to Peter Coors of Coors Beer. Siegal and Coors were friends. In 1984 Coors talked about the takeover to *Winning* magazine:

> Mo Siegal came to me and told me that the race was growing faster than his company was growing, and he wanted somebody to take over as a sponsor, but although he didn't want to hold the race back, he still wanted a local company to take it over so the Classic could be perpetuated. I didn't have to think long before agreeing to be involved, because the opportunity it brought to our company was unique.

Coors hadn't been involved in cycling before, but interest in the sport was growing in America, fuelled first by Jonathan Boyer's success in Europe, then by Greg LeMond's, and at the same time other Americans becoming part of the European pro peloton. That growth received a huge boost in 1984, when American riders dominated the cycling events at the Los Angeles Olympic Games. And at the same time the wider cycling world got its first good look at the Coors Classic, because it was the race most national teams used to hone form before the Olympics.

There was a men's and a women's Coors Classic. The American women were beaten by two of the best in the world, Maria Canins and Jeannie Longo, while the American men's team, who had been racing together in Europe all year, dominated their race. They filled the first three places overall, with Doug Shapiro the winner from Andy Hampsten and Jeff Pierce. Fabio Parra of Colombia, who went on to be a contender in the Tour de France, was fourth. It was a quality field, the racing was exciting, and the roads were stunning; all things that helped with the next step for the race.

In 1985 the Coors Classic went pro, with some of the best teams from Europe entering, including La Vie Claire, with Bernard Hinault and Greg LeMond in its squad. The race started outside Colorado for the first time with a prologue time trial up Telegraph Hill in San Francisco, and the stages were a mix of tough ones through magnificent mountains, and fast city-centre or park criterium races. The formula went down well with the American public, and with the American-based riders, but some of the Europeans didn't like it.

The race format was chosen by race promoter Aisner, who knew Americans liked a spectacular show, which the speed and spectator involvement of criterium racing provides. He also knew that only die-hard cycling fans would stand by the road to wait for the riders to hurtle past on stages through the mountains, and there just weren't enough die-hard fans in America to make lots of stages like that viable.

Aisner had to grab attention, and he had limited time to do it, so he also added extra stunts and a bit of razzmatazz to the criteriums. 'I borrowed things from pro wrestling, from Roller Derby, from lots of different sports. I had to take a guy who was downtown when he came across the race and turn him into a spectator, and then into a cycling fan, and I had forty-five minutes to do it,' he explained.

Open rather than pro is a better description of the 1985 Coors race. The best Eastern bloc national teams were invited. And the doors were thrown open to the European pro teams. Panasonic, Skill, Peugeot and Kwantum, as well as La Vie Claire, took up the challenge. Aisner added some American amateur and professional squads, pro racing having grown quickly in the USA in the wake of LeMond and others' success in Europe, and he had his field.

Hinault had just won his fifth Tour de France, and when interviewed on the eve of the race he said he was in America 'to help Greg LeMond win the Coors Classic'. The team didn't race as La Vie Claire, because its riders were paid 100,000 dollars by Celestial Seasonings to wear kit carrying their brand name, not La Vie Claire's.

Right from the outset Hinault didn't like the criteriums, later saying, 'I have never felt as endangered in the Tour de France as I did in the San Francisco and Sacramento criteriums.' He didn't like the courses, and he especially didn't like the death or glory moves some Americans made in these races. Hinault survived by keeping out of the way in the circuit races, avoiding any kind of jostling to be first into the corners, but he worked hard for LeMond on the road stages, and he helped him fight off a challenge from Andy Hampsten, who was riding for the Levi's Raleigh team, to win the race.

The Coors Classic reached its zenith in 1986, when the world road race championships were held in Colorado Springs, making the Coors Classic the perfect warm-up race for the top pro riders who would contest the worlds. And, just to spice things up, there was a very different dynamic going on between Greg LeMond and Bernard Hinault.

LeMond had just won the Tour de France, with Hinault in second place, but there was simmering bad feeling between the two, with Hinault the villain in LeMond's mind. It didn't affect the welcome Hinault got in San Francisco, though, where thousands lined Telegraph Hill for the prologue time trial, and they rocked the buildings during Hinault's ride.

Not that the Tour de France top two put up much of a performance. Ron Kiefel took his fourth consecutive Coors prologue, with Hinault, whom race director Aisner kept calling Bernie, just about in contention, while LeMond's bike chain derailed during his ride. He had to run up the steepest part of the climb before he could get going again, and he lost 36 seconds.

Fisherman's Wharf hosted the next stage, on a bigger circuit than before, which Hinault liked better. The stage was fast, noisy and proved perfect for the Irish rider, Alan McCormack. McCormack was a great little sprinter who was part of the Sean Kelly and Stephen Roche era. He turned pro for the British Carlton-Weinmann team in 1977, raced for a year in Belgium for Old Lords-Splendor, but then found he liked the fast pro criteriums in North America, and he raced there from 1980 until 1995.

The first proper road stage was 102 miles from Sonoma to Sacramento, between the Valley of the Moon and the Napa Valley wine regions. The pace was brutal. La Vie

Claire went on the offensive, and a big group including LeMond got away, but after 40 miles they were only a couple of minutes clear of a determined chase group that was closing. On hearing this news, LeMond hammered up the next climb, Sage Canyon, until there was just him, Raul Alcala, Bruno Cornillet, Andy Hampsten and Janus Kuum clear. They worked well together, and by the finish had nearly eight minutes' lead, with Cornillet taking the stage.

There were two stages that day, with an evening criterium around the streets of Sacramento, where a puncture cost Phil Anderson two more minutes to add to the seven he lost earlier. He looked totally out of contention overall, so the Australian attacked on the first climb next day, taking some others who were low down the overall standings with him, including Bernard Hinault. The peloton could allow them some time, but it relaxed too much and the break built a lead of 14 minutes. A chase was organised, but it was too late and the lead group finished nine minutes ahead, putting the Norwegian Dag-Otto Lauritzen into the lead.

Hinault had moved up to fourth overall, without contributing a jot to the break that put him there. The race was then air-lifted to Colorado, where Doug Shapiro then Jeff Pierce took over from Lauritzen, with Hinault lurking ominously just behind them. The scene was set for the Vail Pass time trial, where it took Hinault a fraction under 27 minutes to prove he was the strongest in the race. LeMond was 50 seconds behind Hinault in second place, and Hinault took over as race leader.

But a LeMond victory would have made a better story in America, so two days later, when Hinault got in another breakaway that LeMond missed, their manager Paul

Koechli asked him not to contribute. Hinault refused, saying afterwards: 'Paul and I have different perspectives on the race, but since I push the pedals I decide how hard I push them.'

The growing distrust between Hinault and LeMond that had simmered all through the 1986 Tour de France (the story of which will be told in Chapter 18) boiled over on the next stage, a cold, wet and windy one around a circuit in Estes Park, Colorado. LeMond attacked with Raul Alcala, the first Mexican to finish the Tour de France, but once Phil Anderson bridged to them the American stopped working. That was the right thing to do, as Anderson was a threat overall to Hinault, but Hinault didn't trust LeMond. So he attacked.

Hinault chased furiously, in a foul mood too; so foul that when he stopped with a mechanical problem he threw his broken bike to the ground and shouted at Paul Koechli for allowing LeMond to attack. Back in the saddle he pounded up to the break, but once there Hinault let the Italian, Moreno Argentin, ride off and win. Then when Hinault and LeMond crossed the line they dismounted, squared up to each other and had a very public slanging match that ended with LeMond giving Hinault the bent-elbow and clenched-fist salute. Hinault carried on undaunted, winning the final time trial narrowly from LeMond and taking the race overall.

Raul Alcala won the next Coors Classic, but it lacked the drama of 1986, and American cycling really missed Greg LeMond, who was still recovering from his hunting accident (he was accidentally shot by his brother-in-law while they were hunting wild turkeys). There was one more Coors in 1988, which was won by Davis Phinney, and that was it. The race had grown to two weeks long, with merchandising netting 1.5 million dollars for Coors, but it wasn't enough and Coors pulled out. But the Coors Classic spawned other races, and it inspired many young American men and women to start road racing. It also helped in the story of America's first big pro team, 7-Eleven, which was created by Jim Ochowicz, a former speed-skater and cyclist who is still running teams today.

'In 1981 we started a programme to emulate what they had in Europe, a team with a corporate sponsor, all riding the same bikes and wearing the same uniforms, taking part in a programme of races in the USA,' Ochowicz says. The team's first objective was to give the best American riders a platform to work on for the 1984 Olympics, but after the US success in Los Angeles, Ochowicz began looking at Europe, and at the logistics of creating a pro team that could race there at World Tour level. 'I needed a co-sponsor, and I got one in the form of an Italian company called Hoonved, which had already been involved in cycling,' he recalls.

Italian backing brought 7-Eleven a place in the 1985 Giro d'Italia. The team had a difficult spring in Europe, and things weren't going much better in the Giro until Ron Kiefel won a stage. 7-Eleven was getting up to speed. The riders still had a steep learning curve to cope with, and it was made even steeper by a constraint Ochowicz had. '7-Eleven were kind of dragged along by the momentum, they weren't getting any direct benefit from us racing in Europe, although they got lots of residual publicity. I knew that I had to keep the momentum going to keep 7-Eleven interested, so we had to get into the world's biggest bike race, the Tour de France, as soon as possible,' he says.

Ochowicz talked his Italian backers into continuing

with them, then he nagged the Tour de France co-director, Félix Lévitan, into giving 7-Eleven a place in the race. It was a bit last minute; the 7-Eleven riders didn't know if they'd be riding the Tour until June 1986, when Lévitan finally agreed to let them in.

The 1986 Tour de France was a turning point in the race's history. Greg LeMond won, of course, and although they were in the race to learn, 7-Eleven made an impact. Alex Stieda of Canada wore the yellow jersey, the first Canadian and North American to do so, and Davis Phinney won a stage, both early on in the race. But Ochowicz says the team's greatest accomplishment wasn't the yellow jersey or the stage win, it was 'finishing with five men still in the race. By finishing they took us to a whole new level. We were now a serious team who could get through the Tour de France. The Tour is a supreme test, not just for the riders but for the staff as well. There are so many day-to-day things to consider; like where to get gas from, where to get ice for drinks. Once we'd proved we could get through, then we could build on that platform.'

The story of the 1986 Tour de France tends, naturally, to be dominated by the burgeoning LeMond-Hinault rivalry within La Vie Claire, but the team had another top finisher in fourth place overall, and he was American too. His name is Andy Hampsten, and he wasn't from any of the US cycling hot-spots, he was from North Dakota, where as he recalls there weren't many fellow enthusiasts:

The only people with road bikes near me were a group of maybe eight or nine hippies. Some of them had European 10-speeds, and in our town there was one bike shop, and we'd hang around in that. I rode my bike with those guys, exploring my boring little town again and

again. They showed me some useful things, though, like
how to sit on a wheel, but there were so few races, maybe
two or three a year and you'd have to travel hundreds
of miles to get to them. All I could do to get an idea of
what racing was about was listen to these guys translating
French cycling magazines or, just occasionally, when a
copy of *Cycling Weekly* turned up from England.

Then in the summer of 1977, when Hampsten was 15,
he visited England.

My mum's sister married an Englishman, and they lived
in Cambridge with their two daughters, so once every five
years we'd pack up the house and go over there for the
summer. In 1977 me and my elder brother Stephen, who
was also into cycling, went over, and while we were there
we joined the Cambridge Town and County Cycling Club.
We spent all summer riding with them. We were in heaven.
  There was always a ten-mile time trial on Thursday
evenings, and three regular training rides a week. And
there was a guy called Robbie Parker, a great fellow, who
would load us all up, schoolboys and schoolgirls, in his
van and take us off to races up and down the country.
That summer was my introduction to European cycling.
I didn't win anything, I just enjoyed it.

Hampsten started racing in the USA the following year.
'I realised that I really enjoyed the lifestyle, the fact that
I could get out and meet new people, travel lots, sleep
on other people's sofas. Cycling was a good way of doing
the things I wanted to do. I was very shy at the time,
but it gave me that freedom, and some confidence.'
  Three weeks after turning pro in 1985, Hampsten won

a stage in the Giro d'Italia, when he was racing as a guest with the 7-Eleven team. After doing that he was offered a contract with La Vie Claire by Bernard Hinault himself. Then Hampsten won the 1986 Tour of Switzerland, just before Greg LeMond won the Tour de France. So Hampsten was the first American to win a major national professional stage race.

His victory in the 1988 Giro d'Italia means he was the second rider from the USA after LeMond to win a Grand Tour. And after Lance Armstrong's fall, LeMond, Hampsten and Chris Horner (the Vuelta a España in 2013) are the only US cyclists to have won Grand Tours. The Canadian Ryder Hesjedal added to North America's Grand Tour total when he won the 2012 Giro d'Italia.

Hampsten was third in the 1989 Giro d'Italia, but very disappointed when the organisers decided to cancel the scheduled Gavia stage, the Passo di Gavia having provided the foundation of his 1988 victory.

I was completely devastated. I was all ready to go for it again. But my worst memory of that day was driving over the stage route in the team buses in weather that was no worse than the previous year, and seeing hundreds of fans lining the route. They watched us sat in buses not on bicycles, and they'd been waiting for hours. These were people who'd taken the day off work and come from all over Italy to see the stage. The organisers said they couldn't find the equipment necessary to make the stage safe, but that was a lie. I think they just didn't want to repeat what had happened the previous year.

After that Hampsten spent a lot of time working on what he saw as his Achilles heel in Grand Tours, his time trial ability, but it brought him less success than he'd had before. He made a slight improvement against the clock, but it was at the expense of some of his climbing ability. The net result was a couple of difficult years. He put those behind him in 1992, when he returned to focusing on what he was good at.

I was relaxed about the 1992 Tour de France. Miguel Indurain was at his height, and I realised my chance of winning overall wasn't great. There were only two big days in the mountains, so I knew I'd have to concentrate on them. The first day to Sestrière I shattered myself completely to come fifth. I was really at the end of my rope by the end. I could barely walk, but I knew that underneath I was in good shape, and just as importantly everybody else felt the same way as me.

The next day to Alpe d'Huez I started off with my tactical plan, but then I said to myself: Andy, wait, relax, every time you have a plan it goes wrong. I knew that every time I got tensed up something went awry, so I decided to just take each kilometre as it came. And it worked. That attitude works.

His victory at Alpe d'Huez in 1992 was a classic. It's the stage every climber wants to win. 'There were five of us in the move that stayed away,' he recalls.

And I remember thinking, God, I'm actually in the right move for once. I was so amazed. Everybody in the group was willing to work, all five of us totally committed, and we got a minute on the bunch, and then another minute. And then on the Croix de Fer, one guy, Eric Boyer, started attacking. And I was so annoyed that he was playing games, and he could screw the whole thing up by doing so. I mean, what was he going to do: stay away for 50 kilometres to the finish? I rode up to him and started insulting him, riding past him and ridiculing him. I know I shouldn't have done it, but I was really annoyed. After that the Alpe was pretty straightforward. No one had a real advantage over anybody else. I just half wheeled everybody to the top, and won.

Andy Hampsten is still involved in cycling, dividing his time between Tuscany and Boulder; and today in North Dakota, where there was little everyday cycling, and hardly any road racing, when he grew up there, there is the 40-mile Andy Hampsten Bikeway system that thousands of new Dakotan cyclists enjoy.

There are many other brilliant US racers I could write about, all of them adding their own pages to the history of road racing. One of them added lots of pages, but I'll get to Lance Armstrong later. Plenty from Canada too. And it would be wrong not to mention South American riders, and in particular I have to go into a little more detail about Colombia, a country with a massive road racing history.

There are some very good Colombian road racers today, like Nairo Quintana, who won the Giro in 2014 and the Vuelta in 2016, and they are all brilliant mountain climbers. But the Colombian who first thrust this country of climbing kings into the collective consciousness of cycling was Luis Alberto Herrera.

More often known as Lucho, Herrera was born in Fusagasugá, Colombia, in May 1961. He was in the vanguard of Colombian cyclists who came to Europe in numbers during the Eighties. They were mountain-climbing naturals, true climbers in every sense of the word, and Herrera was the best.

To understand him it's good to know a bit about the place where he grew up. Fusagasugá, 65 kilometres south of Bogotá, is a garden town with 134,000 people and an annual average temperature of 20 degrees Celsius. It's hot and hilly, at an altitude of 1,778 metres, and the people there are mad about cycling. The world Herrera grew up in fired his ambition and developed his body into a mountain-climbing machine.

He used his bike for going to school and back, but soon started following the local racers leaving town for the Alto de Rosas pass that leads to Bogotá. They would ride the climb, turn around at the top, freewheel back down and then go up again. Lucho started copying them, stretching his lungs and developing his super-efficient, super-strong but stick-thin body.

Fusagasugá's climate is ideal for commercial flower growing, and Lucho's first job was picking flowers for the many florists in town, earning another nickname, El Jardinero, the little gardener. He rode his bike every day to get to work, and for training afterwards; ever more training. When he started racing, Lucho Herrera was a revelation.

In one of Colombia's biggest races, the RCN Classic in 1981, which was first run the year Herrera was born, he won a stage that climbed the legendary La Linea mountain pass. He was 20 years old and already knocking on the door of the Colombian national team, which started receiving lots of invitations to race in Europe around that time.

Europeans were also racing in Colombia, and in the following year's RCN Classic, Herrera beat some of the best French amateurs to win overall. That got him a place in the national team to take part in the Tour de l'Avenir in France, where he won a stage in the mountains.

Professional road racing went through a rough patch in Europe in the early Eighties. There was a recession and team sponsors became harder to find, so the number of big teams dropped. The Tour de France organisers responded by announcing that the 1983 Tour would be open, meaning amateur national teams, if they were good enough, could take part. The idea was to attract the Russian national team, which dominated amateur road racing at the time. Instead the Tour got Colombian climbers, who'd been waiting for a stage like the Tour de France to perform on.

Lucho Herrera wasn't in the team of ten Colombian riders who were the first amateurs to take part in a modern Tour de France, but the South Americans still made their presence felt. Forty Colombian journalists travelled with the team, and Colombian radio broadcast live commentary back home, even though Tour stages ran through the Colombian night. Thousands of bike fans tuned in to listen to the exploits of their riders, particularly Patrochinio Jiménez, who spent five days in the King of the Mountains jersey before taking second place in that contest, and Edgar Corredor, who finished 16th overall. Even more listened when Herrera rode the 1984 Tour de France.

He looked ill at ease, like a boy who had borrowed his father's bike to pose with his heroes. They looked hewn from rock, he looked like he was made from spun sugar, but he left Frenchman Laurent Fignon, a double Tour de France winner, struggling in his wake as he won stage 17, Grenoble to Alpe d'Huez, by 49 seconds.

The Colombian team was sponsored in 1983 and 1984 by the battery company Varta, who were taking a massive risk because many big Colombian companies had lost money trying to export to Europe. But the gamble paid off, and the publicity Herrera gained through being the first ever Colombian Tour de France stage winner attracted two more companies to sponsor the team in 1985, Café de Colombia and the French bike equipment manufacturer Mavic.

The 1985 Tour team was led by Herrera, and he was backed by several strong riders, including Fabio Parra, who was two years older than Herrera. Parra had finished fifth in the 1985 Vuelta a España, which still started in April back then, and Herrera had won the 1985 Tour of Colombia. The Tour's first mountain stage was stage 11, which went from Pontarlier to Morzine-Avoriaz, a mountain-top finish. Luis Herrera won it from Bernard Hinault, with Pedro Delgado third and Fabio Parra fourth. Herrera led over every climb that day, so he took a commanding lead in the King of the Mountains too.

That must have done the Colombian pair's confidence a power of good, because next day they attacked together. It was a monster stage, 269 kilometres from Morzine to Lans-en-Vercors, with seven mountain passes in it. Herrera and Parra composed a mountain-climbing symphony. Herrera danced uphill as if with wings on his feet. Out of the saddle, in the saddle, it didn't matter, it was pure poetry.

He took maximum points on top of the Col de la Colombière, was then joined by Parra on the descent and they just carried on. Parra won the stage, while Herrera collected so many points he virtually sealed the first Grand Tour King of the Mountains title for Colombia that day. Herrera won another stage in St Etienne, and he finished seventh overall, with Parra just behind him in eighth.

Café de Colombia was joined in Europe by another Colombian team for 1986, although Herrera wasn't at his best that year. It was different in 1987 when he became the first Colombian to win a Grand Tour, by taking the Vuelta a España, and winning the mountains title. He then won his second King of the Mountains in the 1987 Tour de France, and finished fifth overall. Parra was sixth.

For a while it seemed to be only a matter of time before a Colombian would win the Tour de France. The 1987 winner, Stephen Roche, says: 'It was impossible to match Herrera when he attacked, not even the best climbers could do it. All you could do was ride as hard as you dared, and hope he didn't gain too much time. Then you had to beat him by as much as possible in the time trials.'

But a Colombian still hasn't won the Tour. Fabio Parra finished third in 1988, and that was the best until Nairo Quintana's second place in 2015. Colombians went on ripping up the climbs, and Herrera completed a mountains hat-trick by taking the Giro d'Italia climber's prize in 1989. Federico Bahamontes is the only other rider ever to have done that, which is testament to just how good Luis 'Lucho' Herrera was. Up there with Bahamontes, arguably the best climber ever; the Eagle of Toledo and the Little Gardener of Fusagasugá.

18

The Greatest

Boxing has Muhammad Ali, football has Pelé, Formula One has Ayrton Senna. Every sport has its great, one amazing competitor who not only dominated a generation, but stands above all generations because of what they won and the way they won it. In cycling that outstanding person is Eddy Merckx. By any measure, sheer volume of victories or whatever you choose, you come up with Eddy Merckx. There has never been anyone to equal him, and I can't imagine there ever will be.

The biggest testament to Merckx is the calibre of riders he can be compared with and still be judged the best. To select those riders I started at the Second World War and went to the mid-Eighties. That's because by the time normality returned after the conflict, men's road racing had reached maturity in that all the great races were there, and the best tried to race in most of them, doing the monuments, one or two Grand Tours, and the world championships. Then in the second half of the Eighties the sport went through a transition, and the best riders slowly became more specialised. That makes it more difficult to compare riders who came after Merckx with him, and with others from that post-war period, because they don't take on a varied calendar of races now. There are four riders I want to consider before getting to Eddy Merckx, and the first is Fausto Coppi.

Coppi's career was interrupted by the Second World War, broken bones and personal troubles, but he still won the Tour de France twice, the Giro d'Italia and the Giro di Lombardia five times, Milan–San Remo three times, and Paris–Roubaix once, plus many other single-day and stage races. But it wasn't what Coppi won, although his palmarès is prodigious; it was how he won.

There was a time when if Coppi attacked alone he was never caught. Not only that, Coppi just kept widening his gap on the rest. The French journalist René de Latour once said that stopwatches weren't needed to time the gaps that Coppi forged in races, the little hand of a church clock would do. Look at two examples: in his 1952 Tour de France win he was 28 minutes ahead of the next rider, and in the 1953 world professional road race championships in Lugano, Coppi was six minutes and 22 seconds ahead of second place.

And Coppi always raced with great style. At his best he seemed in a state of grace, an azure ship sailing on a celeste sea, where physics no longer applied. You can appreciate something of Coppi from grainy YouTube footage, but instead of trying to describe him from that, here are two quotes from men who saw him at very close quarters.

The first is Jean Bobet, a pro at the same time as Coppi and the brother of Coppi's rival, the triple Tour de France winner Louison Bobet. Jean became a great cycling journalist and writer after his racing career, and this is how he recalled being caught and passed by Fausto Coppi in a time trial stage of the 1953 Tour of Italy: 'One day, in a cloud of golden dust, I saw the sun riding a bicycle between Grosseto and Follonica.'

The other is André Leducq, the 1930 and 1932 Tour de France winner, who for a while after he retired wrote for *Le Miroir des Sports*. This is him describing Coppi in motion in 1952:

> He seems to caress rather than grip the handlebars, while his torso appears fixed to the saddle. His long legs extend to the pedals with the joints of a gazelle. At the end of each pedal stroke his ankle flexes gracefully. It's as if all the moving parts turn in oil. His long face appears like the blade of a knife as he climbs without apparent effort. He rides like a great artist painting a watercolour.

Coppi raced too long and died too young; he was only 40 when a misdiagnosed case of malaria ran untreated and killed him. Thousands turned out for the funeral to bid a final farewell to Il Campionissimo, the champion of champions. That's how Fausto Coppi is still remembered in Italy today.

The next great I'd compare with Merckx is Jacques Anquetil. He was the supreme stage racer between 1957 and 1964, the first five-time Tour de France winner, the first to emulate Fausto Coppi's Giro/Tour double, which he did in 1964, and the first to win all three Grand Tours in his career. At his best, Anquetil was unbeatable. In

1961, when the Tour de France started in his home city of Rouen, Anquetil said he would take the yellow jersey on day one and keep it until the end. He did, and remains one of only four riders ever to do that; and the other three, Ottavio Bottecchia, Nicolas Frantz and Romain Maes, all did it before the Second World War.

Anquetil built his victories on total superiority in time trials, and he is one of the best male time triallists in history. Miguel Indurain is up there with Anquetil, and also won time trials by large margins, but Anquetil won the GP des Nations, the world time trial championships of its era, nine times. Indurain was world time trial champion once, in 1995. Both set new world hour records, another measure of time trial greatness.

Everybody is more than just the sum of their achievements, but Anquetil was particularly complicated and contradictory. He was scientific and superstitious, ruthless and shy, confident yet fixated on being beaten by his closest French rival. There are many well-worn examples of these traits, but they are best heard from someone who knew him well: his right-hand man through Anquetil's glory years, both road captain and close confident – a superb rider too, the 1962 world professional road race champion, Jean Stablinski, whom I interviewed in 2003. These are some of his observations on Jacques Anquetil:

I shared rooms with him many times, shared his greatest moments and his worst. We were close. I analysed him as I analysed all my rivals. I understood him too; I understood when he needed to laugh and when he needed a push. His biggest strength, though, was that his body, his whole system in fact, was tuned to riding a bike. He was a natural. He had a feel for the bike that I have never seen in anyone else. He could tell the correct fit of his bike to the millimetre. He could tell exactly how much pressure was in his tyres. He didn't need a ruler or a gauge, these things were natural to him.

He also had extraordinary powers of recuperation. He could recover while he was racing. In a three-week stage race, normally every stage takes something out of you, even an easy one, but Anquetil could come out of a less important stage in better form than he went in. That is rare. I think that somehow he switched off on those stages to recharge his batteries. It was a problem for us, though, his team-mates, because he could be ambushed by a surprise attack when he went into a torpor like that.

Next was his memory. He remembered every detail of a course and could play it back, like a film in his head. He had it in normal life too; if he went anywhere in his car once, he could go again. He never got lost. He would look over every course for a time trial and remember every detail, and he would decide, even if we were in a car, what gear he would use for each part of the course. And he was always right.

He reconnoitred time trial stages, but we didn't have time to look at the other stages in my day, we had too many races. So Anquetil had a huge collection of maps, and the night before a big stage he would study them, putting all the gradients of the climbs, all the distances and landmarks into his brain. It was like loading information into a computer.

Knowing the course saved him on many occasions, the most famous being on the Puy de Dôme in the 1964 Tour. Look at the film of that. Anquetil never once looks at Poulidor, all he keeps doing is looking up the road, looking how far he has to go and calculating when he can afford to let Poulidor go. He was a calculation machine in a bike race. No matter how hard it was, how bad he felt, Anquetil always knew the figures, knew the angles. He could think clearly and calculate under the most intense pressure.

Another strength was that if Anquetil did not want to be dropped, nobody could drop him. Great climbers like Bahamontes or Charly Gaul could not drop him early on a climb, no matter how hard they went. Later, when he could afford to let them go, he would let them go, but only when he had calculated that they could not gain any more time than he could win back in the time trials. Hanging on like that takes enormous will-power. Anquetil was a very hard man on his bike.

What he couldn't do, though, was sacrifice everything for his bike. He could only work for certain objectives, but he would give everything for them. I only ever trained with him once when he was preparing for a big race. We rode 160 kilometres and hardly spoke. He kept looking at his watch every time we passed a kilometre stone. It was incredible. I was done-in after 30 kilometres and sat behind him the rest of the way, but Anquetil kept pushing, and timing every kilometre. And his wife, Janine, followed us in her car the whole way. But he could not keep that up all year. He couldn't do it because he loved to enjoy himself. He loved to have his friends around him and entertain them, either in a restaurant or at home, although he preferred at home. Anquetil was very timid in public.

And Janine was special. Wives didn't go to races in those days, but Janine went to every race. She spoke up for Jacques with agents, managers and the press, and it was totally accepted. She could walk through the riders' changing rooms and no one batted an eyelid. She took a lot of responsibilities that otherwise would have taken up his time and distracted him. She was a good organiser and a good driver, so she was invaluable to him when he was travelling to all the races we had to ride. We all benefited from that. After the Tour de France we rode many criteriums. It wasn't the team's responsibility to get us to those races, we were riding for ourselves, but for those of us in the same team as Anquetil, Janine would book all the hotel rooms and make all the other arrangements.

But his relationship with Janine also shows up Jacques Anquetil the enigma. This couple, who had done so much together, divorced in the Eighties. Again, Jean Stablinski was there: 'Janine had been married before. She had two children from that marriage, a boy and a girl, who both lived with Jacques and her. One day after we had all stopped racing for quite a few years, we heard that Jacques and Janine were adopting another child. But it turned out that the mother of that child was Janine's daughter, Jacques' step-daughter, and the father was Jacques. No marriage can stand that,' Stablinski says.

Janine left Anquetil when the truth about their 'adopted' child came out. The man who made his own rules had his own morality and seemed unaffected by it. When he started to appear in public with the woman who would be his second wife, who at the time incidentally was married to Janine's son, Barry Hoban saw them at an old pro's reunion and asked Anquetil where Janine was. 'I have changed my life, so I've changed my wife,' was all Anquetil said.

Another facet of Anquetil's character witnessed by Stablinski was the way he dealt with illness, including his stomach cancer, which in 1987 proved fatal:

For years he had an ulcer. I could understand why, because he suffered badly with stress. Before a time trial he would have to go to the toilet two or three times, and sometimes he was sick with nerves. But he never looked after his stomach. He was always rushing around, doing TV, radio, speaking to journalists, doing business. He just lived with it, and put up with the pain when he should have had it attended to.

At home he was never still either. He loved nature, and was fascinated by the stars. He would stay up all night looking at the stars through his telescope, or just walking on his land, sometimes in the rain or snow. That is not good for an ulcer. Anquetil was not afraid of taking risks in life. He once said to me that even in a car crash or plane crash, he knew he would escape with his life. But I know that he was afraid of one thing, he was afraid of cancer.

The way Anquetil discovered he had cancer is a window on his superstitious side. Stablinski again: 'His second wife used tarot cards. Anquetil was fascinated by them, he believed in that kind of thing. One time she was using them with him, and she asked him if anything was wrong with his stomach. "No, nothing more than normal", he said. And she said, "Just go and see a doctor straight away." So he went and he found out he had cancer.'

When he told Stablinski about his illness, Anquetil made no fuss. 'We were at a randonnée in Colmar. Raymond Poulidor was there and a few others. We were talking about this and that, then Anquetil says, "Oh, I have cancer", just like that. But he said that it wasn't a problem, he had seen a professor and he was going to do this and that. Even if he lost his stomach, he said, it wasn't a problem as you can survive without a stomach. It was remarkable, the way he dealt with it; but there you are, he was like that.'

One of my questions to Stablinski was about Anquetil's assertion that he could have won a lot more races if he'd wanted to. He claimed he could have won many classics, a world title, but he didn't because his contract fee was as high as sponsors and promoters could afford. Why should he work harder for the same money? Typical of Anquetil, and it has become a legend, and his victory in the 1966 Liège–Bastogne–Liège is cited as evidence that he could have won anything. This is what Stablinski told me:

> He wanted to win classics and he tried, but he couldn't. I have told you that nobody could drop Anquetil if he did not want to be dropped; well, he couldn't drop the other top riders with an explosive attack. If you gave Anquetil a 50-metre lead you would never see him again. The problem for him was that he could not gain that first 50 metres. When he won Liège, they made a mistake and let him get the gap.

And what about his legendary rivalry with Raymond Poulidor – why did Anquetil single Poulidor out as the man he had to beat, almost to the point of becoming fixated by him? 'It wasn't because he was afraid of Poulidor beating him,' Stablinski reckoned. 'He was a much better rider than Poulidor anyway. Poulidor couldn't beat him. What he was afraid of was Poulidor's popularity, he couldn't understand why Poulidor was so popular when it was Anquetil who always won. That was why he was so much against Poulidor.' Stablinski should know.

There was another factor against Jacques Anquetil winning classics in the Fifties and Sixties, which even if he'd been more explosive would still have stopped him. It's because the classics back then were dominated by a man who had more explosion than an atom bomb. He was Rik Van Looy of Belgium, known as The Emperor, and he's the next of the greats I want to talk about.

Three riders have won every monument of cycling; they are Eddy Merckx, Roger De Vlaeminck and Rik Van Looy, but Van Looy did something nobody else has done: he won every classic as well, which means all five monuments plus Ghent–Wevelgem, La Flèche Wallonne and Paris–Tours. Even Eddy Merckx didn't do that; he didn't win Paris–Tours. That makes Rik Van Looy the all-time king of single-day races.

Van Looy gave me one of the best, certainly most realistic, answers I've ever had from a pro bike racer. When looking back on their careers, I like to ask riders what their favourite victory was. If they're honest the answer can be very revealing. Van Looy's certainly was:

My best victory was my bank account. Paris–Roubaix and being world champion, yes, they're nice, but I'm proudest of the money I made, because it means that I am somebody today. My childhood was tough compared to those of today, but it was typical of my age. My mother died when I was quite young and I grew up unsupervised at times. I often skipped school. I had a paper round, five to six hundred newspapers to be delivered every day, and I did it on a bike that weighed 25 kilos. It took me from six in the morning to midday, so seeing as I'd already missed the morning, sometimes I decided to miss the afternoon at school as well.

But many of the people who I delivered newspapers to were bank managers, lawyers and accountants. People who wouldn't have noticed a boy like me, but now bank managers, lawyers and accountants hold doors open for me. They say, 'Good morning, Mr Van Looy.' And that's because of the money I made from cycling.

As well as all the classics, Rik Van Looy won consecutive world road race titles in 1960 and '61, and took two silver medals. 'Both times beaten by a Belgian,' he says. The first was in Copenhagen in 1956, where Van Looy was beaten by Rik Van Steenbergen in a straight fight, but the second time was anything but straight. In fact, such is its notoriety that the incident sits in the same place in cycling as Diego Maradona's 'Hand of God' goal does in football.

The year was 1963, the place Renaix in Belgium. The race ended in a big group sprint with winner Benoni Beheyt's outstretched hand in contact with the back of Van Looy's jersey. After the finish there was uproar, Van Looy claiming that his Belgian team-mate had pulled him back, but Beheyt saying he had been fending off Van Looy. So was it a push or a pull? 'It was a pull,' Van Looy said to me in 2005, 'and there's another thing about that finish. If I'd known Beheyt was going to sprint, I would have done my sprint differently. In the finale Beheyt told me that he had cramp, and he wouldn't be able to do anything.'

The final master of a generation I'd like to consider in the context of Eddy Merckx before talking about him is Bernard Hinault, known as Le Blaireau, the badger, and the Last Patron of the Peloton, who arrived in men's pro road racing at the age of 20 in 1975 and quickly fought, literally sometimes, his way to the top.

Hinault is from Brittany, and he wanted to win everything, from the Tour de France down to an argument. Those who knew him say that Hinault couldn't take failure, he wouldn't have handled it. In 1971, his first racing season as a 16-year-old novice, he won twelve out of the twenty races he entered. By 1975, with his military service behind him, Hinault was a professional racer with the Gitane-Campagnolo team, under the management of Cyrille Guimard.

In 1977 he won Ghent–Wevelgem and Liège–Bastogne–Liège, then in 1978 he won the Vuelta a España and the Tour de France, both at his first participation. He would win five Tours, another Vuelta, plus a Giro d'Italia treble, as well as more classics. And in the middle of that run he had two lots of time out to get his only weakness, his dodgy knees, sorted.

Cycling was war for Bernard Hinault. Take his second Tour de France victory in 1979. When did you see the yellow jersey win the final stage, the sprinter's stage of all sprinter's stages, on the Champs-Elysées? Hinault did it in 1979. He also won another flat stage the day before.

The 1979 Tour started in Fleurance, close to the foot of the Pyrenees, then had three stages in the mountains; Hinault won two of them. He took the yellow jersey on stage two, and by stage eight was 1 minute and 18 seconds clear of his nearest rival, Joop Zoetemelk. A modest enough gap, but only because Zoetemelk's team, TI-Raleigh, was the best at team time trials, and the 1979 Tour had two in the first eight stages. One was 87.45 kilometres and the other 90.5. Hinault's team, Renault-Gitane, lost 2 minutes and 35 seconds on those two stages. Then Zoetemelk got another leg-up.

Stage nine was a mini Paris–Roubaix, and Zoetemelk

went with an attack made at the very moment Bernard Hinault punctured. There were no 'unwritten rules', no waiting for the yellow jersey that day, and Zoetemelk ended up at the front with some good riders, while Hinault was behind in a group that lost 2 minutes and 30 seconds in short order.

He had little firepower to help, and no team-mates, so he ploughed on alone to the velodrome finish in Roubaix. When he got there, Zoetemelk had the yellow jersey by 2 minutes and 8 seconds, and Hinault was livid. 'Some riders will suffer plenty for what they did today,' he fumed. The stage also set him against Paris–Roubaix for ever. He hated cobbles, hated that race, and even when he won it in 1981 Hinault said: 'You will never make me take back what I have already said about Paris–Roubaix; it's bullshit.'

Two days after the Roubaix stage Hinault won the time trial stage in Brussels. Then he trounced Zoetemelk by 2 minutes and 37 seconds in a mountain time trial in the Alps, taking back the yellow jersey. Zoetemelk put up a fight, winning on Alpe d'Huez, but he got hammered again by Hinault in the final time trial. Hinault won the 1979 Tour by over 13 minutes, although 10 minutes of that time gap came when Zoetemelk was given a time penalty for a positive dope test. Yes, that actually happened in those days, time penalties for doping. The third rider, Joachim Agostinho, finished over 26 minutes behind Hinault.

Hinault dropped out of the 1980 Tour with knee trouble, won it in 1981 and in 1982. He then missed the 1983 Tour, out with another bout of knee problems, probably caused by the prolonged fight he had against a Spanish inter-team combination that had tried to prevent him winning his second Vuelta earlier in the year. He was below his best in 1984, then back to full strength in 1985, when Hinault won his fifth and final Tour. He and his La Vie Claire team-mate, Greg LeMond, who was second overall, were the best two in the race, and the stage was set for LeMond to win in 1986.

It wouldn't be easy. LeMond says that there was an agreement between him and Hinault for the Frenchman to back LeMond. Something that would appear to be true from Hinault's words at the pre-Tour press conference: 'Whoever arrives at the foot of the mountains with the greatest reserves will win this Tour de France,' he said, and 'We won't be giving the Colombians an armchair ride to the Pyrenees.'

Next day Hinault beat LeMond by two seconds in the prologue, but he suffered a setback when he proved weaker than LeMond in the next afternoon's team time trial. The result was that La Vie Claire underperformed, and lost time to rival Laurent Fignon's Renault team. A story circulated that LeMond told CBS Sports that Hinault was deliberately trying to make him lose the Tour. It was nonsense, but gossip soon becomes gospel in the Tour de France press room.

Hinault gained the upper hand when he won the 61-kilometre time trial at Nantes. The only riders close to Hinault's time were a puncture-delayed LeMond and Stephen Roche, while Fignon dropped out of overall contention by losing four minutes. Hinault's pre-Pyrenean strategy had worked perfectly. The Colombian teams were destroyed by the time trials and the extraordinarily fast pace of every road stage. Lucho Herrera did best, but he was eight minutes behind the race leader, Jorgen Pedersen.

Hinault attacked in the Pyrenees, and LeMond finished the first mountain stage in third place, but 4 minutes and 36 seconds behind Hinault. 'That's life,' said a despondent LeMond after the stage. 'I guess I'm going to finish second in the Tour de France again.' The cause of his despair was Hinault breaking away with a big opponent of theirs, Pedro Delgado. It meant LeMond had been trapped by his team-mate.

Some said the Tour was already over after that, but Delgado didn't agree. He said: 'That was only round one; round two starts on stage 13, when the Tourmalet is the first of four mountain passes.' And what a showdown it was. Hinault, wearing the yellow jersey, took the initiative from LeMond again by attacking alone.

He gained almost two minutes after the Tourmalet, and increased that to almost three at the beginning of the Col de Peyresourde, 30 kilometres later. LeMond was really worried now. 'If Hinault had held that lead he would have been eight minutes ahead overall, and the Tour would definitely have been over,' he said after the stage. But Hinault either overestimated his strength and underestimated the strength of his opponents, or he really was setting things up for LeMond by giving their rivals a tough chase.

Under the pressure of Herrera, Robert Millar and Urs Zimmermann, the gap was cut to 25 seconds in 13 kilometres, so Hinault sat up and waited and started the final climb with eight others, including LeMond. On the 16-kilometre ascent to Superbagnères Hinault lost nearly five minutes to LeMond, who won the stage, but Hinault was still in the yellow jersey.

The Alps were next, but LeMond was still depressed after a sleepless night spent worrying about Hinault. 'I felt like quitting the Tour last night,' he told reporters, upset by Hinault joining an attack on the last flat stage just before the Alps. 'Hinault says he did it for the team, but he did it for himself,' LeMond added.

He needn't have worried, Hinault wasn't going well. He was suffering from strained knee ligaments, and he struggled on the penultimate climb of stage 17, the Col d'Izoard. Hinault lost time, and was still climbing when LeMond started the descent to the town of Briançon with only Urs Zimmermann for company.

The last climb to the stage finish was the Col de Granon, and Zimmermann flew up it, but LeMond matched him. Hinault refused to give in, and doggedly climbed between long lines of fans to reach the finish 2 minutes and 21 seconds behind Zimmermann and LeMond. Now LeMond was in yellow, with Hinault third but determined to have the last word.

Next day he attacked on the descent of the Col du Galibier, taking LeMond with him as well as another La Vie Claire rider, the Canadian Steve Bauer, and Pello Ruiz-Cabestany of Spain. Urs Zimmermann chased but almost crashed on a bend trying to stay close to LeMond. He lost 50 metres and his confidence, so he dropped back to the chasing group. That was a mistake.

Bauer and Ruiz-Cabestany both worked hard, but as they began to climb the giant Col de la Croix de Fer they paid for it and fell back. Hinault and LeMond continued with what would become an historic breakaway, where they ended up crossing the finish line at Alpe d'Huez, linked hands raised in victory, having gained five minutes on Zimmermann.

It looked like peace had been declared, but Hinault ripped that notion up during the rest-day press conference.

'The race will not be over until after the time trial at St Etienne,' he said. LeMond really wanted to win in St Etienne to show Hinault who was best, but he went too fast into a tight corner halfway through a 58-kilometre time trial and crashed. LeMond lost half a minute, and a few seconds more when he later had to change bikes because of a damaged brake. He lost the time trial by 25 seconds.

The battle was now over, but Hinault had proved something to himself and his fans. LeMond won, but Hinault could have won too if he'd wanted to and played the race tactically rather than trying to rip it apart for show. Of course he never said that, he said his aggressive tactics were intended to tire LeMond's rivals, so it's just my opinion. I bet I'm right, though. One thing is certain. Bernard Hinault was still the hero in the eyes of the public, and that's what the proud Breton wanted.

And so to Eddy Merckx. He was born at 11 a.m. on 17 June 1945 in a little village called Meenzel-Kiezegem, the eldest child of Jules and Jenny Merckx, and christened Edouard Louis Joseph Merckx. His full title today is Edouard Louis Joseph, Baron Merckx.

Jules Merckx was a hard worker, a man who made a life for his family through total commitment to a grocery shop after the family moved to a Brussels suburb when Eddy was very young. Summer and winter, early every morning he went to the wholesale market in Brussels to buy fruit and vegetables. Then he worked until evening selling, and often into the night doing paperwork and the 1,001 other jobs required to run a small business.

Eddy's mother was a warm kind person, but a fierce fighter who was not afraid to take on the Belgian cycling establishment when she thought her son had been slighted by non-selection for the 1964 Olympic road race, and she won. Merckx turned to his mother when he decided to try to become a professional cyclist, enlisting her help to persuade his father to accept what might appear a perilous venture.

Merckx was a good scholar, but became less interested as he grew older. He would rather play sport; he was very interested in that, and very good at it. He played football for Junior White Star, the football club that later became Racing White and is now called R. W. D. Molenbeek, but cycling was his calling. He followed it on the radio and in newspapers, when no one else in his family did. Merckx can't explain why he was so interested; there were no cyclists in his family, and his parents weren't fans. It just happened.

There was a local racer, Guillaume Michiels, who was a pro, and Merckx knew him because his parents knew Michiels' family. Michiels later became Merckx's masseur and a close friend, but he wasn't the reason Eddy Merckx wanted to race. It came from deep inside him, was something he felt driven to do. He rode unofficial races with his friends, then as soon as he was old enough he took part in his first official race.

That was on 17 July 1961, one month past his 15th birthday. The Belgian debutants category covered the ages of 15 and 16, and racing with the debutants in Laken, another part of Brussels, Merckx came fifth. Thirteen races later, in October the same year, he won his first race and his ambition was set in stone.

The following spring Eddy Merckx won four out of his first five races, then at Easter he told his father he wanted to leave school to train and race so he could become a professional. That wasn't what Jules Merckx had planned for his son, but Eddy's mother worked part-time in their shop and she had to go into hospital for an operation. Merckx senior needed someone to replace her while she recovered, so he allowed Eddy to fill the gap and train and race around his work.

Merckx won almost every time he raced in 1962, often by wide margins, and sometimes Jules Merckx watched him. Then on 16 July he won his first Belgian title in the debutants road race championships. His father had hoped his son might go back to school, but that title and the way Eddy raced meant his talent was obvious even to somebody who knew nothing about cycling. Maybe this was what Eddy Merckx should do with his life, and he received his father's blessing.

Merckx's fame spread quickly. Lots of people gave him advice, but the one he listened to most was a former Tour de France star, Félicien Vervaecke, who became his coach. Merckx didn't need coaching in the full sense of the word; he needed advice and guidance, and the rest was talent.

He also became close to Lucien Acou, another former pro who owned the Café de la Tourelle in the Brussels suburb of Anderlecht. Merckx spent a lot of time with the Acou family and in 1967 he married Lucien's daughter, Claudine.

Shortly after Merckx won the Tour de France for the first time, Acou was interviewed by the British cycling journalist J. B. Wadley, who was after background on Belgium's latest champion. 'Eddy Merckx wasn't coached, he just happened. He happened to have the basic class, happened to be mad on the sport, happened to have the intelligence to mark, learn and inwardly digest what went

on in cycling, and use the knowledge to his advantage,'
Acou told Wadley.

Acou had been a great six-day rider in the Forties and
Fifties, and in the Sixties he was the Belgian national
track coach. He knew Belgium had solid gold with Eddy
Merckx, but he was sensitive to his talent and understood
how best to develop it. He agreed with the solid stipula-
tion made by Félicien Vervaecke that Merckx should not
ride big amateur stage races. It was obvious Merckx could
be a world-class pro, and using his talent in amateur stage
races might be good in the short term for Belgium, but
not in the long term for Eddy Merckx. Anyway, no Belgian
had won the Tour de France since Sylvère Maes in 1939,
and maybe when he developed fully Merckx could be the
next, which would be very good for the country.

Merckx won twenty-eight races in 1963, his first year
competing against senior riders. That put him in line for
Olympic selection in 1964 when the Games were held
in Tokyo, but a problem occurred. The Belgian cycling
squad had a training camp where every rider attending
had a medical examination at the University hospital in
Ghent. The doctor who checked Merckx found something
wrong with his heart. He was off the squad. He wouldn't
be going to the world championships at Sallanches in
France that year, and he wouldn't go to Tokyo.

His mother immediately became suspicious. Her son
was as strong as an ox, a very fit young man. How could
he have a heart problem? She contacted the family doctor
and had him examine Eddy. The doctor found nothing
wrong, so she phoned the man responsible for selecting
the Belgian team, Oscar Daemers. She wanted to know
exactly what this heart problem was.

Daemers told her about the electro-cardiogram done

in Ghent, so Mrs Merckx said her doctor had found nothing, and Daemers called him a quack, then he got cocky. He told Jenny Merckx that perhaps her son wasn't as good a rider as she thought he was. That was a mistake, and he quickly compounded it by telling Mrs Merckx that he might select Eddy for the 100-kilometre team time trial, thinking that would appease her. It only made her even more suspicious. By 1964 Jenny Merckx knew plenty about cycling, and she knew that the 100-kilometre team time trial was one of the most demanding races there was. How could her son do that with his heart problem if he couldn't ride the road race? It didn't add up.

She contacted her doctor and asked him to speak to the doctor who had done the test in Ghent, Dr Marilier. He did, and the truth came out. Dr Marilier admitted he'd been told by Daemers to make a negative report on Eddy. Jenny Merckx then contacted Jean Van Buggenhout, who would later become Eddy Merckx's personal manager and agent. She told him what she'd found out and asked if he would intervene on Eddy's behalf.

Van Buggenhout knew everybody in Belgian cycling, and he knew Oscar Daemers well. Van Buggenhout spoke to Daemers, and Merckx was selected for the road race at both the world championships and the Olympic Games. The Games didn't work well for him. He was caught after trying a lone break near the end, but on a tough course in Sallanches, on a wet September day, Eddy Merckx won his first world title. He was 19 years old.

Within hours of her son pulling on the rainbow jersey, Jenny Merckx received a telegram. It was from Oscar Daemers, and it read: 'Congratulations, Mrs Merckx. Fortunately we took your advice.'

So Merckx had natural talent, he was healthy and he was strong. He had a difficult entry into pro cycling when he fell out with the leader of his first team in 1965, who was the big Belgian star, Rik Van Looy. Merckx thought Van Looy was a bully, because of the way he treated him as a young rider, and Van Looy thought Merckx was a soft Brussels boy who couldn't take a joke. They still don't like each other.

A transfer to Peugeot-BP led to happier times, and Eddy Merckx won his first monument, Milan–San Remo, in 1966, the first of seven, yes seven, victories in that one race. The rest is history, Eddy Merckx pushed the frontiers of what was possible, but how did he do it?

He says that it was simple. He was incredibly strong and cycling was his calling. He was undoubtedly talented, perhaps the most talented male road racer there's ever been, but talent alone is not enough to explain the phenomenon of Eddy Merckx. The next thing he had was a sublime work ethic. Yes, he was talented, but boy did Eddy Merckx polish that talent.

He trained like a maniac. When the Italian coffee machine manufacturer Faema recruited Merckx in 1968, part of the deal was to provide enough cash not only to pay Merckx but to let him build the best team he could. That agreement was preserved when Molteni took over sponsorship of Merckx's team in 1971.

Merckx and his personal manager Jan Van Buggenhout bought the best talent they could, but with one proviso; anybody joining Merckx's team wasn't riding for anybody but Eddy Merckx. The pay was good, but you could forget personal glory. The deal appealed to some, but not everybody he approached, thankfully. Then once the team was assembled there was a pretty tough regime.

He rarely rested in the winter, riding six-day races on the track to keep in trim. 'I put on weight easily, so the races gave me the discipline to stay in shape,' he says. Then training for the road season started on 1 January each year, and it started with a bang. From 1 January every Monday, Wednesday and Friday the team met at his house just outside Brussels for a ride. Most of the team were Belgians, so they were expected to turn up. And the ride plan was simple and unwavering.

Every Monday, Wednesday and Friday, for almost the whole of January the Faema then later the Molteni team rode 200 kilometres together. They rode side by side, swapping riders at the front, and they rode whatever the weather. Rain, hail or sleet, it didn't matter; they rode from Brussels to the East Flanders hills, the Flemish Ardennes, did a big loop of the Tour of Flanders climbs, then rode back to Brussels again. Britain's Barry Hoban says he used to see them:

I'd be out training, but the Flemish Ardennes are a lot nearer to where I lived in Ghent than they are to Brussels. I'd be on my way home and I'd shout, 'Enjoy your 200 kilometres, lads!' taking the mickey a bit, but the training worked. Merckx always had riders around him towards the end of a classic, he always had team-mates who could set the pace and close gaps, setting things up ready for him to attack.

The training group would have a team car following. It carried bike spares, extra clothing and food and drinks because there were never any stops. The car didn't pick up stragglers. Anybody dropped had to make their own way back, then explain to the boss why they were late. And if it rained or if sleet fell, Merckx would just tell the group that it would probably do the same in the Tour of Flanders, so they'd better just get used to it.

Once back at Merckx's place the riders showered and ate, usually the universal Seventies Belgian pro recovery food of hot minestrone soup, and then they dispersed. And in the days they were at home they were expected to do their own training in between the group sessions.

It was a tough regime, but when the season started in February, Merckx and his men were always ready. He was never less than competitive in his favourite first races, the Trofeo Laiguegia, the Monaco GP and the Tour of Sardinia, often winning them. Then Merckx would roar into the classics. Winning Milan–San Remo seven times was no accident; it was based on those Monday, Wednesday and Friday sessions.

Another insight into Merckx's training is provided by what he did in the week before his first Tour de France victory. I'll list it here:

Sunday: Raced in the Belgian National Championships, 264 kilometres.

Monday: Did two races, a 110-kilometre criterium and an evening track meeting.

Tuesday: Raced in a kermesse, but retired after 35 kilometres because he'd been prevented from starting with the rest of the riders by people demanding his autograph.

Wednesday: Training with his team, 180 kilometres.

Thursday: Training on his own, 270 kilometres! (That must have been one of his all-day rides.)

Friday: Behind a Derny for 50 kilometres. (This should have been more, but torrential rain made it too dangerous.)

Saturday: Morning, 40 kilometres fast. Afternoon, 40 kilometres easy. Evening, the prologue of the Tour de France.

So Eddy Merckx did the work, but he was also driven. He raced on average every three days, so when you look at his win total he won a race every ten days. And if that didn't happen he worried and couldn't sleep. During those periods of victory drought, however brief, Merckx would obsess about everything to do with cycling. His wife says that sometimes she would wake on nights he was at home and notice he was no longer in bed, and she would find him in his garage workshop, tinkering with his bike.

Merckx was an excellent mechanic, and as a junior rider he took his bike to pieces just to find out how many separate parts it was made from. Through his professional career he had 200 tyres stored in a dark dry place in his garage. Doing that to race tyres in those days made the rubber go extra hard, so it helped prevent punctures. He had at least 20 bikes on the go at once, constantly tried new saddles and handlebars, and kept adjusting the positions of both. No possible gain was too small to consider. Eddy Merckx practised marginal gains forty years before Sir David Brailsford even thought of the phrase he came up with in 2010.

Merckx paid attention to his nutrition, and his weight was important to him. Power to weight ratio is now seen as crucial in road racing, but Merckx understood this years ago. He says it was something he learned in the Faema team, the first one built around him.

I always had a good appetite, and until I joined Faema I ate well, thinking that I'd burned lots of energy so I had to eat a lot to replace it. I ate anything too. But that was the Belgian way then; in Italy they were different. Vittorio Adorni was the most experienced rider in Faema, a very good one too with a long career, and he taught me about nutrition, about what was in different foods and when to eat them. Above all he taught me to control what I ate, and not eat indiscriminately.

And then there were Merckx's teams. He also had invaluable help from a hand-picked and dedicated team. 'That's the thing about Eddy Merckx that gets forgotten,' says Britain's Barry Hoban. 'He was the greatest, but he also had the greatest team. He had riders who could win big races, but they rode for him, and they did it knowing they'd never have the chance of winning, because Merckx wanted to win everything. He offered me a place in his team once, and although the money was good I said thanks but no thanks.'

Eddy Merckx is the best of all time because he was the perfect storm for his opposition. He had incredible natural ability, and the perfect physique for cycling: a big chest, long legs, a powerful back and a solid core. He exuded natural strength, the rest he did himself through incredible drive, dedication and intelligence. He wanted to win everything and he was prepared to work harder than anyone to do it. I'll end this chapter with a little story told to me by one of his biggest rivals in single-day races, a rock-hard Flemish rider, who was also prepared to push the limits, called Frans Verbeek.

The early seventies were the hardest era to win but the easiest to get in the winning break, you just watched Eddy Merckx and went when he did. He was so talented, he had so much class. I hadn't got big class like Merckx, but I had the work ethic. I did the training, as much training as it was possible to do. My thought was if I can't out-class Merckx I'll out-work him, and I started training even longer and harder.

Then one day I was doing a ride from where we are now, not far from Leuven, right down to Marche-en-Famenne, close to the Luxembourg border, and back again. It's nearly 300 kilometres there and back, so I set off early, before any pro cyclist I knew would be out on the road.

I was feeling good, I was up and riding before anybody else, riding longer than anybody else, so I'd be stronger than anybody else; that was my reasoning. Then I saw someone pedalling towards me. It was Eddy Merckx. Oh no, I thought. I was sure I was out before anybody, but here was Merckx; he trained this early too.

I figured that was my advantage gone so I started going out even earlier after that, at five fifteen in the morning, when it was still dark. Merckx had everything, he had class and he had the work ethic, and he wanted to win everything. That's why he was the best. That's why he won so much.

19

Dark Side of the Road

It's not possible to write a book about road racing without talking about doping. It has been part of the sport for so long, seen as a necessity in the early days but as a blight today. What started out as help to endure awful conditions in early long races was hijacked by ambition and the drive to get an edge over the rest, or at least not wanting to give any advantage away. And that fuelled the use of performance-enhancing drugs through the years. There are other factors too, and whole books have been written on doping in sport, but I have to end this one with a brief look at the history of doping in road racing.

Going back to the early days, races tried to outdo each other in distance and severity to attract attention. The long races were a testing ground for bicycles as well as cyclists, so bicycle manufacturers hired the strongest riders, hoping to showcase the durability of their products through race victories. The strongest could earn good money, which made the sport attractive to tough working-class men because, in a similar way to boxing, cycling could get them out of the mines and the factories and lead to prosperity and a better life. To help the riders do that, men called trainers in the USA and UK, or *soigneurs* (carers) in Europe, became part of the sport.

Trainers had ways and means of helping riders perform better, and not just by prescribing training sessions or adjusting their diet. The best trainers worked for a share of the rider's winnings, so the higher a rider finished in a race the more the trainer earned. Some trainers used chemical substances to revive tired riders. These substances included nitroglycerine, which was used in Victorian medicine as a heart stimulant, but was also said to improve an athlete's breathing. Strychnine, in very small doses, improved muscle tone. Cocaine was used to perk up tired riders. And none of it was illegal; instead, such substances were thought to be a necessary part of racing.

In 1896 a Welshman, Arthur Linton, won Bordeaux–Paris. He was trained by a former top-class runner called James Edward 'Choppy' Warburton. Warburton was famous for a black doctor's bag he carried everywhere with him. It held the various potions he used to revive and rejuvenate his athletes. At Tours, just over halfway through Bordeaux–Paris, Linton was described as coming through the control point in the lead but 'with glassy eyes and tottering limbs and in a high state of nervous excitement'.

He staggered on, just about maintaining his lead, but later, at Orleans, he stopped again. He was in a really bad way and on the verge of collapse. According to reports, Warburton delved into his black bag and administered various substances to Linton. He rallied instantly, then gained 18 more minutes on the second-placed rider by the time he reached Paris.

Linton died a few months later at the age of 24. The cause of death was typhoid. Even young people as fit and strong as Linton died of typhoid in those days, but the long-distance road races of his era required almost superhuman exertion. What toll did that take on competitors? Especially those who had been boosted by some sort of stimulant to carry on when their natural body systems were trying to close down, perhaps to protect them. But there was pressure to perform, and more than just personal pressure to win and make a better life, for the outcome of races could affect hundreds of people working for a bicycle manufacturer. In many ways pro road racing was made for doping.

In a way it's understandable. Doping occurs in other sports too, and not always because of money and outside pressure, but for glory, for winning, and not necessarily winning big, just winning. That's certainly true in cycling. Just look at the crop of amateurs caught doping recently in races that, in many cases, hardly anyone has ever heard of. And then there's the human need for drugs. I'll never forget the great Italian coach, Aldo Sassi, a man of high principles himself, pointing this out to me during an interview: 'Humans are hardwired to take drugs. We have a headache so we reach for Aspirin; if we are tired we drink a strong coffee. We have always done this, so it's no surprise that sports people should reach for drugs. In a way it's human nature.'

Whether the wider general public knew about doping

in road racing before the 1924 Tour de France is unclear, but they certainly heard about it then. Upset by the draconian rules enforced by the race organisers, the 1923 Tour de France winner Henri Pélissier abandoned the 1924 race in Normandy. Along with his brother Francis and another rider, Maurice Ville, they stopped mid-stage in Coutances, and sat down in a café, where they were joined by Albert Londres.

Londres was a serious writer who didn't normally cover sport, but he was interested in the phenomenon of the Tour de France. He wanted to know why riders would take part in such an extreme race, and he wanted to understand the attraction the Tour held for people. What he got in Coutances was a tirade of complaints about the organisation and their rules from Ville and the Pélissiers, then Henri Pélissier turned out his pockets.

'We suffer from the start to the end. You want to know how we keep going? Here …, Pélissier said, and he pushed a tube across the table towards Londres. 'That's cocaine for our eyes,' he said. Then he produced another tube, saying, 'This is chloroform for our gums. And pills, we keep going on dynamite.' Pélissier showed Londres three boxes of pills he had, and the other two riders fished three identical boxes out of their jersey pockets.

Londres reported these revelations in his newspaper article, which the riders in question later tried to play down, claiming they were just winding the journalist up. But that's an excuse. It's not clear what the pills were, but they weren't sweets, that's for sure.

After that it became accepted that many professional cyclists used drugs. Strychnine was probably the strongest, but anything that could numb the pain or give a buzz was used. It was common practice for riders to soak cloths in ethanol to wear around their necks. The cloths helped cool them down, but the ethanol fumes acted as a stimulant as well. Riders carried small bottles containing ether to sniff for a buzz when they needed it, a practice that went on into the Fifties.

The use of stimulants was so widespread that when the Tour de France changed its rules in 1930, allowing only national teams to compete instead of trade-sponsored ones, the organisers listed what they would and wouldn't supply to the riders in the race rule book. It warned that drugs were one of the things the organisers wouldn't provide, the inference being that if they needed them riders had to bring their own.

The purpose of all early drugs used in cycling was to dull pain, fend off drowsiness or provide a little buzz or a kick. A bigger kick came from a drug group called amphetamines, which have a therapeutic purpose, and they are still given to some Attention Deficit Disorder sufferers. Amphetamines were given as stimulants to soldiers in the Second World War, and they were prescribed in Europe quite freely for many years after, even for things as trivial as helping somebody lose weight, or helping students concentrate when they studied. They were certainly used widely by cyclists from the Forties onwards.

Amphetamines improve cognition and memory. For athletes they increased alertness, which has an effect on improving stamina. They also make a rider feel good, so they can push harder. However, they impair judgement, and high doses can lead to muscle breakdown, behaviour disorders, and a serious rise in body temperature.

Amphetamines were called La Bomba in Italy, and Fausto Coppi was interviewed on TV once and asked if he had ever taken La Bomba. 'Only when necessary,' he

replied. Asked to clarify what he meant by when necessary, Coppi said, 'Almost always.'

But some riders overdid their use. Several cases of
strange behaviour and even collapse were attributed to
amphetamine use. And amphetamines were the reason
why the cycling authorities began to consider their position regarding the use of drugs in the sport. Anonymous
tests carried out in Belgium, designed to determine the
extent of drug use in 1965, found that 37 per cent of
pro racers were using amphetamines.

In 1966 their use was outlawed for the first time, and
the first drugs tests in professional cycling were carried
out during the Tour de France. All they did was spark a
protest from the riders, who held a strike. Then in 1967
Tom Simpson died in the Tour de France, and traces of
amphetamine were found in his body and an empty
amphetamine container was found in his racing jersey
pockets.

This was serious. It can't be said absolutely that the
drugs caused Simpson's death. Indeed, anecdotal evidence
from people who were inside the Tour at that time claims
that the autopsy – the report was destroyed some years
ago in accordance with French law – put his death down
to a cardiac arrest, to which amphetamines could have
been a contributory factor. It was a hot day, and Simpson
was suffering from a stomach virus. He had drunk very
little water, and was very dehydrated. Those factors
contributed too, and some of them could have been
exacerbated by amphetamine use.

There is no doubt that Tom Simpson used amphetamines, but his fellow riders put his death down to other
causes, and many who were using them just carried on
doing so. The five-time Tour de France winner Jacques

Anquetil, who was quite open about his use of drugs, even suggested that the new drugs tests might have caused Simpson to use something riskier.

That was an extreme view, but Simpson's death didn't change much; pro cycling carried on as it had done. If anything, riders upped the ante and started using steroids and hormone treatments. Almost everything used before steroids had been a psychological drug, taken to pep the users up and make them feel better. Steroids and hormones were physiological drugs, which helped riders build muscle, recover quickly and train and ride harder.

Cortisone and corticosteroids were widely used. The 1975 Tour de France winner Bernard Thévenet says that cortisone ruined his health, and there are others who are ill today due to its use but won't talk about it. The doping effects of cortisone are not fully understood. Science says it helps widen airways and reduces pain, and coupled with steady exercise it is very effective for weight loss. However, those who have used cortisone, and more so corticosteroids, say that they have similar effects to testosterone.

Testosterone is a male sex hormone that, among other things, is involved in muscle growth. It is powerful stuff, and its concentration in the body falls off during a long stage race or during prolonged bouts of heavy training. That's why its use in cycling grew, and it was a long time before an effective test for artificial testosterone was perfected. Human growth hormone was also abused for similar reasons.

That was another problem. Every time a test for a banned substance was found, riders would switch to another product, often with doctors helping them. And for a while some riders even carried on taking stuff that would show up, and then cheated the dope tests which were carried out on urine samples. Blood testing was still some way off.

The most famous incident of cheating a dope test occurred during the 1978 Tour de France, when the race leader Michel Pollentier tried to pass off a urine sample given to him by somebody else as his sample. The urine had been in a condom kept under Pollentier's armpit, so it stayed warm. The condom was then connected by a tube that led to the underside of his penis.

In those days riders providing urine samples were allowed to stay dressed, pull down the front of their shorts and pee into the sample bottle. Unfortunately one of the other riders selected for testing with Pollentier found his tube had detached from his penis, so he began fumbling around in his shorts to find it. The doctor supervising the test became suspicious. He asked the rider to lift his jersey and the DIY urine delivery kit was found. He then asked Pollentier to lift his jersey and found a similar set-up. Pollentier was thrown off the Tour.

Riders who used these devices called them pears, because of the shape the condom went when full of urine. They were common enough to become the subject of jokes. One rider who used one to mask the fact that he'd taken cortisone was found guilty of taking amphetamine. What he'd done was ask a team mechanic to supply a sample of urine, which they placed in a 'pear' device, but what the mechanic forgot to tell the rider was that he'd taken amphetamine to help him stay awake during a long drive through the previous night. There was another story, a joke this time, about a rider who was told that his urine sample was clear of banned substances but that he was pregnant.

Then there was blood doping, or blood transfusions – it wasn't called blood doping until the process was banned. The process involves removing blood, usually 500cc, well before a big race, storing it so the cells stay alive and in good condition, then transfusing it back before a target race. The transfusion then provides 500cc worth of extra red blood cells, which contain oxygen-carrying haemoglobin molecules that deliver oxygen to working muscles. So, if you increase the number of red cells you increase the amount of oxygen available for the muscles to use.

Delivering more oxygen is one of the prime objectives of endurance training, and a prime limiter of performance. Blood transfusions were used in sport from the late Sixties, but the process wasn't banned until 1986. It was a procedure, one that some athletes and cyclists freely admitted to while others were cagey about it, but it was still an allowed procedure until 1986.

The Finish athlete Kaarlo Maanika admitted using the technique in 1980 when he took a bronze medal in the 5,000 metres and silver in the 10,000 metres at the Moscow Olympic Games. Joop Zoetemelk was prescribed blood transfusions in 1976, but he was anaemic as a result of injuries sustained in a bad crash in 1974, after which he contracted meningitis. Pat McDonough of the US Olympic cycling team that dominated the 1984 Los Angeles Games admitted using blood manipulation. The same goes for Francesco Moser in his preparation for a successful attack on Eddy Merckx's hour record in 1984. There were others who were open about it, and probably a lot more who didn't want to talk.

And so it went on. The drugs changed, but riders' preparedness to take them didn't. It wasn't every rider, but still a good few, and that was especially true of Grand Tour contenders, for whom doping with things like testosterone, steroids and human growth hormone was particularly effective and gave a significant advantage.

But there was another way of thinking in pro cycling that fuelled the continuous drive to dope as well. Many riders were convinced, or had convinced themselves, that doping was a requirement, just to get through gruelling races like the Tour de France. They referred to doing without drugs as riding on bread and water. For many, doping was part of the badge of being a pro racer, or even a shared naughtiness that had to be shielded from the public.

This is the Australian Allan Peiper talking in 2005 about his early experiences as a professional rider with the Peugeot team in the Eighties. It's a window on what it was like for hundreds of new professionals at that time, and how many came to see doping as part of the game.

I thought I had been looking after myself, and in my first pro year I turned up at the pre-season training camp with my garlic pills and wheat germ capsules, but the first thing I learned was how to use a needle. Not for doping, but for vitamin injections, because it was felt then that if you needed vitamins it's more effective to inject them.

The whole thing was treated as a sort of initiation rite. Everyone would be in the soigneur's room and you had to inject yourself in the backside while they all watched you. And you couldn't throw the needle in, you had to push it in slowly so that you could feel it going through each layer. The guys would be lying around on beds and sprawled on chairs, laughing at your discomfort.

Now, to people not involved in cycle sport, that might

sound a bit frightening, but it was part of your job. Your job was to be in as good a condition as possible, and it was your responsibility to ensure that. Injecting vitamins was part of making sure you were the best you could be. Taking tablets just wouldn't do it, because your body might not take up the vitamin; the tablet has to be digested and the digestive system might not even absorb the vitamin. With an injection, especially intravenously, your body has no choice but to absorb it.

I still didn't take it on board at the start. I rode my first Tour de France in 1984 on nothing, no vitamins. I rode on bread and water for the whole way basically, and I think it was probably one of the worst things I could ever have done. It took me months to get over it, because the more your blood values fall – iron levels, vitamins, minerals and hormones – the less well your body runs and you damage it.

Of course, I'm not trying to say there were no drugs in cycling; I'm not blind. Right from my first year I heard guys discussing taking amphetamines, although I didn't get involved with it. To be honest, I saw the whole thing as a joke. To me the guys were like kids in the playground; you weren't allowed to have lollies at school, but you had them in your pocket anyway and ate them when the teacher wasn't looking.

That's what the atmosphere was like when I turned pro. There were controls at some races, but not at others, and the guys all knew where and when they were. They would be in the changing rooms like naughty schoolboys, talking about a race in France next week, a 'Chaudière' race. *Chaudière* is the French word for a heater, meaning these were hot races, where you could get a charge and use amphetamines.

I'm comparing the guys to schoolboys, because it's the only way I can get across how drugs were viewed. Of course the consequences of taking drugs were not the same as the consequences of a schoolboy prank. A lot of lives got messed up by amphetamines. There were even guys I raced with who ended up in psychiatric hospitals, because their addiction got out of control. That's the danger, and it's an unseen danger; it might have seemed a joke back then in the Eighties, but it is a dangerous joke. Or was a dangerous joke; it's not any more because amphetamines are out of place in this era, but they were the stage setter for what happened next.

There was also a body of doctors who were prepared to help riders dope, eventually earning a great deal of money as doping became more sophisticated. Some doctors sympathised with the belief held by many pros for a long time that drugs supported their health in Grand Tours, that riding a Grand Tour without medical support, a euphemism for doping, was bad for a rider's health. As cycling moved on through the Eighties these doctors slowly became involved with the teams, and with individual riders.

Then in the early Nineties a drug entered cycling that is the dictionary definition of performance-enhancing. Synthetic EPO was developed to help cancer patients produce red blood cells when natural mechanisms are too stressed to do it to the level the body requires. Red blood cells carry inhaled oxygen to the muscles, where the oxygen is used with glucose to produce energy.

It's like a car, where the fuel ignites in the presence of oxygen. Deliver more oxygen, with a turbocharger for example, and the car's engine is more powerful. EPO is a human turbocharger. If synthetic EPO is injected into a healthy human it can boost their red blood cells so they deliver 10 per cent more oxygen to their muscles. Ten per cent more oxygen roughly translates into 10 per cent more power. It was like blood doping but without the inconvenience of a transfusion.

The argument that pros had used to justify drug use to themselves, that you need drugs to get through long races because cycling is very hard, didn't wash with EPO. Using EPO wasn't coping with a tough sport, it was cheating, although as we'll see, that didn't stop the drug's use spreading rapidly. And EPO produced some quite strange results.

Bjarne Riis wasn't a bad rider, but he wasn't a natural-born winner either, and his victory in the 1996 Tour de France shocked a lot of people. He didn't set the world alight when he turned pro, although he had fearsome ambition and drive, and he is very intelligent. He slowly turned himself year by year into a better rider, winning bigger and bigger races until he eventually won the Tour de France.

Later, though, Riis was forced to tell the truth about his victory. He'd been named by others involved with the team he raced for, T-Mobile, who had admitted doping. Riis's position became untenable and he admitted using EPO to win the 1996 Tour de France, underlining what most people suspected. There was even a black joke inside cycling in which Riis was referred to as Mr 60 Percent.

That name came about because there was no test for the presence of artificial EPO in the body until 2000, so when its use was first suspected by the cycling authorities they began to test the rider's red blood cell count, which is expressed as a percentage reading called a haematocrit. A tested rider whose haematocrit exceeded 50 per cent would be prevented from racing by the UCI on health grounds until it fell below that mark. It's obvious then why Riis was called Mr 60 Percent.

Nowadays each top-level rider has a blood passport, with the results of haematocrit and other tests taken at regular intervals entered in it. The result is a profile of their blood values over an extended period, and if anomalies turn up on a test the rider is investigated thoroughly until an explanation is established. That explanation can be deemed satisfactory, that the fluctuation was caused by illness or an accident, for example, but in the absence of a satisfactory explanation the rider is presumed to have doped.

The reason the authorities took haematocrit readings and called them 'health checks' instead of drugs tests, flags up the other problem with EPO. Apart from the fact that taking it is cheating, it can be dangerous. The normal haematocrit range lies between the high 30s and high 40s per cent. At over 50 per cent the blood starts to become thicker. Factor in dehydration from heavy exercise, which lowers blood plasma volume, and red blood cell concentration rises even more, leading to the danger of blood clots and heart failure. There's no evidence that Riis ever actually had a reading as high as 60 per cent, but anyone boosting to that level would be taking a huge risk with their health and could die.

Some riders might have died as a result of taking EPO, but no big-name pros. And this flags up another danger of doping: if done by experts it can be relatively safe, but EPO could be bought on the internet and self-administered. In the Nineties a number of good amateur racers and second-level pros simply died in their sleep. It wasn't the reason for every death, but the suspicion is that some were possibly due to taking EPO.

EPO users must keep their blood diluted enough to cope with the extra cells. This requires expert help and advice, as well as specialist equipment like mobile centrifuges to monitor red cell concentration. To be safe, it requires a doctor, and the number of medical practitioners who began to oversee the training and preparation of pro bike riders increased during the Nineties. That was no coincidence.

It's true that being trained by a doctor doesn't mean a rider is doping. Many doctors who worked in cycling in the worst days of doping, the Nineties and early Noughties, did so in strict accordance with the rules on doping. Doctors are necessary on teams to treat the riders and staff in case of illness, and medical doctors are in a unique position to help teams plan a rider's training and racing programme.

Still, a doctor who knew his or her stuff could make big money from doping in sport, and maybe still can, and this needs to be watched out for constantly. If it became known that a number of riders from different teams were seeing one doctor it would raise suspicion now. And many teams don't allow riders to consult anyone outside of their own personnel. While the money must be a temptation in itself for doctors, Allan Peiper reckons that there's more:

I think some doctors get a bit of a God complex. It's like with surgeons; they come up with procedures that defy nature. You know, where you get a patient who is so ill that it looks impossible for them to survive, but the surgeon says: 'Now hang on, if I do this and this', and they save their lives. That must be a buzz, it must be addictive, and in a way when doctors get involved in doping I think they get the same kick by saying, 'Okay, nature says you can go this fast, and do this and this. But I can change that, I can make you go that fast and do more.' I think they get into that and get a kick from it.

Of course very little of this was known for certain outside of pro cycling in the early Nineties. The pro peloton ran like a secret society, and what happened inside it stayed inside it. It was ruled by omertà, the law of silence. There was plenty of chatter within the peloton about everything that concerned it, but the chatter had to stay there. Anyone who spoke out was vilified. It meant that, guilty or innocent, most pros stayed silent.

Those who didn't dope tried to put it out of their minds. This was a necessary survival tactic, because if they let it in, then in their minds they would always be beaten by the dopers. And that's another reason, and quite a considerable and understandable one too, why innocent riders were reluctant to talk about it. Talking forced them to think about doping. Better to shut it out and keep it there. Good performers in sports can do that; they can compartmentalise their lives and put things in a place and leave them there. They do it with pain, for example.

And there was no test for EPO until 2000, so nobody got caught. Some young riders and other anti-drugs campaigners did try to draw attention to the fact that doping had got out of control, but in the main nobody was listening, or they didn't want to listen. Then something happened to take pro cycling and the policing of doping temporarily out of the hands of the usual authorities. No one is absolutely sure why it happened, but perhaps the authorities outside of the sport thought that doping had become so prevalent it needed sorting out.

Willy Voet, a Belgian who lived in France, was a soigneur who had worked in cycling for a very long time. He had good hands and a deep understanding of the sport, so he worked with some of the best, and he knew every trick in the book. He was also a good man to have on your side in a murky world; trustworthy and dependable, and with a Machiavellian belief that the ends always justified the means.

A few days before the start of the 1998 Tour de France in Dublin, Voet travelled from his home in the Alps to Paris to pick up a car supplied by the Tour organisers that his team would use on the race. He then set off on a rambling journey to Belgium, which included a visit to Switzerland, calling at various places along the way to pick up supplies for his team, which was sponsored by the watch manufacturer Festina.

In Belgium he visited the team's doctor, Dr Rijckaert, to collect some medical drips. The plan was to set off next day for the French port of Calais, then drive across England, through Wales, and from there take another ferry to Ireland. Rijckaert knew exactly what Voet had in his car, so advised him not to cross into France by the E17 coastal motorway, but go by the back roads.

Theoretically there are no borders in the Schengen countries of Europe, but customs officers still patrol them. They still stop people, and regularly turn up loads of smuggled cigarettes or booze or recreational drugs, or people being trafficked. They carry out a few random stop-and-checks, but most customs activity is intelligence led. They swap information with officials from other countries and choose the right moment to stop someone, when whatever or whoever they are looking for is with them.

Voet knew the back roads of Flanders like the back of his hand, and he decided to cross the border into France at Neuville-en-Ferrain. Normally you would never even see a customs vehicle at such a crossing, but on 8 July the place was swarming with them, and they stopped Voet. They didn't even look at him, they just asked him to open up his car, give them the keys, and stay put. An armed officer watched him while the rest searched the car. What they found was 234 doses of EPO, 160 of testosterone, 80 bottles of growth hormone, and lots of blood-thinning tablets. Voet was arrested, and pro cycling's big secret was out.

Voet sang like a canary. He'd been involved in doping riders for years, and he wasn't alone. What's more, he told the authorities that Festina had an internal doping programme to which the riders chipped in a part of their salaries. And it was all done under the expert supervision of Dr Rijckaert. It wasn't compulsory, but the best riders and those who wanted to support them in big races were in it.

When the 1998 Tour reached mainland Europe more raids were carried out, teams were quizzed by the police, and at the end of the first week the Tour de France organisers threw the Festina team off the race. At first the other riders protested. They talked about the dignity of their profession being violated. But as more revelations came out, as more riders were questioned, products seized and teams put under investigation, their protestations sounded increasingly hollow. The race was won by Marco Pantani.

Pantani's victory was the first Italian Tour victory for over thirty years, it was as brave and as classy as any in the race's long history, and he also did the double – he'd already won the Giro d'Italia that year. Pantani is the last rider ever to have achieved that Giro-Tour double too, but in retrospect it was a footnote to the 1998 Tour de France. Doping was the story, and Pantani would soon become part of it, his career and personal life slipping into a tail-spin that saw him die alone in a hotel room in 2004 after a cocaine overdose.

A doping arms race was going on in cycling, and although the cycling authorities were testing, they had ignored signs of its escalation. Not deliberately perhaps, but they were definitely in collective denial. A few brave riders spoke out. Gilles Delion at the beginning of the Nineties was one, but few listened, they weren't ready then. Some didn't want to believe what Delion was saying; others thought it was an exaggeration. Some of his fellow riders even suggested that the only reason Delion talked so much about drugs was that he wasn't good enough. But he won the Giro di Lombardia in 1990, so that just wasn't true.

A few years later people listened to Christophe Bassons. He was a French pro with Festina. He wasn't racing in the 1998 Tour, partly because as a first year pro he didn't have the form or experience to be selected, but possibly because he refused to join Dr Rijckaert's programme. He just said no, but during the 1998 Tour he said yes to every interview he could. He became something of a hero, although his racing career eventually ended because he'd broken the vow of silence about drugs. Bassons found little support from his fellow riders.

You might wonder why the riders let this happen. Why

didn't more of them say something, the ones who weren't doping, as Bassons did? Or why didn't they leave the sport? But that's the problem with highly motivated athletes. They are driven, they want to win, and they want to take responsibility for their talent. The money, too, is no small factor. Imagine a young rider going back to the housing estate he grew up on, back to the factory he worked at, and telling his mates he gave up his £300,000 a year job because he didn't want to take a few drugs.

And all the time these riders were being told by people they respected – team managers, doctors and people who'd been in cycling for a long time – that doping was okay. It was what a serious pro did. Many were told that it was better for your health than racing on the euphemism of bread and water. Not everyone in cycling held those beliefs, but there were enough.

Riders with talent want to explore it. Very few set out wanting to take drugs to help them win, but many decided it was their only option. If they didn't they would never be as good as they could be, they would never have the glory or the money they could have. Some probably told themselves that by doping they were doing the best they could for their families. And for others it was simply the desire to win, to be somebody, to be admired, adored even. It's easy to judge the conduct of others, but less so if you face the same circumstances and choices as they face.

Cycling was in a bad place in 1998, but there was more to come. Lance Armstrong had joined the US Postal team. He didn't ride the Tour de France that year, but he'd recovered from cancer, and picked up new determination. He was coming back, and he was coming back with a grudge. Instead of stopping after Festina, doping carried on regardless and arguably got worse.

Armstrong won an unprecedented seven Tours de France, but as he did so rumours of doping turned into accusations, which Armstrong came down on like a ton of bricks. No matter who said what, he went for them, including fellow riders.

Riders in the Tour knew the truth. Of course the ones doing the same or similar to Armstrong weren't going to say anything, it wasn't in their interests to do so. And the vast majority of those who didn't dope wouldn't speak out either. That's one of the hardest things to understand about this period. Even riders with not a blemish, not a suspicion to their name, guys who could have got a lot better results if they had doped, even they wouldn't speak out. They feared the backlash if they did – the treatment Christophe Bassons got.

Bassons rode the 1999 Tour de France, the first of Armstrong's seven victories, and while on the race he wrote a column for the newspaper *Le Parisien*. In it he said that the Festina affair hadn't changed anything, but instead of getting behind what he said, by stage ten, from Sestrière to Alpe d'Huez, few of his fellow riders were speaking to him.

So he decided to ride ahead of the ambling peloton during the very early part of the stage. Then, he told BBC 5 Live in 2012:

All the teams started riding together to catch me, and when they did they all rode by staring at me. Then Lance Armstrong reached me. He grabbed me by the shoulder, because he knew that everyone would be watching, and he knew that at that moment he could show everyone he was the boss. He said what I was saying wasn't true, what I was saying was bad for cycling, that I mustn't say it, that I had no right to be a professional cyclist, that I should quit cycling, that I should quit the Tour, and he finished by saying fuck you. I was depressed for six months. I was crying all of the time. I was in a really bad way.

Bassons also said that Armstrong asked him why he was speaking out. 'I told him that I'm thinking of the next generation of riders. Then he said, "Why don't you leave, then?"' Armstrong has since confirmed the story, but during the 1999 Tour, on the main evening news on TF1, a French TV station, Armstrong called Bassons out, saying: 'His accusations aren't good for cycling, for his team, for me, for anybody. If he thinks cycling works like that, he's wrong and he would be better off going home.'

Bassons was shunned by other riders. While giving a television interview later on in the 1999 Tour de France, he says that a passing rider from his own team had said: 'Watch what you say.' Bassons felt totally isolated, and shortly after that interview he left the Tour. In 2012 he told the BBC:

The team doctor comforted me. We often talked together about the problem of doping, and we share the same ideas. I got to sleep, but a bit after midnight I could no longer sleep because of my worries.

I went out into the corridor. I phoned my coach, Antoine Vayer, and Pascale, my wife. At 5.30 a.m. I had my breakfast and I packed my case. I crossed with Marc [Madiot, his team manager] and he said I was letting the team down. He said a rider could leave the race if he had cracked physically, but he couldn't accept that one can crack mentally. I said goodbye to everyone, but one rider didn't even look at me and he refused to shake my hand. That hurt.

And so it went on, all through Armstrong's run until he won his seventh Tour in 2005. Then into retirement and through his comeback in 2009 and 2010, accusations were hurled at Armstrong and he batted them away. There was no smoking gun, because those who'd seen it weren't speaking. They were Armstrong's team-mates, and they weren't making accusations even though some of them had moved on, felt the rough end of Armstrong's lash, and in many cases had been caught doping in other teams. But in 2010, one of them did talk.

Another American rider, Floyd Landis, tested positive for performance-enhancing drugs directly after his victory in the 2006 Tour de France. He was disqualified and later banned from the sport. After years of mounting a vigorous legal defence, Landis finally admitted doping between 2002 and 2006. During part of that time Landis was a member of the US Postal team, and he had worked hard on his bike in support of Armstrong in races.

That was one bombshell, but the next one had a much louder bang. Landis accused Lance Armstrong and several key members of the US Postal team of doping, with the knowledge and assistance of the team manager Johan Bruyneel and other members of staff. And Landis sent his accusations, backed by eyewitness accounts, by e-mail to senior cycling and anti-doping officials.

He had been trying to make his way back into cycling, and had tried to enter the Amgen Tour of California, but was refused by its organiser Andrew Messick. Landis released his accusations to the media in May 2010, while the Tour of California was going on. Lance Armstrong was one of the riders in the race.

Armstrong reacted as you might expect, controlling the narrative by trying to diminish Landis and place him where cycling had pushed him, firmly on the outside. Johan Bruyneel did the same. They said that Landis had asked for a place on their new team, RadioShack, and his accusations were made because they wouldn't give him one. However, other former US Postal riders also named by Landis were ominously quiet.

At first some fans and people inside cycling didn't like what Landis had done, but now the overwhelming feeling is that he did the sport a favour. Even people with no vested interest in covering up the past thought that for him to be believed, the time for Landis to speak was in 2006, and doing it now was just revenge because he couldn't get back into the sport. But what they didn't know was that Landis's revelations were detailed and extensive.

The American authorities took them very seriously. They started a federal enquiry into the activities of the US Postal team to establish if those involved had misappropriated United States government money. It wasn't a doping investigation, but it looked to see if government money, i.e. the sponsorship funds the US Postal Service gave the company running the cycling team, Tailwind Sports, had been used to fund a doping programme. That could have constituted fraud against the government.

The World Anti-Doping Agency also widened an enquiry they were involved in to encompass what Landis alleged, but it was the US Food and Drugs Administration who first had a go at the riders named by Landis. Their enquiry was led by special agent Jeff Novitzky, and by the federal prosecutor Doug Millar. Millar convened a grand jury in Los Angeles, and they started asking questions and making enquiries. The riders Landis accused were subpoenaed, one by one, and they were treated as witnesses. The grand jury never asked to speak to Armstrong or to Bruyneel.

This was serious. Lie to a grand jury and the consequences are grave. Faced with the reality of going to prison, the US Postal riders questioned had no safe option but to tell the truth. And it was a tidal wave of truth that could wash away anything, including Lance Armstrong. Novitzky and Millar had already worked on the BALCO laboratory case, a business that was supplying anabolic steroids to athletes. The baseball player Barry Bonds and Olympic gold medal-winning sprinter Marion Jones both lied to that enquiry, and they both ended up in deep trouble.

Novitzky was also involved in an ongoing enquiry into cycling after performance-enhancing drugs were found in an apartment in California rented by an American pro racer, Kayle Leogrande. Through that enquiry Novitzky had built a working relationship with Travis Tygart of the United States Anti-Doping Agency (USADA). Tygart also received Landis's e-mails. He and Landis spoke at length, and Landis told him about his doping with the US Postal team, and what others had done. Landis also filed a False Claims Act lawsuit against Tailwind Sports. That case is still rattling on.

Novitzky and Millar used the full power of the law and tracked down and subpoenaed all the witnesses they needed. They did it slowly and methodically, and behind closed doors. The truth came out. Novitzky travelled to Europe to check facts and seek further evidence. It was rumoured that indictments were on their way. Then, on 3 February 2012, a US attorney called André Birotte Jr issued a press release saying that his office was 'closing an investigation of federal criminal conduct by members and associates of a professional cycling team owned in part by Lance Armstrong'.

This was another bombshell, and a very different one. It looked for a while that Armstrong had dodged a missile, never mind a bullet, but he hadn't. While the government enquiry was going on, USADA had done one of its own, hearing evidence from the same witnesses, who, now they had told the truth once, found it easy to do so again. Some even said it was therapeutic. USADA built a case against Armstrong, which he knew. But when the government dropped its case, after hiring expensive lawyers and spin doctors during it, Armstrong said he wouldn't defend himself any longer. USADA could do whatever it liked.

It was his last attempt to control the narrative, but it was thwarted when USADA published a document called the Reasoned Decision of the United States Anti-Doping Agency on Disqualification and Ineligibility. The main decision was to strip Lance Armstrong of all achievements from 1998, including his seven Tour de France victories, and to suspend him for life from competing in all sports that follow the WADA code.

The UCI upheld the decision, and it decided not to promote any rider to first place in the Tours that Armstrong lost. Armstrong didn't appeal, and although he has made confessions since, notably to TV audiences with Oprah Winfrey, he hasn't yet given detailed testimony about his drug use.

In short, while agreeing that what he did was wrong, including his bad treatment of individuals, Armstrong says that at the time he saw no other way of giving himself a chance of winning the Tour de France. 'I went and looked up the definition of cheat, and the definition is to gain an advantage on a rival or foe. I didn't view it that way. I viewed it as a level playing field,' he told Winfrey. There's little doubt he still believes that. He also said that he owed a lot of people apologies, people he tried to intimidate or to hurt. He has been in communication with several of them, and made a public apology to Christophe Bassons.

At the beginning the Reasoned Decision states that none of its evidence was obtained from the federal authorities, that it all came from 'Mr Armstrong's former team-mates and employees of the US Postal and Discovery Channel cycling teams'.

The document presents evidence and refers to testimony that proves Armstrong's involvement and participation in doping from 1998 until 2011. It does the same to prove the involvement of Dr Garcia, Dr Michele Ferrari and Johan Bruyneel, and that of other US Postal team employees Dr Pedro Celaya and José Marti.

Then it goes on to say how Armstrong and his team-mates avoided providing positive drugs tests. For a start, Armstrong was never tested as many times as he claimed. One former team-mate, Tyler Hamilton, testified that the various drugs-testing agencies' out-of-competition testing was not sufficiently robust to catch offending riders. If he thought he might provide a positive sample when a tester called, Hamilton wouldn't answer the door, and the tester didn't always record a missed test.

There was also testimony from US Postal riders that

Johan Bruyneel seemed to have information about when drugs tests would be carried out at races. The riders would also get advance notice of out-of-competition tests, or team staff would delay a tester to buy enough time for saline drips to be used to lower haematocrit readings. The team also knew where to train to avoid out-of-competition tests.

The riders knew exactly how long it took for traces of detectable drugs to be flushed from their system. They micro-dosed with EPO, used testosterone in oil or limited use of patches to cut the likelihood of a positive test. Furthermore, when an EPO test was perfected, Dr Ferrari worked out how to frustrate it by stimulating natural EPO production using a hypoxic chamber. They also went back to using blood transfusions in response to the EPO detection test, because until 2005 there was no methodology for detecting blood doping or human growth hormone. And the team's doctors also used groundless exemption certificates to cover cortisone use.

The Reasoned Decision produced evidence of Armstrong's efforts to suppress the truth about his anti-doping violations, and how he tried to prevent witnesses from testifying by intimidation. Tyler Hamilton testified that he was told by Armstrong at a chance meeting in Aspen in 2011, 'When you get on the witness stand, we are going to fucking tear you apart. You are going to look like an idiot. I'm going to make your life a living fucking hell.' The report also concluded that at one time or another Armstrong made direct or implied threats to team-mates and staff whenever they spoke out about doping in the team.

The Reasoned Decision made grim reading, but is men's professional road racing clean now? I say men's road racing specifically, because there has been nowhere near the number of doping convictions in woman's racing, although there have been some. It's not guilt-free.

The only realistic answer to the question is that we don't know. If it is happening, only those doing it and those helping them would know for sure. But comparing this generation with those from a long and chequered past, there are reasons to hope that men's top-level pro road racing is largely clean, and doping certainly less prevalent.

One reason for hope is that *omertà* appears to have been broken, in that riders will talk to journalists and others about doping today, whereas many of them were reluctant to do so in the past. A lot of people who were involved in doping don't work in cycling now. There may still be people in the sport who have things to hide. And some say that it was wrong to strip Lance Armstrong of his results, when there is little doubt that those of other dopers are still on the record books. But men's road racing feels better since that happened. As Lance Armstrong once said when somebody accused him of doping, 'Extraordinary accusations require extraordinary proof.' Well, extraordinary violation requires extraordinary punishment. And the message that even the best will be brought down if they dope is a strong one.

There are still suspicions and grey areas. The use of Therapeutic Exemption Certificates (TUEs), which allow a rider to take a banned substance and still race if there is a medical need to take it, is under the spotlight. There's a suspicion that TUEs could have been abused in that the medical condition has been used as an excuse to use a banned substance for a performance-enhancing reason. That accusation was certainly at the heart of recent inquiry into Team Sky, but the team denies any wrongdoing and the doping authorities found no evidence of any, although the team's medical record keeping was highly criticised. The whole question of how TUEs are granted is now under review. Rightly so, because top teams will push things. They will go up to the letter of the rule book; in fact, some think it is their job to do that, because if they don't, others will. It's possible that some might try to manipulate ethical grey areas, so the authorities need to look harder at that. Policing the top of professional cycling, indeed all sport, must be thorough and executed without fear of favour.

The sport does look more believable, too. Extraordinary performances still happen, but they are not as common-place as they were. Meanwhile we must also guard against jumping to the conclusion that extraordinary perfor-mance is always due to doping. It's the nature of sport to excel. And records have always been broken as the understanding of how to train and prepare deepens and becomes clearer with time. There have certainly been a lot of advances in sports science recently.

There are worries, stories of undetectable substances and even suspicions about motors in bikes. And no matter how far-fetched they sound they should be considered, and the authorities must take action to police them. Some riders of both sexes have been tempted to cheat when they think they can get away with it, and no doubt others will be in the future; it's part of the human psyche. Plus there are a worrying number of cases where amateurs have been caught taking drugs. It's not always for money; winning casts a spell of its own.

The answer is I don't know if cycling is clean now, and it's foolhardy to say things like the new generation of riders we have now won't dope because they are better educated. I've seen that put forward recently as a reason to believe in clean road racing today, and in my opinion it doesn't hold water. Ambition doesn't just belong to the disadvantaged, and better education doesn't necessarily mean better ethics.

One thing I do know is that you will go dizzy trying to find an answer to whether any sport is clean from the outside. We must try to trust the people who run sport, and they must do everything they can to keep that trust. They haven't always done that in the past. Road racing is still a beautiful sport, and I thoroughly enjoyed taking part in it at my own low level, and will never tire of watching it at its highest level. I've also met many wonderful people through the sport. I hope that road racing continues to captivate people like me for many years to come.

Acknowledgements

I'd like to thank all the professional road racers who have given me insight into their world and shared their experiences, particularly Barry Hoban. Also the late Aldo Sassi for sharing some of his deep understanding of the physical demands of road racing.

Thanks to Simon Richardson, editor of *Cycling Weekly*, for letting me quote from the excellent, long-gone, *Sporting Cyclist* magazine, and to the late JB 'Jock' Wadley for his writing in that publication. Also to Mike Breckon for letting me share his experiences of racing in Brittany.

The excellent Myles Archibald came up with the idea to write this book, commissioned it and even thought up the title, so big thanks to him, but also to all those involved in the editing and publishing of it, especially Steve Dobell and Julia Koppitz.

Thanks to my agent Robert Dudley, and last but by no means least to my wife Kathleen, who has to read first drafts of anything I write, despite having heard it all before.

INDEX